The Triathletes

THE
TRIATHLETES

A SEASON IN THE LIVES OF FOUR WOMEN IN THE TOUGHEST SPORT OF ALL

Jeff Cook

ST. MARTIN'S PRESS NEW YORK

Design by Judith Christensen
Production Editor: Suzanne Magida
Production Manager: Marni Siskind

Library of Congress Cataloging-in-Publication Data
Cook, Jeff
    The triathletes : a season in the lives of four women in the
toughest sport of all / Jeff Cook.
        p. cm.
    ISBN 0-312-08184-7
    1. Triathlon. 2. Women athletes. I. Title.
GV1060.73.C66 1992
796.4—dc20   92-24050
                                                                  CIP

First Edition: October 1992
10 9 8 7 6 5 4 3 2 1

Contents

◆

Acknowledgments

Several remarkable athletes opened their lives to my reporting, thereby making this book possible, so I must first acknowledge their courage. Although being written about is flattering at the outset, in the long haul, it is work. I believe that Julie Wilson, Kirsten Hanssen, Jan Ripple, and the many others who spoke to me so candidly and so often did so because they felt that a chronicle of their experiences, from the glorious to the grim, could be useful to others who might seek a career in athletics. I cannot speak for them, of course, but this is my belief. I thank them for the many courtesies they, their families, and friends showed me during my three years work on this book.

I also wish to recognize the contributions of Laurie Samuelson, Colleen Cannon, Luanne Park, Terry Schneider, Erin Baker, Beth Mitchell, Paula Johnson, Julie Moss, and Karen Smyers. All are fine athletes (and books in themselves) and each lent precious insight into top-level triathlon.

Many outstanding male triathletes also gave generously of their time and knowledge. In particular, I would like to recognize the influence of Dave Scott and thank him again for his patience and work on my behalf.

Several experts helped me through difficult areas of research: Dr. Maria Root of the University of Washington; Dr. Pam Douglas of Harvard Medical School; Dr. Bob Laird, Medical Director for the Hawaiian Ironman; Lew Kidder, publisher of *Triathlon Today*; Rob Newby-Fraser; Jane Gindin; Dr. Rosemary Agostini; Dr. Robert Voy, former Chief Medical Officer of the United States Olympic Committee; and Dr. Mary O'Toole of the University of Tennessee.

In the trade, Sharon Carson has my enduring thanks for reading the first pages and not laughing. Philip Turner also greatly encouraged me in the early going. I thank my agent, John Ware, who helped me shape a decent book proposal, and Michael Sagalyn, for buying the book. My most recent editor, David Sobel, nudged me onto the high road during the final edit and Eric Wybenga gave courteous and professional help throughout.

My father Chet Cook, my sister Sue, and my friend Kevin were always there to listen, as were Richard Miller, Katie Weiss, Bob Cumbow, Dee Oliver, Bev, Wally, Jenny, Susie, and Rebecca. My daughter Cameron made the book better just by being herself, but especially by sharing her abundant, kinetic joy. And certainly, had it not been for the love, insight, and support of my wife, Jan Salisbury, this book would never have been dared, let alone completed.

The Triathletes

PROLOGUE

◆

*T*his is the true story of a small group of professional female triathletes. The book primarily covers the 1989 triathlon season, a period of approximately ten months. The story ends at the 1989 Hawaiian Ironman Triathlon, the eleventh running of the world's toughest and most fiercely contested endurance event: 140 miles of swimming, cycling, and running done back-to-back-to-back.

The women I encountered at the top of long-distance triathlon were routinely lean, broad-shouldered, and exceptionally strong. More often than not, their bodies bore scars from past bike crashes. They were highly competitive, and self-disciplined; most were well schooled in scientific training techniques. They had firm handshakes and the kind of agility that people notice. They were certainly not exemplars of the "round of body, gentle of mind" female archetype of yore, but, on the other end of the spectrum, had taken the contemporary model of feminine fitness to the extreme.

Despite living far outside the "traditional" feminine mainstream, the women of this book personify a virtue long believed to characterize the female sex: the ability to persevere.

That women are better constituted than men to endure hardship and pain is a belief that goes far back in history. Is this merely a stereotype that has contributed to centuries of female subordination, or is there some truth to it? Since assembling circuit boards and typing memos from dawn till dusk are not "natural" activities, scientists have looked elsewhere for clues to female durability. Because only women give birth to children and because doing so involves a great deal of pain, scientists recently decided to test a hypothesis every midwife knows to be true: Women are better equipped to withstand pain than men. They found that women, as a group, have a higher tolerance of pain than do men. That is to say, given the same aversive physical stimuli and the same ranking scale, women tend to rate their level of discomfort lower than will men.

Women seem better able than men to withstand psychic distress as well. All things being equal, women secrete less epinephrine (a kind of adrenaline) under stress than men. One test of this involved measuring epinephrine levels of both men and women after groups of each were subjected to repeated attempts to draw blood. The results suggested that women were more likely than men to say to themselves, "Hang in there, you can take it."

Despite mounting scientific evidence to the contrary, the world of athletics has long denied the physical and psychological durability of women. Time and again, sports officials—not all of them men—have refused to acknowledge that women can withstand the prolonged stresses involved in endurance competition. Although women had been running marathons previously for decades without widespread calamity, it was not until 1984 that women were allowed to run the 26.2 mile distance in the Olympics. Some would blame a handful of far away, sexist patriarchies for what now seems an obvious injustice. However, even in the United States, a belief in female frailty has only recently begun to give way. Until 1958, the longest track and field event open to women was the 440 yard dash. Even as late as 1967, the prestigious Boston Marathon was officially closed to women. That was the year Kathy

Switzer entered as 'K. Switzer' and ran the distance incognito. In that same year, the official world's marathon record for women was three hours and seventeen minutes. Less than twenty years later, women are running the marathon nearly *an hour faster.*

Even in sports where women have distinct physiological advantages over men, bans against female participation have persisted. For example, in open-water swimming, a woman's extra layer of subcutaneous fat can provide vital insulation and helpful buoyancy. Partially because of this (but mainly because she is an outstanding swimmer) Penny Dean of California has held the record for swimming the English Channel (twenty-one miles not counting the effects of currents) since 1978. No man (of any size) has ever done it faster.

Ironically, the longest swimming race open to women in the 1988 Olympics was 400 meters. Four months prior to these Games, Janet Evans, with no visible fat on her body, swam 1500 meters freestyle in a time that would have won every men's Olympic 1500 meter freestyle race up to 1972.

If women had the kind of coaching, encouragement, and financial support that sports officials, the public, and sponsors so willingly lavish on men, would the best women endurance athletes beat the best men? It's an interesting question, but not one this book seeks to answer. It is intrinsically demeaning to women to require them to better or equal male performances in order for their achievements to have value. That Ann Trason beat the former record holder (male) by four miles in the 1989 National TAC/USA twenty-four-hour foot race does not make her accomplishment any greater. But it does make it newsworthy. How did she do it? people ask. A popular answer going around at the time was that women are better than men at converting fat stores to muscle energy. And, the argument continued, since women carry larger stores of fat than do men, Trason—a woman—would have a natural advantage in a race of exceptionally long duration. But all experiments testing this "natural fat-burner" hypothesis have so far not shown women to be any more efficient at or prone to burning fat (over carbohydrates, if available—and they were in this race) than were men.

If endurance is nature's special gift to women, the powers behind traditional organized athletics have done little to provide a proper showcase.

Triathlon, however, is not a traditional sport. Unlike endurance running, cycling, and virtually all the ball sports, triathlon has never been closed to women. Since its inception in the late 1970s, triathlons of every distance have been open to and, for the most part, encouraging of women. And the effects have been breathtaking. For example, top female finishers in Ironman distance triathlons are running the closing marathon fifteen minutes faster than the records set for the women's marathon in the late 1960s—yet the triathletes are doing it immediately after they've swum two and a half miles and cycled a hundred and twelve.

Though the focus of this book is female triathlon, it is interesting to note the opportunities for male/female comparison that this sport offers. From the beginning of triathlon, women have competed alongside men over the same courses at the same time, under the same conditions, and subject to the same rules. Nonetheless, by sticking to the personal stories of four women, the book is able to move beyond hearsay, myth, and scientific tidbits to deal thoroughly with the question "Just what is endurance and how well are women equipped to pursue it as an occupation?"

The three years I spent researching and writing this book yielded many surprises. An amateur triathlete myself, I was not a complete novice to the sport, but as I spent time around the women of this book—watched them race, trained with them, listened to them talk—I realized how little I actually knew about endurance training, and even about professional competition. Most of these women knew more about nutrition, biomechanics, weight training, cardiovascular conditioning, muscle chemistry, racing strategy, and the equipment involved in three sports than most kinesiology graduates. Certainly they knew far more than I had picked up in three years as an amateur triathlete and ten years as an amateur runner with four marathons and dozens of lesser races under my aging feet. Ironically, however, none of these women had benefit of anything near the level of technical, emotional, and financial support routinely provided every second-string player in the PAC-10 college football conference.

I was also surprised by how little they knew about—or communicated with—one another. There was no "sorority of struggle," no "sisters in pain" high-fiving their way through murderous workouts. Instead, I encountered fierce competitors who lived and trained in relative isolation. If they spent time in each other's company, it was almost always at races, where prerace conversations were brief and guarded and where postrace talk was preempted by the pressing need each felt to return home and prepare for the next encounter. I found deep reservoirs of mutual respect among the top professional women, but few close friendships.

Finally, the business side of sports was new to me. When I began my research I, like most Americans, suffered from the romantic delusion that how far one goes in sports depends totally on one's own natural abilities and the strength of one's desire. I found there's a lot more to it than that.

How and why, out of fifty or so women who raced triathlons professionally in 1989, did I select just four on whom to focus the book? My criteria had as much to do with drama and continuity as anything. Of the fifteen hundred triathlons held in the United States in 1989, only one race had the feeling of a final, all-important championship, and that was the Hawaiian Ironman. The women I chose had each decided at the beginning of the season that the Ironman would be her most important race. And each had a credible chance of winning it. After this, I looked for women whose competitive paths met often enough during the season prior to the Ironman that their relative strengths and weaknesses could be compared. From there, I looked for qualities vital to the contemporary, professional athlete—natural ability, discipline, competitiveness, fair play, and business savvy.

And I looked for opposites: the champion versus the underdog; the rising star versus the falling star; the proponent of multiple, over-distance workouts versus the believer in reduced mileage and speed work; the woman who lived with her children and husband versus the single woman living alone; the hedonist (if there is such a thing in endurance athletics) versus the ascetic; the optimist versus the cynic; the well-sponsored versus the self-sponsored. Finally there was the matter of proximity and access.

By far the biggest problem I had while working on this book was maintaining emotional distance from my subjects. I felt from the beginning an immediate and perhaps unhealthy empathy for each of the main characters. I cared for and rooted for them all and was thus constantly torn because I knew only one of them, if any, could win the Ironman. To compensate, I struggled to present each character in a neutral but frank and honest light and to keep her story untainted by my approval or disapproval. I wanted to tell their stories, not my own. To the extent that I did this too well, the book may be faulted as lacking a point of view. I wanted the book to be a portrait, not an argument. But when the book recounts behavior that seemed to me clearly self-destructive or unfair to others, I hope my perspective is clear.

Lastly, I must admit that as a fortyish, long-married man, and father as well, I was often embarrassed when people asked me what I was writing about. I would frequently answer that I was writing about a bunch of young, beautiful women who raced long and hard under the hot sun, nearly naked. Hearing this, people would quickly glance at my balding head and laugh; and I would be relieved, feeling somehow exonerated.

If I had to give a serious answer, I'd say I deeply admired these women—was awed by them in fact—and felt compelled to tell others what I saw while pursuing the fittest women on earth.

CHAPTER 1.

IRONMAN EVE

◆

*T*he Olympic Marathon, Le Tour de France, The English Channel Swim—each has been called the ultimate test of athletic endurance. In the hyperinflated 1980s, that test was the Hawaiian Ironman Triathlon.

The Ironman race was conceived and first organized by John Collins, then a commander in the U.S. Navy living on Oahu, Hawaii. During visits to the San Diego area in the mid-1970s, Collins had seen a number of swim-bike-run races called triathlons. Though very new, triathlon had acquired a reputation as the latest challenge for jaded marathoners and competitive swimmers. It occurred to Collins that a swim-bike-run triathlon of heroic proportions might settle a long-running debate over which athlete—the swimmer, the cyclist, or the runner—was the fittest.

The distances and location of the first Ironman fell together quickly in Collins's mind in January of 1977: The race would combine the distances and the routes, more or less, of the best known endurance contests in Hawaii—the 2.4 mile Waikiki Rough Water swim, the annual bike race around Oahu of approximately 112 miles, and the 26.2 mile Honolulu Marathon run.

The first Ironman race, in which the winner would receive a home-soldered statue made of nuts and bolts, took place on February 18, 1978. Eleven men, including Collins, started the race and eleven finished. The winner was Gordon Haller. His time: eleven hours and forty-six minutes. No women raced that first year.

Collins's preposterous dare grew quickly into an annual athletic Woodstock for endurance enthusiasts worldwide. To accommodate the burgeoning number of contestants, spectators who came to see them, and friends who came to support them, the Ironman venue was moved in 1981 from Oahu to the Big Island of Hawaii. The format remained unchanged: 2.4 mile swim, 112 mile bike, 26.2 mile run—in that order. The one-wave swim start, in which all contestants take off together, was also retained. Consequently, as the number of competitors swelled to more than a thousand, the start in Kailua Bay became a water-borne stampede—more like the running of the bulls in Pamplona than the stately departure of a big-city marathon.

Since the number of would-be iron men and women was soon significantly larger than the number who could be marshaled, watered, and treated in the medical tents on race day, a system of qualifying events was cobbled together from "lesser" triathlons held primarily in the United States, Australia, Germany, Japan, France, and Great Britain. An athlete could qualify for the Ironman by placing in the top three at one of these races or, alternatively, by placing highly in his or her sex and age group. Starting in 1988, a lottery was used to award a small number of entry slots. Top finishers in the previous year's Ironman were automatically qualified.

There were eleven age groups recognized at the Ironman, starting with 18–24, and ending with 70 +. There were two divisions—men and women. In 1989, 1,275 of the estimated 1.2 million triathletes worldwide were invited to race in the October 14 Ironman.

Over the years, the Ironman evolved into three races inside the larger whole. First was the race to finish. Hundreds of competitors had only one goal—cover the distance before the midnight cutoff, seventeen hours after the start. They weren't trying to beat anybody, just their own limits. No one who trained seriously for the Ironman ever underestimated the difficulty of covering the distance.

A second race developed among amateurs vying for a top finish against competitors of the same sex and age. Although no prize money was awarded for age-group victories, competition within the age-groupers was tough across the board, and was particularly fierce among the young. In 1989, after ten hours of racing, only three minutes separated first place from third among the 25–29-year-old women; the top three men of that age group finished within twenty-three seconds of each other.

The main event, of course, was the race to win.

Those who aspired to win the Ironman in 1989 were not weekend athletes who trained for the race on a beer bet. Neither were they world-class marathoners or cyclists who'd taken the summer to learn to swim; nor were they ex-channel swimmers who'd grown tired of the grease. The best triathletes, men and women of extraordinary ability and discipline, trained year-round in all three sports and raced in upward of twenty triathlons over eight months. The Ironman was the richest race and it came at the end of the season.

First-time observers at the Ironman often said before the race that they wondered how it could be done at all. After seeing it, they wondered how it could be raced so fast. Most of all, they were surprised by the women. They'd never seen women so lean, so strong, so tough—and so competitive. And they didn't know what to make of it.

The first woman to enter the race was Lyn Lamaire. She finished the 1979 race in twelve hours and fifty-five minutes. In 1988, Paula Newby-Fraser went nearly four hours faster, winning the women's division in nine hours and fifty-five seconds and placing eleventh overall in a field of 1,200. The next fifty women across the line *all* finished faster than the male victor of the first Ironman.

October 13, 1989. Kailua-Kona, Hawaii

The athletes began arriving at the seawall behind the King Kamehameha Hotel just after dawn, intending to swim in Kailua Bay as they'd done all week. But on this day, the day before the race, they weren't coming to train—it was too late for that. They'd come instead to relax, and find confidence in their preparation.

Clumps of spectators began to form along the seawall as the male and female athletes stripped off their warm-ups and set them in tidy piles on the Kailua pier. They were all muscular and lean, richly tanned, and youthful in appearance, though some were pushing seventy (away).

A few paused to pose and stretch in the waking sun, but most walked quickly to the stone stairway in the seawall, then stepped gingerly down to the chocolate beach. After donning caps and goggles, they slipped into the turquoise shallows and began to swim out into the blue Pacific with a powerful, rolling freestyle.

The swimming ceased by midday, when most of the athletes were in their rented rooms making final repairs and adjustments to their bikes. Though the race would not start until seven the next morning, all bikes had to be relinquished to race officials later that afternoon—1,275 bikes take a while to rack. As the athletes prepared, the crowd of fans grew larger in anticipation of their return to the bike racks on the pier.

By three in the afternoon, several hundred fans had gathered at the seawall and several hundred more bled down the avenues to where the shore drive met the pier. Many fans wore shorts and caps of the latest colors—neon pink and fluorescent lime—colors that made the heat of the day, which was considerable, only hotter. The tropical air was heavy with humidity. For the relief of shade, many crowded under the big banyan tree, loud with squawking birds, that grew up from the asphalt next to the hotel.

Above and beside the crowded street, workers hurried to erect the announcer's tower, the photography bleachers, the medical tent. Dozens of fat, black electrical cords lay across the road from the hotel to the finish area under the tower. There weren't many kids around, just a few infants in sun bonnets that read "Iron Baby."

Around 4:20 P.M., someone yelled, "It's Scott," and the crowd compressed.

Six-time winner Dave Scott appears in the crowd like a hologram, pushing a light bike and an aura. The crowd parts in his path, and fills in behind. He releases his bike to race officials and appears to levitate to the banyan tree for shade and autographs. A dapple of sun splashes across his face. His eyes are swimming-pool blue and his face is serene, despite the jostling of the crowd and the live possibility that someone will step on his uncommon feet.

Other top men arrive: Mark Allen ... Greg Welch ... Kenny Glah ... Wolfgang Dittrich ... Scott Tinley. They continue to stride through the crowd, pushing their bicycles with bony fingers curled around their handlebar stems. Muscles and tendons pop up from their forearms. Their postures are perfect. Most wear caps or visors with stiff bills that shade their faces down to their sun-baked lips. Their bodies are brown; all the top men are tan Caucasians with the weathered skin of surfers. Their legs have been shaved smooth to enhance their feel for the water and to make scrapes easier to manage. From neck to ankle they are lavish in muscles, not bulging with the cartoon balloons of power-lifters, but sheathed with the elongated ovoids of anatomy texts. They all wear running shoes with spongy tongues; their laces are not tied in bows but lie pinched off inside tiny plastic barrels.

Of the top women, Kirsten Hanssen arrives first, still mounted on her bike. Hanssen is of Scandinavian descent, fine and fair, a waif so lean that one can see her muscles move her bones. Her triangular back is a collage of moving plates covered with gold skin drawn tight as stretched rubber. On the bike she seems anything but frail; she's all over it like a spider on a web of steel, her limbs not much bigger than the frame tubes. The machine seems a piece of her, her legs coupling to the crank arms like connecting rods to drive wheels.

Deftly, she clicks her right shoe from the pedal cleat and stands propped to the right, her bike heeled over. She is approached immediately by fans who adore her and wish her good luck and ask her to sign their shirts, programs, even water bottles. The twang in Kirsten's soprano is pure Kansas charm as she says, "Why sure I will. Thank yew. Thank yew *so* much." Still strapped to her head is a blue, teardrop-shaped helmet. The big end curves around her forehead and tapers back to a point at the base of her neck. The damp hair curling out below her ears suggests that she's been out riding—hard. Down the lens of her sunglasses, a band of rainbow-colored polycarbonate, lays a wide ridge of sweat.

The crowd knows Kirsten as a sprint-distance champion who attempted the Ironman for the first time the previous year; she finished third wearing a cast on her left forearm—the same one she wore on the swim. As she reaches out for the programs, small rips widen under the right arm seam of her blue, sleeveless racing suit. Loose stitching shows around her sponsor's logo—TIMEX—evoking the tag line: ("Takes a licking and keeps on ticking"). Kirsten removes her helmet and sunglasses, then writes variations of "Praise the Lord" and "God Bless You" with her autograph.

As Kirsten approaches the check-in gate, cheers and clapping erupt all around, but the fans are looking past her. She smiles gamely, glances over her shoulder, and sees the reigning champion, Paula Newby-Fraser, pushing a small-wheeled bike. Mounted behind her on a motorbike, Murphy Reinschreiber, her agent and manager, covers her back.

Paula glows, walks slowly, laughs freely, and tucks her lower lip under her grin. She thrusts her palm up and waves to each side. Her underarms are bare and a rusty scab lays thick and cracking over her right elbow. She has wide, dark eyebrows and thick, dark-chocolate hair, layered on the sides and brushed back to a shoulderlength mane that falls from a cord knotted tight at the base of her skull. Her dark pigmentation stands in noteworthy contrast to the largely fair-haired athletes who dominate the scene. Where Kirsten's teeth are broad and white as a vicar's collar, Paula's are narrow and shorter, but her smile is equally wide and warm. Her oval face is led by a slightly reddish nose that rounds down at the tip; her ears tip slightly forward. She has a gentle earthiness to her and, for a world-class athlete, she is unimposing in stature. None of the other women have bothered much with jewelry, but Paula is well accessorized. Her nails are long, silver, and end in definite points that say, "Don't crowd me." Following a recent fad of the Southern California beach culture, Paula's wrists are circled by friendship bracelets made of knotted embroidery thread. Rings are scattered over several fingers. Hoops and gold studs glint from her left earlobe, four altogether. Four more are pegged to her right ear, including a dangling gold ankh, the Egyptian sign of life. A small jade Buddha swings over her freckled chest; it hangs just above her sponsor's name—Aerodynamics—which shows prominently in white on her U-neck, magenta skin suit.

"I'm a firm believah in pyramid powah," she said. "Me mum made the one under me bed." To Americans unfamiliar with the South African accent, she sounds British, slightly cockney. Her phrasing is precise, but her comments are vintage, new-age California.

As Paula works the crowd, it's tempting to conclude that her accoutrements—jewelry, nails, ankh, Buddha—are part of the show. Murphy, a quick, fast-talking man in smokey horn-rimmed sunglasses, agrees, saying, "Yeah, she likes those things. But I suppose if you took them all away from her, she wouldn't be too upset."

Surrounded by the reverent throng, Newby-Fraser is regally graceful, pleasant as tea on a tray, a levelheaded young woman who, she says, "started running only a short time ago simply to lose weight, and anyone can do it." Those who saw her win the Ironman in 1988, however, remember something else: a salt-dripping, wind-sucking metabolic furnace—an aerobic miracle unfolding by hours.

Paula gives her bike to the handlers at the checkpoint where she is joined by her triathlete boyfriend, Paul Huddle. Together they work the crowd to the seawall, descend to the beach, and strip to their suits. Murphy, Paul's agent too, takes their sheddings. The couple hold hands, wave good-bye, then plunge into the Pacific side-by-side for a leisurely swim down the coast.

Jan Ripple, a crowd favorite, is conspicuously absent from the procession of top women. She sent her bike to the pier in the care of her husband, Steve, and remains holed up in her condo, ducking reporters.

Lying on her bed, dressed in a pink muscle blouse and shorts, Jan reads through letters of encouragement from her children's classmates while a bedside boom box fills the room with gospel music. Ripple is compact, strong, and vital, the sort of woman who might spend her day swinging a hammer or climbing utility poles. Her sleeveless top accents the strong cut of her shoulders and the steep arch of her biceps. The other women pros ask for small or medium race shirts, but Ripple always checks the box marked "XL."

Dark blue shadowing deepens her already-large eyes. Her hair is blond and fluffy; it falls to just above her large shoulders. In contrast, her face is small and finely featured. Her legs are littered with patches of scar tissue from bicycle spills, translucent skin that shines like wax paper inlay on her leathery knees and wide, brown shins. Her calves are the size of junior footballs. Blue veins web up the backside of her forearms. As she sings along to the music, her voice is southern: lilting, but strong and a bit ragged, like a blues singer's scorched by bourbon.

Other professional triathletes often refer to Ripple as the oldest "girl" on the circuit, as if a thirty-four-year-old mother of three can be called a girl. Everything about her speaks of two people expressed through one athlete's body. She's half southern belle, half wrecking ball—a unique and magnificent combination.

Jan is happy to be alone. The media barrage through the

week had made her nervous. "ABC wants a comeback," she sighs. "They're pressing me."

Reporters like Jan Ripple. They understand her, she's a good story: "After two valiant, but failed attempts to win the toughest race in the world, Jan Ripple—mother of three, daughter of LSU sports legend Bob Meador and wife of former LSU football hero Steve Ripple—returns to Hawaii in the best shape of her life determined to break Paula Newby-Fraser."

Back on the pier, Julie Wilson guides her bike through the crowd. A few fans point to her race number, knowing that the "27" on the white card below the seat meant she finished twenty-seventh overall last year. (Paula's number is "11"; and Kirsten's, "26.") Apart from the significance of the number, Wilson's just a young woman pushing a bike. There's no teardrop helmet ("It's back in the room"), no skin suit ("Too hot"), no waving to yelling fans ("I'd be embarrassed"), no sponsor's logo across her chest ("Someday"). She lacks the trappings, but not the preparation.

Earlier that day, Wilson cleaned her bike. She soaked the chain in kerosene and did the same to the freewheel and both derailleurs. She tightened nuts and oiled all moving parts. She took her race wheels from a plastic shipping carton, held them by the hubs, and spun them, watching for wobble. Satisfied, she removed the sturdy training wheels from the bike frame and put them safely away. Then she put the race wheels between the forks and tightened the quick-release levers.

She shoved a hundred pounds or so of air in the tires with her hand pump. She'd race at a higher pressure, but, not wanting to risk a premature blowout, would wait until race day to pump up. She adjusted the brakes, checked the tension on the seat-post nut, and wrenched every which way on the handlebars.

Julie took the bike onto the road and ran through the gears. The rear derailleur moved well as she shifted up and down the cluster of gears on the rear axle; the chain hopped smartly and grabbed without a stammer. She shifted onto the big chainring, felt the resistance, and bore down, gripping her aerodynamic handlebars hard. Under Julie's power the bike spun like a gyroscope, quiet and fast; her flat racing spokes cut the thick air like blades. She checked the half-dollar sized computer on her handlebars—rpms, elapsed time, and speed. It all worked. She coasted off the shore drive back into the parking lot. The freewheel clicked like a fishing reel spewing line to a marlin.

Back inside, Julie fastened her race number behind the seat, then changed into bermuda shorts and a snappy T-shirt she'd found at the mall. She told her husband, Jim, that it was time to go. They locked up and headed for the pier.

As Wilson approaches the checkpoint, her expression is poker tight and her face flat except for her squint-pinched cheeks and the sunburnt tip of her nose. She wears no make-up. Her hair is honey-blond, short in front and tied back in a wide braid. Her blue eyes are narrow set and her eyebrows shoot away from the thin bridge of her nose; the combination gives her an unnerving intensity. She's pretty, but she'd blush to hear it. Her fingers are long-boned and big knuckled, better for carpentry than embroidery.

Though she does her best to look placid, she's nervous and worn out from the waiting. She needs a big win or a paying job. She has no endorsement contracts, no money sponsors, no college degree; just Jim, her husband, who ambles a few yards away with a video camera perched on his shoulder. When she finds him in the crowd, her pressed lips echo his earlier assessment of the race. "It's like having a normal job and working a whole year, every day, without getting paid," Jim Wilson had said with little inflection. "Then you're told, 'Come to work on Saturday and if you do a perfect job, you'll get paid for the year. But if you mess up, then you won't get paid and you'll be fired.' Most people can't handle that, can't put themselves on the line that way. It's too much pressure. Everybody has off days—days you don't feel good, days your car blows up or your cat dies or something happens so you can't do your best. In normal jobs, that's okay; it's good enough. But in this sport, it's not good enough. Not for Julie. If she doesn't have a perfect race, she's out."

Julie likes the way Jim put things. "He's so logical," she says. "I get all confused and get upset real easy. But then Jim talks to me and it puts things in perspective. He's always been that way, even when we were kids."

Julie hands her bike forward to an official and watches it go. When she is satisfied, she looks at Jim and jerks her thumb to say, "Let's get out of here."

She walks away relieved, thinking, "Finally we get to race this darn thing."

The crowd began to thin after six, leaving a long line of amateurs chatting toward the check-in gate. Under the banyan tree, a spectator put her hands on her hips and announced to no one in particular, "This isn't a race. It's an illness." And she had a point. But to most of the assembled triathletes, the Ironman was less illness than cure, something done to get well and, without doubt, to satisfy a habit.

CHAPTER 2.

THE GLIMMER

◆

*W*hen Julie Wilson arrived to race the Ironman that October of 1989, she had thirty-seven professional races behind her, including two fourth-place finishes at the Ironman: in 1987 and again in 1988. She'd finished every race she entered, placed first in seven, and had rarely come in out of the top ten. She was a long-course specialist, preferring races that took between four and ten hours to complete.

In a sport sometimes likened to running the top of a picket fence to see who could fall off last, Julie's record drew respect. She'd never been penalized or disqualified for rules violations; she'd never quit from pain, anger, disappointment, or mishap. Whenever she raced, Julie Wilson would go hard and she would finish; of that her opponents were certain.

But finishing, even placing, was not enough for Julie Wilson after she raced the Australian World Cup held in April of 1988. After Australia, she had to win and not just any race would do; it had to be the Ironman.

April, 1988. Surfer's Paradise, Australia

The World Cup of 1988 was a big-money event held on the eastern coast, about an hour and a half by car south of Brisbane. With a prize purse of $234,000, it was the richest race since the triathalon's inception in the mid-'70s. A Japanese construction conglomerate, "The Daikyo Group," had built much of Surfer's Paradise, the host city, including a massive housing development inland, in the Robina district. It surprised no one that the bike course wove past the many FOR SALE signs in Daikyo's Robina. The finish area for the race was the clubhouse parking lot of a golf course built by Daikyo.

The 1988 World Cup was one of the few triathlons, apart from the Hawaiian Ironman, where good prize money went deeper than first place. A third-place finish was worth $10,000, enough for a round-trip ticket to Australia from anywhere in the northern hemisphere, with enough left over to resupply and transport the athlete to the next race. For competitors like Wilson, who raced without cash sponsors or appearance money, the race offered a good chance to break even.

The other draw was the course itself. It was long, hot, and hilly—home for a distance specialist and no place for a sprinter. To most triathletes, a sprint was any race that could be won in two and a half hours or less. For the women, these races were contested at a pace roughly equivalent to a 35-minute 10k run. It wasn't all out, like a 100 yard dash in which all power comes from chemicals stored in the muscles, but it was very fast indeed, and much faster than most entrants to the sport thought possible—even after seeing it done.

The most common triathlon format calls for a 1500 meter swim (.93 mile), followed by a 40 kilometer bike leg (24.8 miles), and ending with a 10 kilometer run (6.2 miles). The clock runs continuously and everyone either starts at once or in staggered bursts of a hundred or so. Such races take approximately a quarter of the time of an Ironman distance event to complete and are the backbone of the sport at the amateur level and are often called USTS (United States Triathlon Series) races or, more wishfully, races of the Olympic distance. Although triathlon is not in the Olympic Games, strong efforts have been made since the mid-1980s to include it, at least as a demonstration sport.

Julie Wilson typically finished USTS distance races somewhere between four and six minutes after the winner. She could stay with the leaders through the swim and bike, but would be passed before the finish by a few good runners. Julie realized during the 1987 season that she wasn't a sprinter. "By the time those races are over," she said, "I'm just getting warmed up." Wilson decided to concentrate instead on long-distance events after placing fourth at the '87 Ironman. "I was the first American woman finisher and I've never felt that good in my life. I can close my eyes today and still see myself running down that hill into Kona."

The Australian World Cup course was about three times the distance of a USTS event and the terrain it covered was as tough as the distance, suiting Wilson's training and temperament perfectly. She came to the race in peak condition—uninjured, strong, and confident.

The swim course in Australia was just shy of two miles. Staged in saltwater, there were currents to sap the undertrained and a stiff chop to harry those who could breathe only to one side. The bike course was eighty miles long. What a touring cyclist would reserve two days to complete, the top triathletes would cover in four hours or less. Julie figured the rolling hills out in the bush would give her a chance to build a needed lead on the good runners.

In this regard, she was thinking mainly of the Puntous Twins, sometimes called the Twinkies. The Puntous Twins were nicknamed not for what they ate, but for coming always as a pair and speaking with fluffy, French-accented giggles. Julie liked the twins: "They're such good sports; funny, too."

Both Patricia and Sylvianne Puntous were contenders on the bike, but on the run they were lethal, Sylvianne in particular, who set the pace for the pair. In the closing miles, they'd come from behind, Sylvianne two strides in front of Patricia, and when they'd pass, their beaten competitor would tumble two places in the rankings. Lean, strong, and long, the Puntous sisters consistently posted the quickest run times in long-course races, or did until Paula Newby-Fraser and Erin Baker approached their potential.

Newby-Fraser had not entered the race in Australia, but Baker had.

Erin Baker came from a large, blue-collar family in Christchurch, New Zealand. Rugged, abrupt, and redheaded, she'd raced triathlons since 1984, mainly in Europe, New Zealand, and Australia. Her record was that of a natural at her peak: In four years, racing all distances, she'd never placed lower than second.

Julie Wilson respected Erin Baker for her athletic ability and she shared Baker's work ethic. But she'd wince when Erin denigrated a competitor or complained about sponsor mistreatment and exploitation of the pro women. Erin bluntly spoke her mind and this annoyed people, particularly Paula Newby-Fraser, against whom Baker once refused to compete because, as Baker put it, "I don't think South Africans should be allowed to race in this sport." Baker quieted on the subject when she was convinced that Newby-Fraser—a child of South African citizens and resident of South Africa from age four through twenty-four—was not technically "from" South Africa because she carried a passport from Zimbabwe, her birth country. Although Erin Baker would likely never hold a job in public relations, her athletic ability was unmatched and a good measure of her cockiness seemed to Julie well-earned. Baker and the Puntous Twins were tough competitors, serious athletes, and fair. Anyone who beat them or even led them for a while had to be one of the best.

Only the best would do well in Australia; the course and conditions would see to that. The three-kilometer swim would take place in a tidal lagoon called the Broadwater, a four-mile U of brackish, lukewarm water opening to the ocean. It ran north-south between the mainland and the spit where the high-rise vacation hotels of Surfer's Paradise faced the northern Tasman Sea.

The triathletes would enter the water from the southern mainland and head north up the Broadwater, against the incoming tide. About twenty-six hundred yards (a mile and a half) from the start, the course took a left to the shore, a half mile away. On the shore was a parking lot where racing bikes waited, racked in race number order. There were three hundred bikes in the racks.

Race day broke cloudy at 6:50 A.M. The light was still dim as Julie stood on the beach waiting for the gun to pop. She looked out over the still, gray water. The pack of competitors—large enough to fill a good sized movie house—was strung along the shore in the shape of a squashed pyramid, forty bodies wide and ten deep in the middle. They would start simultaneously, all rushing, hurdling, then diving into the water at once.

Julie staked out a position in the middle of the front row, three strides from the water.

Every fast swimmer wanted to get to the water first, not just to avoid the wicked thrashing of the pack, but also to control a line of calm water. Nothing was faster than deep, still water, nothing except water directly behind a faster swimmer, which was good work if you could get it. The front row was the domain of ham-shouldered swimming specialists and the true contenders. The front row also drew packs of posturing young men reveling in their physical being. They talked of being "awesome" in the water and riding "radical" bikes. Although these "way cool killer dudes" would, like everyone else, be spread over miles of rolling hills after the first two hours, they still presented a competitive obstacle in the early stages. They could be particularly troublesome to the women pros who stood, on average, five inches shorter and forty to fifty pounds lighter.

Julie Wilson wasn't intimidated. She drew herself up to her full height and, to make herself bigger still, put her hands on her hips. She expected trouble in the closing moments before the gun and she got it. "Guys were just *pushing* me around . . .

and they were really tall." The skirmish became more intense as the last seconds were counted down and Julie was blocked. She didn't say anything, but she knew what to do.

When the gun fired, the big guys burst away from the pack, taking long, hurdling strides into the water. Julie hung on their backs like a fullback going up the middle behind an offensive line. "I ran down behind and when they hit the water, I grabbed both those guys' wet suits at the shoulder and"—Julie grimaced, growled, and threw her clenched fists out to the sides—"I shoved them apart and jetted up the middle. When I hit the water, I was flying."

Julie went with the leaders under the Southport Bridge. She heard someone's head thunk against a concrete piling. Beyond the bridge she established her line to the far buoy. She concentrated on holding a pace she could only feel, not calculate, for there were no mile markers and no time to look at a watch. Her pace was fast enough to exit the water in sight of the leaders, but not so fast as to tire her too soon into the six hours of biking and running to come. The rolling glide of her freestyle stroke propelled her at the rate of one hundred yards every minute and twenty seconds. An excellent adult swimmer at the community pool can do a few hundred yards at this pace. Julie and the top pros would hold a 1:20 pace or better for thirty-five hundred yards.

The tidal current stiffened toward the middle of the Broadwater, where the South Pacific tide flowed deepest. Competitors who'd blundered into the teeth of it slapped forward at a diminishing rate, the weaker ones resembling wind-up bath toys stroking ever more slowly against the tub wall. Sighted from shore, some were moving backward. Race attendants in kayaks herded clumps away from the currents while lifeboats fished others out. Once a shoulder to shoulder mob on shore, the pack was now shaped like an arrow pulled from both ends. The leaders stretched the point while the main shaft lengthened and the stragglers fell farther behind.

Thirty-five minutes and twenty-six hundred yards into the swim, Julie slapped along in a kind of trance. She was highly aware of a select group of inputs—her breathing, her stroke, and the ache in her shoulders as she caught the water with her plunging hands and swept it back under her flat stomach. She exhaled hard, blowing holes in the chop, then relaxed her throat and let the air rush in before turning her head back down.

The natural sorting by ability had once again superseded the explosive disorder of the start and put Julie near the swiftest women of the day: the Puntous Twins. Julie saw them under-water, the yellow side panels of their matching wet suits gleaming in the gray turbulence.

Julie had not seen Erin Baker since the beach. But that meant nothing. She might be two hundred meters ahead or drafting on Julie's toes. Short of turning around, there was no way to find out until they were all on bikes.

Suddenly, the flashing Puntous Twins were gone. Sylvianne had surged and pulled out beyond Julie's sight while Patricia had drifted back. Julie rounded the northernmost buoy and looked up to establish her line to the balloon archway that marked the swim finish some five hundred meters distant. She had seven minutes left in the water and she began thinking again, reviewing her race plan: basically, to ride as hard as she could for four hours.

Sylvianne Puntous was jamming her numb feet into her bike shoes when Julie rose from the water and ran up the indoor-outdoor carpeting that had been laid on the beach as an exit ramp. Julie's arm, chest, and back muscles—her deltoids and lats particularly—were gorged with blood from their long ex-ertion, giving her the shape of a running heart. She ran stiffly to her transition bag that hung in the pro racks next to her bike. Sylvianne rode out of the transition area as Julie sat down to pull a race jersey over her one-piece swimsuit. Julie's race number was secured to her jersey by stitches that ran com-pletely around the perimeter of the six-by-ten-inch emblem. "I took needle and thread with." (Wilson usually omits the *me* after *with*.) "I don't like my numbers to flop around." She was the only competitor to have sewn on her race number.

Wilson mopped her feet and pushed them, sockless, into her white cycling shoes. They were the cleated kind made to lock directly onto the pedal posts. She slid on her eyeshield (it was red, chosen to increase road definition in cloudy weather), strapped down her white Styrofoam helmet, grabbed her bike by its white saddle and silver stem, lifted the contraption out of the blocks, straddled it, locked onto the right pedal post with a popping sound, cranked around the chainring a couple times, popped onto the left pedal post . . . and was gone. Her transition from water creature to road warrior had taken less than two minutes.

Julie didn't bother with cycling gloves. "They're too hot," she said, and they take too much time to put on," she reasoned. But most long-distance triathletes do wear them, not just for the cushioning but for the protection they provide in a fall. When rider and bike part company at speed, the cyclist's first reaction is to reach out to "catch" the fall. Consequently, the most common biking injuries, apart from road rash or, more colorfully, "street pizzas," are skinned palms and broken wrists.

Julie was familiar with falling. She'd come off her bike three weeks earlier on St. Croix but had been lucky to get away with only scrapes. "I decided at the beginning of the season that I could either keep racing conservatively—and place in the bottom of the top ten—or take more risks. I decided to test the edge and race as aggressively as I could."

Her decision was having the desired effect. Julie passed Sylvianne within five miles and took the lead. Racing under the palms down the spit of land, she crouched forward, making herself small to the onrushing air. She rested her elbows on the crossbar pads, lay her forearms up the U-shaped tube that jutted out over her front wheel, and curled her hands around the end.

Julie passed the resorts by the sea and licked through residential Robina, taking turns at speed, laying the bike over, her weight on the outside pedal, her inside knee aimed at the apex.

Minutes later, she sped through the bush. Horse pastures lined with split-rail fences and eucalyptus trees came and went;

then came hills like waves, close and repeating. Riding the hills well took concentration and a large measure of guts. "You had to be able to look at those hills and *know* that on *this* hill you're lookin' at a forty-two-tooth front gear and a fifteen-tooth back. All I could think of at the top was, shift onto that big ring as soon as you can." Coming off the flats, she lunged uphill, spinning her last big gear hard before dropping fast into the lower ranges. Working the steeper grades, she stood out of the saddle, shoving down on the pedals while pulling up on the bars. Downhill she spun 80, 90, 100, 110 revolutions per minute in her big gears until she bounced on the saddle, then she drew her knees tight to the top tube and stretched out farther on the aerobars ... 30, 35, 40, 45 miles per hour. "I like hills," she said, "they separate the weenies from the buns."

The roadway was rough, with a pebbly surface that served to vibrate and, sometimes, punch the riders. The shaking came principally up the front forks—which held the front wheel by the hubs—then passed through Julie's hands and forearms and into her neck and shoulders. Her sunglasses bounced on her nose. Thirty-five miles out, Julie was building her lead. She knew Erin Baker was behind her—spectators with radios had told her that—but she didn't know exactly how far. This was thrilling and terrifying both. Erin was a fearless cyclist, well schooled in the highly technical courses in Europe. What's more, Erin could run. Julie knew Erin could finish the swim three minutes behind, lose ten more on the bike, and still pass her before the finish of the 18.6 mile run. Baker was that strong, good enough to be considered a contender for New Zealand's Olympic marathon team. "Oy simplee wunt ta bee the beast," she'd say. Baker was dubbed "the animal" by the leading triathlon publication—a backhanded compliment and a sign that the triathlon community was not quite prepared to accept such an aggressive champion.

About halfway into the eighty-mile course, Wilson was alone and riding hard to the crest of a long grade. As the gritty pavement began to level under her wheels, she settled back down into the saddle and spun out of her small chainring as fast as she could, anxious to get onto the big forward gear, the fifty-three-tooth ring. Without looking, she reached down with her left hand and pushed the shift lever down hard with her thumb. The front derailleur shoved the chain off the small chainring and toward the large. The chain was halfway across the gap when Julie's front wheel hit something—a stone, a stick. Her bike hopped and came down hard. Instead of grabbing the teeth of the large chainring, the chain flew over the big ring altogether and looped around Julie's spinning right foot. She was thrown to the road at twenty-five miles per hour.

As she hit, Julie kept her head and hands high and she landed hard on her right forearm, then slid. Small pieces of gravel dug to the bone in her elbow; then her right hip landed and the rushing pavement scraped off about twenty square inches of flesh. When it was over, she noticed a bloody gash from her right knee to her ankle but had no idea how it happened. Adrenaline kept her out of shock. She sat up and at first felt no pain. Then she remembered where she was. Oh, God, she thought, we've spent $3,000 to get here. I can't quit!

Julie saw her bike and limped to where it had stopped bouncing. The machine appeared considerably better off than she, except that the rear derailleur was bent inward toward the frame—a serious problem on a course that required frequent shifting. She grabbed it with bare fingers and bent it back into position as best she could.

Julie remounted and headed for the finish, forty miles away. The bike worked well except for the rear derailleur, which hopped a few teeth each time she changed gears. Twice she pulled to the shoulder and wrenched on the derailleur. It was during her second stop that Erin went by.

Julie gave chase. Anger fueled her pursuit as much as her fear of facing bills with no money. Endorphins dulled her pain somewhat, but soon her elbow began to ache from the swelling. From time to time she sprayed water on her road burns to wash away the stinging salt of her sweat. She rode hard and caught Erin. For a while, they rode side-by-side but twenty miles from the bike-to-run transition, Baker surged and Wilson had to let her go.

Wilson rolled into the area three minutes behind Baker.

Every triathlete dreads the transition from biking to running because it is so painful. On the bike, back muscles stretch and hip flexors—the muscles that lift the legs toward the chest—tighten. The quadriceps and gluteus muscles provide the bulk of the cyclist's locomotive power.

Within two minutes or less, all that is changed. Underused stomach muscles and overused back muscles must suddenly work in tandem to hold the body erect so that it can run. The heart must suddenly work harder to pump blood higher to the head. Hamstrings and calf muscles—virtually unused on the swim and only secondary power sources on the bike—must be fueled with glucose and brought on line. The body resists this changeover with pain, gasping, and a deadness in the legs. Gradually, over the first mile or two, the legs stretch out, the heart and lungs catch up and the athlete is presented with the new demands of distance running.

Baker was one of the few who could get off the bike after a tough ride and still run fast, right from the start. True to form, she blew out of the bike racks at six minutes, forty-five seconds per mile—quick enough to drop a Japanese camera crew in the first hundred yards. Her quickness off the bike demoralized anyone close enough to see her run out, head high, arms pumping, her big quads arched and shining on every footfall.

Julie was in too much pain to be demoralized. Besides that, she was still in second place. She'd ridden the bike course only five minutes slower than Baker, and nearly fifteen minutes faster than the Puntous Twins. She had a shot at some good money if only she could hold together.

"My most serious problem was my elbow," she remembers. "I was certain I'd broken it. It ached and swelled and I couldn't bend it. But I run with it pretty much locked anyway, so I could manage. The scrapes on my leg hurt worse than my elbow. The sweat stung so badly. But I just kept squirting them with water I got at the aid stations. I knew I was so fired up with adrenaline that I didn't feel as much pain as I would later."

Blood dripping from her elbow painted a perfect arc from the top of her race number to her hip.

When Julie Wilson ran into the finish area at the golf club and rocked down the finish chute, spectators gasped at the blood trickling down her shin and the rawness of her ripped hip. "I'm okay," she said in a thin voice to the handlers who rushed out to grab her. "But my elbow's pretty bad."

Julie ran the 18.6 miles in just under two and a half hours; only Sylvianne and Patricia Puntous—two of the best runners in the sport—beat her on the run. And Julie finished fourth.

As race officials took Julie to the medical tent, Erin basked under the palmy skies and spoke with characteristic pith. "I don't like to win because someone's fallen or had a puncture. It was unlucky for her. She's a terrific competitor, just the kind of girl I like to race."

Wilson spent the night in the county hospital, collected her $8,000 in winnings, and squirmed through the nineteen-hour flight home.

She thought of herself then as a professional athlete traveling the world, challenging the leaders and holding her own. She'd proven herself a contender and felt she couldn't quit until she'd won a major race. She was so close.

The crash in Australia set the tone for the balance of Wilson's 1988 season. Her cuts and scrapes healed, but lingering tendinitis pain in her right leg slowed her running and prevented her from drinking the glory she'd only tasted in the spring.

That summer she continued to train and race. She won some long-distance events, chiefly in the Northwest, but avoided the short-course circuit. Each week in training, she rode her red, aluminum-framed bike about three hundred miles and swam twelve; the intensity and duration of her workouts accelerated through August and September. Running on the roads was predictably painful, so she relocated her workouts to the pool, where she ran in the water. This provided an aerobic workout without jarring, but it did not provide the confidence needed to withstand the real thing. To compromise, she ran in the water through the week, but did her long runs—her weekly twenty milers—on the track. A cinder track is softer than the road, but then, twenty miles on a regulation track is eighty times around. "I took my radio, my cooler, and Mandy [her cocker spaniel] with. Oh yeah, I grabbed a long stick too. Every fourth time around I scratched a mark in the dirt. That was one mile."

The racing season passed in a long wince, ending, as it always did, with the Ironman in October. Her legs, chiefly her right, did not recover during the season. She knew that further injury was likely if she did the Ironman. The marathon was her most fearful concern because it would involve hours of pain—pain of the kind she was having little success managing in training. Her feet and quads hurt on every foot strike when she ran. She iced, received frequent massage, got new orthotics, and took massive doses of non-steroidal anti-inflammatories, and nothing relieved it.

There were other reasons not to go. Two weeks in Hawaii would be expensive and she had no reason to believe she would place in the money. The options remaining were to either pull out or race with pain. A professional athlete does not, Julie believed, pull out of the biggest event in the sport because something hurts. If you're a professional athlete, something always hurts.

October, 1988. Kailua-Kona, Hawaii

Her race plan was simple—get through the swim, go as hard as possible on the bike, then take stock. If she could run after that, fine. If she couldn't, then she'd get in the car and go back to the condo knowing she'd tried her best. It was a good plan and it worked until Julie got off the bike in third place, behind Paula Newby-Fraser and Erin Baker. Julie jogged to the women's changing tent. The pain was still there, but so was Kirsten Hanssen, behind her somewhere on the bike course. Julie knew Kirsten was racing injured as well, and she knew Kirsten would not quit—certainly not after Newby-Fraser's agent had said of her, "They're going to have to haul her off the course in a basket." Hanssen was racing with a blue cast on her still-fractured left wrist. "It did hamper my feel for the water," Kirsten later acknowledged, "but nobody crowded me either."

Julie's legs felt stiff and sore but she got into her running shoes anyway and headed up the hill to the Queen K highway. Her brain told her to quit around mile four; the pain was increasing and weariness flooded her body. But Kirsten Hanssen was bearing down on her like a manic Barbie doll and there were more like her farther back. How could she come this far and quit? What made good sense back in her bedroom in Seattle made no sense now. Just keep going, she told herself. It wasn't in Julie's character to quit from pain. She remembered her father grimacing from a shoulder injury while he pounded nails into sheetrock. "Come on, Dad, why don't you quit and sit down here on the couch," she asked.

Her father said, "Nah, it'll still hurt when I stop. Might as well keep at it."

Julie kept at it, but still, Hanssen ran by at mile seven. Six others—all of whom would eventually finish in the top ten—came closer every minute, but none of them caught her. Julie finished fourth in a silent triumph of will.

Meanwhile, Newby-Fraser set a new course record of nine hours and one minute. She trounced Erin Baker, embarrassed most of the male professionals, and finished eleventh overall. Newby-Fraser was the Queen of Kona and no one could stop talking about her or what she'd done.

That night, Julie's husband, Jim, took her in his arms and carried her up the steps to their second-floor rental. The evening breeze off the Pacific was calming and the steady crunch of the breakers below took Julie's mind off the aching. Her ordeal was over. Everything was fine again but for the crummy truth that there are no cash bonuses, sponsorship deals, or endorsement contracts for gutsy fourth-place finishers. Not in triathlon anyway. Julie knew this was "only business" and was not a judgment against her, personally. But in her heart, she felt shame, and anger and puzzlement as well. "Dave Scott, Tinley, and them ... after racing at their absolute edge for eight hours ... they can barely lift their feet crossing the finish," she said. "How can Paula have enough left to leap over the finish line and walk around all night? It just doesn't add up."

After the World Cup, Julie believed that if she worked hard enough, her effort would inevitably result in recognition and financial success. After the '88 Ironman, she didn't know what to think. Newby-Fraser's win had upped the ante just when her hand was weakest. She didn't fold, but was determined instead to bring more resources into play.

CHAPTER 3.

PRE-SEASON

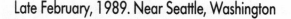

Late February, 1989. Near Seattle, Washington

*I*t was 5:30 A.M. when Julie Wilson reached for her watch on the night table. She lay still and took her pulse: fifty-six beats a minute. Okay, she thought, but a little high. Julie got up, walked into the bathroom, and stood on the scale: 117 pounds. Too heavy, she thought, though by conventional standards, at five-foot-five-inches tall, Wilson was on the medical borderline between "healthy" and "underweight." As an endurance athlete, Wilson did not feel obsessed with leanness as much as rightfully concerned. She wanted to race at 110 pounds; that, she decided, would give her the highest ratio of power to weight. I've got to start eating better, she thought, and she began dressing to run in the rain.

Dressed in synthetic underwear and running shorts, Julie went to the small room off the kitchen which served as living room, family room, TV room, and home for her bike and training stand ("It feels close in here," Julie would say). She stretched out briefly, then got down on all fours and called to her cocker spaniel. "Mandy, come here, girl." Mandy wiggled alongside until Julie said, "Up girl." Mandy jumped onto Julie's back and stood there sheepishly until Julie let her down.

Julie pulled on her rain suit and sat at the table to tie her running shoes. The gray table and chairs, part of a 1950s dinette set handed down from her parents, had tubular chrome legs. Fluffy kapok showed through the clear tape that spanned rips in the plastic seats. Greaseless bike parts and an assortment of paper lay on the table—a set of brakes, a discount bike catalogue, a *Runner's World* magazine, and some correspondence between Jim and a race director ·concerning a triathlon overseas.

The table, the chairs, the orange sofa covered with Mandy's blanket—all of it had been pressed into service when Julie and Jim were married ten years before. For eight years, this one-bedroom basement apartment just south of the airport had been home. All their discretionary income went into Julie's career.

Rain had fallen nearly every day for three months, and every day the clouds seemed closer to the ground. For the first two months, Julie had despised it. But now she saw it as just another of the hardships that would ultimately make her tougher than the others. As she opened the door to the cold, she thought of Paula Newby-Fraser and the sun queens of San Diego; she saw them loping down the blond foothills to the blue Pacific for a morning dip.

"Be a good girl," Julie said to Mandy, then she closed the steel security door behind her and pumped up the steps. Her rain suit swished in the dark as she splashed across the streaming blacktop. She remembered to push her ponytail under her cap. Even in the rain, she had more trouble when her hair swung free—catcalls and cars coming too close mostly—but every so often something more menacing. Every woman runs with fear, and though Julie had never been assaulted, her awareness of danger was acute because her principal training area was where the still-at-large Green River serial killer has left many bodies, one of which Julie saw during a training run as it was hauled out of the river.

Julie deals with her fears with a mixture of caution and gallows humor. She laughs when she tells of the following incident: In 1988, she was running before dawn in thick fog when a car went slowly past and stopped ahead, hidden by the fog. She couldn't see it, but she heard its loud muffler fade, then go silent. Suddenly, a man burst out of the fog, sprinting straight for her. She turned and ran faster than she'd ever run before, straight back to the apartment. She rushed into her bedroom and shook her sleeping husband. "Jim . . . Jim," she yelled, "Wake up. There's a man chasing me down on Military Road."

Jim struggled awake. "Okay, okay," he said, "Go over and run on Pacific Boulevard."

Jim was aware of the risks, but believed Julie could outrun, outsmart, and outfight most guys. Jim joked about making a sign for Julie to hang round her neck. He told her it would say, "Warning: I've got PMS and a bike pump." As her coach and manager, a job he'd taken on four years back, it was one way of telling Julie, "You're tougher than they are." As her husband, Jim raised the idea of buying a cellular phone for her to carry on her bike since she often rode far out into the country, alone. The phone idea died, partly for lack of money, and largely because Julie liked being alone. She didn't want to hear the phone ring in the middle of 40 mph descent.

Jim Wilson knew there was no stopping Julie from training; it was her job, her career, her dream. Jim was Julie's sponsor, coach, and best friend and husband. They first met in elementary school, but took little notice of each other. He was just the quiet son of her sixth-grade teacher, Mrs. Wilson, whom Julie remembers as a resolute disciplinarian and stalwart of the Church of the Nazarene. Mrs. Wilson was not, Jim recalls, warm or nurturing. "My grandma on my mom's side was cold and mechanical in her approach to correct child rearing. Mom tried to be just like her and she succeeded." Jim and his brother Jerry looked elsewhere for warmth, sometimes to their father, but more often to their uncle Harold, who lived next door and worked in the sugar factory like most everyone else in Nyssa, Oregon.

Jim admired Julie from the beginning but began taking longer looks when he was sixteen. He was on the football team and Julie was a cheerleader and, as things happen, they took to meeting after practice. Jim was drawn to Julie's will as much as to her vibrant good looks. She was self-disciplined and virtuous. She went to church. And she made him laugh.

With Jim, Julie felt secure, her fears of the larger world soothed by his matter-of-fact outlook. He was, like her father, a hard worker. Julie sensed that he would do nothing halfway, that he would drive himself to distinction, and, like herself, be modest in success. "He was a moral person and very religious. I knew I couldn't be with anyone who wasn't," Julie recalls. When they could, they drove out in the red stone canyons of the Owyhee river, although neither had much free time.

Julie spent summers at the Nyssa pool where, each day, she swam four hours with the swim team, taught two sets of lessons, and spent four hours lifeguarding. Jim starred in high school sports year-round—football, basketball, baseball. Then there was church, which Jim's mother made sure he visited often. Her plan for Jim was that he would study religion at Northwest Nazarene College and enter the ministry thereafter.

Julie graduated before Jim and entered Northwest Nazarene in the fall of 1974; she studied to be a dental assistant and commuted from home. She did not date and, while working for an oral surgeon, waited through the next year for Jim (two years younger) to finish high school. They married when Jim graduated; Julie was twenty, Jim was eighteen. They moved from Nyssa to an apartment in nearby Nampa, Idaho, home of Northwest Nazarene College. "I was Jim's wife," she recalls "that's all."

Within the year, Jim cracked. "He rejected everything he'd been taught in church," Julie recounts. "He dropped out of his ministry classes. It was like our whole world ended. Jim was my anchor and when he dropped the church, we just drifted. It was the worst year of my life."

While Jim struggled with his soul, Julie lost weight. Perhaps she could get the old Jim back if she was smaller, thinner; she didn't know. Her weight and her diet had always been of paramount concern, but now it just seemed more important than ever to have control.

Gradually, Jim regained his spiritual composure, though not his faith. Julie could live with that. He was still her best friend, and with his regained self-assurance, still her guide. Jim changed his major from seminary to electrical engineering and Julie sought help from a nutritionist.

By the early 1980s, Jim had graduated and accepted a job with Boeing. They moved west and settled into an apartment south of the Seattle airport. Jim worked as computer engineer and Julie went to work again as a dental assistant. She swam when she could and did a little running. They lived an isolated life.

When Julie considered triathlon racing, it was at the suggestion of Linda Edgar, a top-level marathoner who also held the record for the 50 kilometer run (31 miles). Edgar introduced herself to Julie in the pool after noting Julie's smooth freestyle and powerful butterfly. Edgar had been doing triathlons to improve her strength and was spending time in the pool to recover from running injuries. She was a dedicated athlete. When she told Julie that she could do very well in triathlon, Julie was flattered, but skeptical.

Jim was all for it. "Jim kind of pushed me into it," Julie remembers. "He said he had his chance once and blew it. He said that I had my chance now and that if I didn't take it, it would be gone forever." When Jim told her this, she heard his regret as much as his encouragement. Jim had turned down athletic scholarships after high school—as much to marry her as to follow his mother's wishes. Although she did not feel blamed, Julie heard in Jim's voice a yearning to compete again. They were a team and Jim wanted to play. She did, too.

At the time, Julie was scraping teeth for a dentist who enjoyed making Julie the butt of his put-the-patient-at-ease jokes.

Julie quietly endured it, but was too proud to take it for long. She hoped triathlon might be a way out of this demeaning work—a way to achieve distinction through her own efforts. She had a great fear of normalcy, or, as she put it, "of growing up and finding out I'm just like everybody else."

Julie was the last of three children born to Andy (also called Henry) and Thelma Anderson. Like her and Jim, Julie's parents had known one another since early childhood and neither had ever considered marrying anyone else. After Julie was born in 1958, the family moved from New Plymouth, Idaho to Nyssa, a working town whose name was an acronym, some said, for the New York Sheep Shipping Association, a company that owned thousands of grazing sheep in the surrounding area.

Julie's parents expected responsible, moral behavior from their children and they got it. "I was the kid that every parent wanted to have. I didn't drink or smoke and I didn't know anything about drugs. I don't think there were drugs at our high school. Bein' an example to others, that was real important to Mom—bein' someone others could look up to—she's what you'd call a perfectionist."

"Dad's way of doing things," Julie continued, "was to just hurry and get it done. With Mom it was, do it over and over 'til it's perfect. I came out more like my dad. I have to finish things." But Julie was, by Jim's accounting, a combination of both. Whatever she attempted, she had to finish *and* do perfectly. It was not surprising that, as a child, Julie tended toward isolation.

A rigid and perfectionist attitude toward earthly affairs was common among those who lived near the Snake River. Spiritually, Mormonism and conservative offshoots of the Methodist Church dominate the region. The Wilsons belonged to The First Christian Church—a close relative of the Church of the Nazarene. Julie attended services there on Sunday, went to youth group on Wednesday, and sang in the choir. She knew of no other life.

"Julie was a terribly bashful girl when she was young," said

Thelma. "She preferred the company of animals to all but a few children. She had her horse, her dog, and chicks that she'd smuggle home in her shirt from the hatching rooms at the Feed and Seed." A typical afternoon for Julie would include a bike ride out to Cow Hollow, where her horse was stabled. She would go riding, often alone and usually up to Stallion Hill. Other days she'd stay around home with her dog and tend her pigeons.

Julie doesn't remember much about childhood with her two brothers—they were eight and ten years older—except for Jerry's struggle to rehabilitate his right arm after a crippling bout with polio. She watched him work out with weights and thought that the body was a traitorous thing that could, at any moment, turn on its occupant. Best get the most out of it, she thought, while it worked.

One brother married early and left. The other joined the Navy and left. Her brothers gone, her father at work, and her mother busy with sewing or church, Julie was left to find her own diversions.

Lorinda Baker changed everything.

"The first time I saw Julie," Lorinda recalls, "she was ten or eleven. She wasn't on the team, just swimming with her friends, but I thought instantly that someday she'd go to the Olympics. You know how you can just tell? I'm certain she could have made the Olympics. I knew it in my blood."

It was 1969. Lorinda was nineteen and swam for Brigham Young University. Her times in the breast stroke were good enough to take her to the NCAA finals in 1971. Lorinda lived in Ontario but drove the forty miles down to Nyssa to coach the summer swim league.

The swim facility in Nyssa is a cinder-block shower house and a twenty-five-yard outdoor pool that remains covered most of the year. It is the only pool in town. In summer, it's an oasis in a desert of blowing dust and hot sun. In the small park adjacent, a hundred yards from the pool deck, a mothballed Super

Sabre jet soars overhead on an upswept pedestal, inspiring childhood dreams of power and flight.

Julie vividly remembers the day she met Lorinda. "I was just a scrawny little kid then and I practiced with Mel Calhoun's baseball team. Mel was the pool manager and he knew me—well, everybody knew everybody in Nyssa. We played hardball, I pitched ... could knock anybody into home, too. I could do everything any boy could do—and better—but I didn't stay with the team. Before our first game I was so scared about going in front of all those people and parents that I pretended I was sick so I didn't have to go. When I didn't go back to practice the next day, Mel took me to see Lorinda."

Lorinda was in the guard tower when Mel came around the shower house with a downcast little blond girl following behind. Lorinda remembers looking down at Julie from the tower. "I asked her if she'd like to join the swim club and she said, 'No, ma'am. I wouldn't be interested in that.' I looked at her and I told her like a mother, 'Sometimes we're given a talent, Julie. And if we don't use it, we'll regret it very much later on.' Well, Julie left, but what I said must've haunted her. She came back the next day and told me she wanted to swim."

"I didn't want to swim with the club," Julie recalls, "because it involved bein' in front of people and dealin' with people. But Lorinda was so neat; she was like a big sister to me. I thought she was so ... I don't know the word for it. I thought she was IT."

Lorinda felt the same way about Julie. "She conditioned very quickly. We only swam for nine weeks, and by the third week she was in top shape. She had gorgeous shoulders. A beautiful stroke. She had a prowess, like she was fightin' people. When she was standing there on the blocks you could feel the other swimmers giving way."

Because Nyssa was a good day's drive from Oregon's big swim meets, the Nyssa team competed frequently in Idaho and went to the state championships there. Julie won the Idaho State championships several years running in several events, setting records in the freestyle sprints. At 14 years old, Julie

swam the 50 yard freestyle in 27 seconds. At the time the
women's world record for the 50 free was less than 4 seconds
faster.

Julie remembers trips to Boise, Payette, Nampa, and Moscow
as big-city adventures. "The first time I went to State, I'd just
turned thirteen ... we went to Moscow, Idaho. This beautiful
pool, I mean I'd never seen a pool like that before. It was just
... big ... and they had the electronic timers and pads on the
sides of the pool ... touch plates ... all that stuff. They had
starting blocks, too—not the boxes you carry over and set
down, but real starting blocks!"

"At Nyssa, we didn't have a pace clock. Lorinda used a stopwatch. And none of us kids wore goggles. I'd come home after
a day in the pool and my eyes were all red and puffy. Mom
would pour milk in them."

Julie approached swimming not just with fervor, but with a
personal discipline that coach Lorinda thought unusual for a
thirteen-year-old. "For example," she said, "unlike the other
kids, Julie was always mindful about nutrition. She always
had a set diet to follow. If we were out of town at a meet,
she brought her own food. If she didn't have what she needed,
she had her parents go get it. Julie had to have her chicken-
noodle soup."

Sometimes Julie would ride to meets and room with Lorinda,
even though her parents went along, too. This special attention
gave her strength to overcome her paralyzing shyness.

"I was so scared at meets, so nervous. I don't think anyone
really knew how hard it was for me. I'd tell Lorinda, 'I'm
scared,' and she'd tell me it was going to be all right, that I
could do it. I remember swimmin' an event and I did good and
she came over to me and patted me on the back and gave me
a hug. That's all it took. I'd do anything for Lorinda."

"It was Lorinda," Julie knows, "who planted the seed in me;
she was the one who first gave me the idea I could be a professional athlete. She was the one who taught me how to push
hard ... to know that when you're in oxygen debt and everything aches, that it's good."

"I loved those kids," recalls Lorinda. "Who knows where they came from? I guess they just came up out of the dirt somewhere."

Julie was fifteen when Lorinda went away on a six-month mission for the Mormon Church, leaving in the middle of Julie's most successful swimming season, the summer of 1972. In the fall, school doctors heard a loud murmur in Julie's heart and told her to take it easy. Over the fall and winter, her discipline with her diet broke and she gained twenty pounds. She was teased and it hurt. "I'd been eating junk, the standard teenage diet. I got up to a hundred and thirty-seven pounds, really chunky. But I was just getting interested in boys and wanted to be a cheerleader. So I started watching my nutrition real careful and with all the exercise, began losing weight fast. People would tell me, 'Gee you look good,' and I thought if I lost a little more I'd look better. I got down to a hundred and five, a hundred and ten."

In the spring of 1972, when Julie turned fourteen, an angiogram discovered the cause of Julie's heart murmur—one of her aortic valves had a nicked edge. It was not life-threatening and Julie was told she could continue swimming and go as far as her heart would take her. Julie had fretted all winter that she might never be able to swim "ever again." Now she was jubilant and determined to achieve full mastery over her body.

Lorinda returned the next summer and watched Julie shrink. "Julie had gotten a little plump and then, that summer, she suddenly lost over twenty pounds. It was scary, anorexic-like. At the beginning of the summer, her nylon racing suit fit fine. At the end of the summer, it just hung on her. That was the year her concentration broke."

"Lorinda and I had an argument," Julie remembers. "Lorinda, she told me that I was wasting my talent, that she really thought that if I worked hard and got even better coaching, that I could make the Olympics. People don't just say that to you. I always remembered that, that someone believed in me."

Athletic greatness requires more than encouragement. When

the summer program ended, the nearest pool was forty minutes east, in Payette, Idaho. Thelma drove Julie there a few times and waited during the two-hour swim practice. But soon mother and daughter decided it was best for Julie to pursue a normal life on dry land. And for a while, she did.

Today, her mother looks back and sighs, "People around here now say, 'What a change. As shy a girl as she was, how did she ever get into this triathlon world?'"

Julie finished her run that rainy February morning and shed her wet clothes. By the time she'd eaten, finished some housework, and called Jim, it 10:30 A.M. and time for a fifty-mile bike workout.

It was still raining and not above forty-five degrees, so she put on dry long underwear, wool socks, two wool sweaters, some heavy-weather leggings of black nylon, and a slick yellow Gore-Tex jacket with Velcro to wrap the sleeves tight over her mittens. The layers would hold the heat even when wet and this was critical because Julie carried less than 10 percent body fat, and was easily chilled. She'd trained her body to dissipate heat, not conserve it. The last thing she put on before leaving the apartment was a coat of Vaseline on her cheeks and chin.

Around her chest she'd strapped the sending unit of a heart-rate monitor. The display unit was taped on her handlebars next to a cycling computer that showed her rpms, speed, mileage, and elapsed time. She pushed the start buttons of both, whipped up the hillside parking lot, and headed out into the Green River Valley.

On the bike, Julie did not concentrate excessively on technique. Cycling purists, who preach an even application of power around the chainring, would call her a bit of a plunger, someone who favors the downstroke. Julie was not blind to efficiency, she simply put more stock in power-to-weight. A zealot about maintenance, she could strip a bike to the frame, clean, and reassemble it herself. She could reach back, find the space in the frame above her rear brake, and lay her right palm over her spinning rear tire to sweep away anything that might cause a puncture; she didn't have to look back to do it.

She'd even practiced falling. She laughs, "Yeah, when I got my first new triathlon bike, Jim said, 'If you're gonna race a bike, you've got to know how to fall off.' You're not supposed to stop yourself with your hands is the idea. So we went out to a field and that's what I did; I practiced falling off without using my hands." Julie thought it was excessive at the time, but knew later that the reflexes acquired in that field had saved her race in Australia.

On this day, Julie's durability would again be tested by rain and hills. The gloom and persistence of the rain that winter had at first depressed her, but the more it rained—twenty-eight days straight in one stretch—the more Julie began to count each bike session as a triumph of discipline. Julie relished hill work for similar reasons. She would pick a mile-long grade, ride into the sticky web of gravity, then struggle out, and do it again and again. The concentration and intensity of hill work served to cleanse her mind of self-doubts; the sessions left her proud, but very tired. When Julie returned, she ate, then napped for ninety minutes. At 3:30 P.M. she got up to eat her dinner—70 percent complex carbohydrates, 20 percent protein, and 10 percent fat—alone. After calling Jim at work, she grabbed her swim bag and drove a small, white Honda to the pool where she joined the afternoon practice of a high school swim team. The kids were fast and goofy and gave Julie a cheerful buoyancy she was unable to manufacture herself. Workouts were tough, but the structure and the cheekiness of the kids made the yardage (five thousand, or two hundred lengths of the twenty-five-yard pool) go by quickly.

When Julie returned home, it was dark and still raining. Jim was not back from Boeing and would not return till after seven. It had been a typical, preseason training day: eight miles of running, fifty miles on the bike, and about three miles in the pool. It was a regime that would devastate a simple marathoner, or swimmer. And most elite cyclists would no doubt drown before finishing five thousand yards. Julie Wilson had trained for roughly eighteen years to build an aerobic system capable of doing it all—and not just once, but for days at end.

Julie grabbed a bagel from the cupboard and held it between her teeth as she filled a cooler with ice and cold water. She carried the cooler to the couch and sat down. One at a time, she lifted her feet over the lip and lowered them into the frozen, burning slush. She said to Mandy, "You can bet those California girls were out there today," and then she rested, eager to tell Jim how well she'd done on the hills.

CHAPTER 4.

Dancing on the Threshold

◆

Late February, 1989. Outside San Antonio, Texas

As Julie Wilson iced her aching ankles outside Seattle that February evening, Paula Newby-Fraser, number-one female tri-athlete in the world, sipped a beer in the bar of John New-combe's Tennis Ranch, thirty miles outside San Antonio, Texas. Although Newby-Fraser lived in Encinitas, California, the epi-center of the Southern California triathlon culture, of which she is the reigning female star, she would be at Newcombe's for two weeks, working as one of five celebrity instructors in-volved in a training camp for amateur triathletes.

More than any other woman, Newby-Fraser represented to Julie Wilson the Southern California triathlon crowd and what she called "the hoopla" and "endless strutting around." Wilson had once been to San Diego for a race and had felt unwelcome there and very much an outsider to what most non-California triathletes perceived to be a snobbish clique. To Wilson and many others, Southern California triathlon is run more like a family business than a sport. As for the athletes themselves, Wilson disapproved of what she called their "house hopping habits." "There's a lot of triathlete divorces down there. For me," she says, "marriage is more important than triathlon." She is certain that if she had moved there to train—as many thought she should to increase her visibility to sponsors—her marriage would have collapsed.

Paula Newby-Fraser embraced the California life-style. She was single and preferred it that way, though Paul Huddle, also a triathlon professional, was her steady companion. Despite an affectionate and supportive relationship with Huddle, Newby-Fraser was known to make comments about other male athletes that Paula's British forebears would call randy. Huddle didn't seem to mind, but more than a few women pros were startled by Newby-Fraser's jocular sexuality, particularly the married ones. Most took it for what it was—playful talk. But Wilson was offended.

Paula Newby-Fraser likes to push limits and in that sense is a prototypical Californian. As if to confirm it, she often says that the woman she most admires is Madonna—not Madonna, mother of Jesus, but Madonna Ciccione, mother of makeover, the twenty-nine-year-old "nobody" from Michigan who'd built herself from parts into an international rock star. To Newby-Fraser, Madonna represents a glorious plasticity of personal identity—the possibility of throwing aside every shameful, ugly, or merely inconvenient thing about oneself and forging a new identity.

Paula Newby-Fraser was twenty-four when she emigrated, alone, from South Africa to the United States in 1986. She had no relatives in the States, but was well off and had the means to return to South Africa if things didn't work out.

About her past, Newby-Fraser is secretive. From birth to her U.S. debut in triathlon twenty-three years later, Paula Newby-Fraser was a child of privilege inside two economically segregated and racist police states: first Rhodesia (now Zimbabwe), then South Africa. She learned quickly that there was no advantage—in the United States anyway—to spreading around any details, however exculpatory.

Paula Newby-Fraser entered the United States in Honolulu in October of 1985, traveling on a Zimbabwe passport. Born in Zimbabwe to South African nationals, she had her choice of either a South African passport or one from Zimbabwe. She chose Zimbabwe. After 1985, the Zimbabwe government disallowed those holding Zimbabwe passports from also claiming South African citizenship.

At the time she arrived in the United States and up until quite recently, South African athletes were banned from most international sporting competitions. Prior to Barcelona in 1992, the last Olympic Games open to South African athletes were held in Rome in 1960, two years before Paula's birth. Paula circumvented the bans—and to some extent, the stigma attached to them—by using a Zimbabwe passport.

Paula Jane Newby-Fraser was born in Salisbury, Rhodesia (now Harrare, Zimbabwe) on June 2, 1962, the second child of Brian and Betty Newby-Fraser, South African citizens born themselves of South African citizens. The Newby-Frasers' South African lineage went back to the turn of the century. They were of British ancestry, members of the 40 percent of the white population of South Africa that was not Dutch Afrikaans.

Brian and Betty moved from Durban, South Africa, to Rhodesia in the 1950s. There they had two children, Stuart before Paula. Brian was a businessman and Betty worked at the university. He was a status-quo conservative, she a progressive liberal.

Paula's first cousin remembers going to parties with Betty in 1963. "Betty knew just about every black person in town," he said, "that just wasn't proper then for a white person." Brian was uncomfortable with his wife's political activism. People had been jailed in Rhodesia and South Africa—indefinitely and without formal charges—for less. Additionally, he had no patience for the idea that the Bantu could ever run a government.

When Paula was four, her family fled Rhodesia and the racial and political crisis fomenting under British renegade Prime Min. Ian D. Smith. Brian and Betty believed their children's future would not be bright in Smith's police state—perhaps darker in the turmoil that would follow his eventual decline.

They were right. Roughly a year later, in 1968, Rhodesia was expelled from the community of nations by a British blockade and a harsh United Nations censure. The Newby-Frasers returned to Durban, South Africa, where they had roots. A busy port on the Indian Ocean, Durban is the largest city in Natal province (former home of the Zulu empire). When Paula was a girl, Durban held three-quarters of a million people.

Back home, the Newby-Frasers prospered financially. Father Brian's many commercial enterprises supported a generous life-style. His successful industrial painting business allowed him to retire in his early fifties. Paula's mother worked as an instructor of sociology at the University of Natal in Durban, a racially integrated school of five thousand students at the time. (The school also housed an all-black medical school.)

Betty pushed Paula and Stewart through years of swimming, ballet, and karate classes. "Betty drove both Paula and Stewart very, very hard," remembers Rob, Paula's first cousin, "but I don't know why except that Betty had been an only child and was extremely disciplined and intelligent. I'd say Paula got the discipline and intelligence from her mother and her warmth from her father."

Paula swam competitively from age four through sixteen; she swam through childhood, puberty, and adolescence. In between, she took a rigorous course of ballet lessons. It shows today in her effortless good posture and fluid technique in all the triathlon sports.

Like Julie Wilson, Paula won meets and set records, primarily in freestyle. For academics, Paula attended a girls school in the finest part of Durban. There was no television set in her home.

Paula was sixteen when she graduated from high school in 1979, whereupon she stopped swimming entirely. She couldn't go any higher as an amateur and nobody, she was certain, could make a living as a professional freestyle sprinter.

Paula and her brother were teenagers when her parents separated after years of unresolved disagreement over political and social issues. Betty took the kids and moved to a Durban suburb called Cowie's Hill, one of a string of small towns hug-

ging the road that twists through the foothills to Pietermar-
itzburg.

In climate and geology, Cowie's Hill is much like San Diego;
both are on the thirtieth parallel, one north, one south. The
residents of Cowie's Hill are blessed with an ideal climate
where temperatures are rarely lower than sixty and rarely
higher than eighty.

In the fall of 1979, on the heels of high school, Paula entered
the University of Natal on King George V Avenue, where her
mother taught in the sociology department. Paula says she
"partied" through college and did nothing for fitness. She took
courses exclusively in psychology, sociology, and anthropol-
ogy. Consistently a B-minus student who gained her highest
marks in psychology, Paula was awarded a bachelor of social
science degree in 1981. She received a postgraduate diploma
in applied social science in 1983. Thirsty for independence,
action, and enterprise, she took an entry-level job with a marketing research company and began running "to lose weight."
With a childhood of athletics behind her, she conditioned
quickly. At the urging of her fiancé, she bought a bike in December of 1984 and did her first triathlon near Cowie's Hill,
"the triathlon capital of South Africa," in January of 1985. She
won. Paula raced twice more in South Africa and won an entry
slot and an airline ticket for the 1985 Hawaiian Ironman to be
held that coming October. She left early. For the next eight
months prior to the Ironman, Paula traveled through Great
Britain and Europe. She "hung out" with her boyfriend and
raced three more times.

Paula's training for the 1985 Ironman was pitifully inadequate by standards used then—and now, for that matter. Each
week during the year prior to the race, she'd averaged no more
than a hundred miles on the bike, five thousand yards in the
pool, and "maybe" twenty miles of running. Most pros at the
time were following the marathoner's rule of three times the
race distance each week, or three times Paula's amount.

When Paula placed third that year (in a time of ten hours
and forty minutes), the triathlon world built by Californians

was shaken. Most old-timers thought her success was a fluke. They didn't believe anyone could do so well with so little training. Such an entrant could compete well for a few hours, they felt, but not that hard all day. As often happens when an unknown athlete has an amazing debut, rumors of ill-gotten gains began to circulate. But it was hard to imagine a motive for anything unsavory or unfair—Paula had no sponsors to please and no prize money to win. There had never been a prize purse at the Ironman and there wouldn't be until the following year.

After Ironman '85, Paula didn't return directly to South Africa but instead flew to San Diego for a vacation. She found a climate like home and a similar culture as well: like Durban, San Diego was once owned by people of color, whose ancestors now arrive by bus to do the cooking and cleaning of the moneyed white settlers. The main difference was the lack of violence, which so horribly permeated daily affairs in South Africa.

After a short trip to South Africa to collect her things, Paula moved to San Diego. Her boyfriend, with whom she'd been traveling, stayed behind to satisfy his South African military requirement. Paula shared living quarters with various athletes and hoped for good winnings. Her visitor's visa did not allow her to work.

Paula settled twenty-five miles north of San Diego, in Encinitas, close to where the first triathlons were contested around 1974. North County San Diego—as residents call it—had been the incubation chamber for what Newby-Fraser's agent, Murphy Reinschreiber, likes to call, "the world's sexiest sport."

San Diego was the business hub, and the string of beach communities dotting the interstate north to San Clemente (Cardiff-by-the-Sea, Encinitas, Leucadia, Carlsbad, Oceanside) housed the human resources—the world's greatest concentration of sweaty dreamers, all chasing a living from triathlon competition. On any sunny day throughout the 1980s, packs of young men—aspiring triathletes all—could be seen pumping their racing bikes up and down the Pacific Coast Highway. The original handful of agents—Charlie Graves, Murphy Reinschreiber, and Lloyd Peters (who would become Paula's first agent)—also lived in North County San Diego. They were the first to call Nike and say, in essence, "My guy's going to hammer the Horny Toad Triathlon next week. For two hundred dollars he'll wear your shoes . . . if he can keep the shoes." Agents and their acts trained together and lived together. They shared food, equipment, and rent. Nobody was into equity.

Back when it all started, triathlon was little more than a beach game. North County was largely rural and the towns along the coast restful. Kids who went to high school with Julie Moss (Ironman '82 legend) at Carlsbad High used to ride their horses just off the shoulder of Interstate 5. The park rangers who patrolled the beaches didn't wear guns then, but were thinking about it; kids unhinged by angel dust and PCP were becoming more common—and considerably more dangerous—than skinny-dippers and drunks.

Tillie Follander, Carlsbad High class of 1974, remembers, "It was still pretty kicked back. But a lot of kids didn't make it. Drugs mainly. What I remember most about my fifteen-year high school reunion is this guy standing up and reading all about these kids in my class who'd killed themselves. Today everybody is so tense."

The original triathlon community was swept along with success in the early 1980s when a new generation of young athletes—raised on MTV, prosperity, and high technology—arrived carrying credit cards. What began as fun, these consumers took seriously. The old guard might have been social innovators, but the new crowd was into technology, and fashion. Within two years they created a national market for sunglasses of multicolored polycarbonate, aerodynamic handlebars and disc wheels, carbon-fiber frame sets, and teardrop helmets—anything to go faster while looking better. A good rule of thumb was to figure that beyond the minimum expenditure of a thousand dollars just to get started triathloning, each additional hundred dollars spent on equipment would cut one's finish time by at least a minute. But even after $3,000 wisely spent, training and genetics still remained the keys to success.

Unlike Los Angeles, where fitness meant wearing a warm-up suit to the mall, in San Diego, people like "working out." And nobody worked out harder, longer, or in as many ways as the triathlete. The resident professionals became icons of the Southern California fitness culture. It was into this stew of fitness and fame that Newby-Fraser cast her ambitions.

When she first arrived, Newby-Fraser was astounded to hear people say they made a living off triathlon. She saw only "a collection of almost-failed single-sport athletes" who were ruining their health through excessive and ill-designed training. If there really was a living to be made, Paula was certain she could do as well as any of them. Much of what Paula heard—that *lots* of pros were making more than $100,000 a year—was wishful exaggeration.

Her first full season, 1986, went poorly. Through the summer she raced well, but inconsistently and with no big wins. Then, in October, she won the Ironman—sort of. Paula crossed the finish line three minutes *after* veteran Patricia Puntous, but Puntous was disqualified—for following another cyclist too closely (drafting)—and Paula was elevated to first. It was victory, but it wasn't sweet. The Puntous sisters were well liked and Newby-Fraser was still the outsider. The heartbreaking disappointment of Puntous, sobbing in the arms of her twin sister, diluted the happiness for Newby-Fraser.

In the winter of 1986–1987, Paula was approached by two entrepreneurs. Lloyd Peters was one, a young ex-race director from Pennsylvania then working for CAT Sports, the privately held company that ran the USTS. The other was Ron Smith, a fifty-year-old triathlete, ex-Navy underwater demolition team (UDT) diver and founder of The Chart House restaurant chain. Peters and Smith said they were starting the "United States Triathlon Training Center" at the Olympic Resort in Carlsbad, Ca. Essentially, it was a training-assistance and athlete-marketing venture. Six triathletes joined. Paula was one and Paul Huddle,

who would become her closest companion and training partner, was another. "It sounded," said Huddle, "a lot better than
it was."

"Basically," recalls Peters, "Ron [Smith] just wanted to train.
He wanted me to handle the business end. He got some money
from one of Dominelli's old investors" [which Smith denies].
Jerry Dominelli and his wife, Nancy Hoover, ran a house-of-
cards investment scheme based in San Diego in the early
1980s. Dominelli and Hoover—whose son, George, was an excellent triathlete who knew most of the top pros—lavishly supported a team of triathletes until the cards fell. Both Dominelli
and Hoover were convicted of fraud.

"My job," continued Peters, "was to help with anything that
needed doing outside of training—but mainly I tried to get
them sponsors. Every athlete needs an agent. No athlete is
comfortable calling a sponsor and saying, 'I'm good. You
should pay me to race for you.' Which is exactly what you
have to do."

Even with Peters representing her, Paula didn't sell. "No one
wanted anything to do with an Ironman winner from South
Africa," recalled Peters. "I called Nike. . . . I called all the regular players and they all said the same thing: They weren't interested." The U.S. Triathlon Training Center evaporated within a
year.

But training and racing went on. Newby-Fraser raced without popular distinction in the regular 1987 season. Consistently trailing national champion and born-again Christian
Kirsten Hanssen, Paula seemed doomed to walk-ons at the
awards ceremonies. She held her envelope with $300 inside
while Kirsten, clutching her four grand, gushed and thanked
God.

At the 1987 Ironman, Paula finished a full hour faster than
she had two years earlier. But so did Erin Baker and Sylvianne
Puntous. Paula placed third and returned to South Africa, dis-
heartened. Paula's father met her at the airport and when she
stepped off the ramp, he said, "You look a half a stone [seven

pounds] light." He was certain Paula would have won had she retained more weight.

Paula agreed. On her return to San Diego, she changed her diet. She also changed agents, dropping Lloyd Peters in favor of Murphy Reinschreiber, an attorney who'd been one of the original professional triathletes. Murphy headed the triathlon's first national rules organization—the USTA; he was well connected, reassuring, and looking for athletes. "When Paula turned up on my doorstep," Murphy said, "she'd been the victim of some bad training advice. I helped get her feet back under her and get her training organized."

Paula threw out the "mega-mileage and rinsed cottage cheese," saying, "I tried the Dave Scott diet [vegetarian] and followed his rabbit eating habits. My blood pressure dropped and I became anemic." She stuck to her own brand of training, which emphasized speed and rest.

Murphy sought a steady sponsor for Paula, but it wasn't easy. No women other than Kirsten Hanssen, the Puntous sisters, and Julie Moss had ever made any money in triathlons. And then there was the South Africa problem. To deal with that, Murphy assured sponsors and race directors that the announcer need never say, "Paula Newby-Fraser from South Africa."

"She's from Zimbabwe," Murphy said. "She's a Zimbabwe citizen." Nobody knew Zimbabwe from Pago Pago but they sensed Paula's poise and willingness to sell. Guided by Murphy and her own athletic acumen, Paula found a formula that worked.

The turning point was in 1988. With the sport's best sprinters out for half the season, Paula collected enough top-three finishes to win the United States Triathlon Series (USTS) championship. With races open to the public in ten major cities across the country, the USTS was both farm league and major pro circuit, the race distance a standardized 1.5 kilometer swim (0.93 miles), 40k bike (24.8 miles), and 10k run (6.2 miles).

Paula built both speed and endurance steadily from spring

to fall; her best day was October 22, the day of the 1988 Ironman. Her swim was solid, she broke the race open on the bike, and then dropped her last rival for good by running a 3:07 marathon, one of the day's fastest by man or woman. Never had so many people seen a woman go that hard for that long. She passed scores of men who considered themselves to be among the best athletes in the world.

If Paula Newby-Fraser of Zimbabwe was not then the best female endurance athlete that ever lived, which she likely was, she was certainly the best on television. She could face the camera and spontaneously compose a grammatically correct English sentence. She did not stammer, gush, or scold. She was humble in victory and noble in defeat—a champion. She immediately lost her outsider's status with triathlon's hoi palloi, bearing out again Liz Taylor's observation that, "There's no deodorant like success."

By late February 1989, the glow of her Ironman win had faded and Paula faced a new season and high expectations. She was ten pounds over her race weight and had yet to begin serious training for the '89 season. In the six weeks since January, she'd spent her weekends standing around the sports-apparel sections of Southern California department and sporting-goods stores promoting workout clothes while answering questions like: "How did it feel to beat your boyfriend at the Ironman?" (A: "I kept hoping it wasn't him.") and "Are you married?" (A: "After I tell people what I do, the first thing they ask me is, 'Are you married.' Why is that?") Selling the sponsor's product was what Murphy, her agent, liked to call a responsibility. "The day of athlete as billboard," Murphy would say, "is over." Appearances, product demos, prerace clinics, press conferences, sponsor parties, awards banquets—it was all part of Paula's job now. Compared to the Saturday-afternoon demo, instructing at Newcombe's camp wasn't a bad gig as far as triathlon went. And compared to tennis, that wasn't very far.

Newcombe's Tennis Ranch—a thoroughly Texan complex of ranch house, residence suites, pool, and tennis courts—was built by John Newcombe, an Australian tennis player successful in the 1970s. In 1975, when most winners of major triathlons took home only bragging rights and sore muscles, John Newcombe played one set of tennis against Jimmy Connors for a winner-take-all prize of half a million dollars. (Newcombe lost.) The sweep of Newcombe's ranch only underscored the commercial impoverishment of triathlon, a sport in which the richest event divided $284,000 among thirty competitors. The poor-relation status of triathlon to the "ball" sports was a sore point to Dave Scott, another of the camp's celebrity instructors. Six-time winner of the Hawaiian Ironman, Scott was certainly the best known, and highest paid triathlete. He was an expectant father as well and when an amateur asked Scott what he would do to develop his child's athletic ability, Scott said, "Throw some tennis balls in his crib."

Other instructors at the camp included Newby-Fraser's rival, former two-time national triathlon champion Kirsten Hanssen from Denver, Colorado, and John Howard, the premier U.S. road racing cyclist in the 1970s. Howard cycled for the U.S. in two Olympic games and won a gold medal at the Pan Am Games. Howard also held the record for the highest speed ever attained on a bike (152.284 mph). In 1981, Howard won the Ironman.

Triathlon amateurs tended to be well-off and white, and so were Newcombe's campers. They came from jet cockpits, engineering stations, operating rooms, law offices, sole proprietorships, corporate headquarters, and all manner of upper–middle class, hard-driving enterprises. For many, triathlon was either an alter occupation or an escape. And it could be, every triathlete agreed, a psycho-physical addiction. One camper spoke of a friend who'd quit triathlon after his four-year-old son told him he'd kiss his daddy more if he didn't always taste like sweat.

There were a third of a million amateur triathletes in the United States in 1989 and the campers at Newcombe's mirrored the statistical profile: median household income, $55,000; average age, thirty-four; sex, male (80 percent); education, college graduate (80 percent). They paid entry fees of $35 to $250 for the Hawaiian Ironman per race. In 1989, it was unlikely that even fifteen triathlon professionals in the United States managed to earn through prize earnings and endorsement contracts anywhere near as much as the average amateur took home from a desk job.

Two campers at Newcombe's were not amateurs, however, but Japanese professionals sent by their sponsor (maker of a Japanese electrolyte replacement drink) to participate fully, take notes, and bring the concept back to Japan (as with the transistor and the automobile).

Mitsuhiro "Mikki" Yamamoto and Tomohisa "Tomo" Umezawa had just come the long way from Tokyo when they rolled their bikes into the conference center. Tomo was built like a middle-weight wrestler, but he understood no English and arrived hungry and tired. His condition seemed to worsen through the week. Tomo's teammate, Mikki, was a foot taller, conversant in English, and considerably more alert. Mikki was the captain of the party and kept Tomo awake during lectures on nutrition. Mikki was a diligent triathlon team captain, but he was not humorless. Befitting the stereotype of Japanese Gadgetman, his bike had gadgets upon gizmos, including a duplicate set of brake levers installed far forward on his aerobars—apparently to allow him to brake without rising from the stretched-out, praying mantis position. When asked why he needed two sets of brakes, Mikki just smiled and said, "I ride Tokyo."

A tall, gold-skinned man with brilliant white teeth, Mikki had jet black hair and 6 percent body fat. He was an excellent triathlete, a little weak on the swim, but a contender. He'd finished sixteenth at the 1988 Ironman and hoped to do better in 1989. He was anxious to improve and eager, as all triathletes are, to have any part of his athletic capacity tested. Mikki was particularly looking forward to the anaerobic threshold test, or AT for short.

To serious triathletes, AT is more important than the venerable concept of VO2-max, which had been used for many years as the ultimate measure of aerobic fitness among runners. VO2-max is the maximum amount of oxygen a person can pull from the air in a minute. It is expressed in milliliters of oxygen used per kilogram of body weight per minute.

An elite marathoner would be expected to have a VO2-max around sixty-five to seventy milliliters/kilogram/minute; a twenty-five-year-old recreational runner would be expected to have a VO2-max around fifty-five; an active, lean woman of sixty-five years in good cardiovascular condition, around forty-five.

VO2-max is tested by increasing the exercise demand on an individual (most commonly done on a treadmill), while measuring the amount of oxygen they take in, but don't exhale. A person's VO2-max depends on three things. First, their cardiovascular system, which determines how much oxygen can get to individual muscle cells. The second variable is weight. Losing weight will automatically increase one's VO2-max. The third factor is how much oxygen the muscles can actually demand. The more muscle mass that can be called into action by the nervous system, the more oxygen that can be demanded. All three variables can be affected positively by training, thus increasing VO2-max.

Cross-country skiers usually post the highest VO2-maxes—in the mid seventies—because so many of their skeletal muscles are used simultaneously. Elite runners come next, around sixty-five, then top cyclists at about sixty, and then top swimmers at fifty-five.

By 1989, the few tests done on elite triathletes showed that they had, with some notable exceptions, VO2-maxes just shy of elite marathoners. When tested swimming, of course, the runners would fall far behind triathletes because their upper bodies are more lightly muscled.

Thus, VO2-max represents the maximum rate, or top speed, at which a given athlete can consume oxygen.

But for anyone racing for hours, top speed is not as important as top *sustainable* speed. And that is what AT is supposed to indicate—how fast for how long.

An athlete crosses over his or her anaerobic threshold when

demands on the muscles are so great that aerobic (with oxygen) respiration is no longer capable of supplying the chemical fuels the muscles need to contract. Principally, the fuel required is adenosine triphosphate, or ATP. Enough ATP can be stored in the muscles and the liver to power short bursts of effort, as in a 100 yard dash. Longer efforts require the body to manufacture ATP, which it does inside the muscle cells themselves, using oxygen and glucose or, if it must, oxygen and fats. Under submaximal muscle demands, oxygen and glucose carried by the bloodstream into the muscle are transformed by a series of chemical interactions into ATP, CO_2, water, and small amounts of lactic acid. The ATP allows potential chemical energy contained within the muscle fibers to be transformed into the mechanical energy of muscle contraction by a fascinating, yet complex process. Suffice it to say, without ATP, muscles simply will not contract, no matter how forcefully the nervous system tells them to. In fact, without ATP, very few cellular functions can take place at all.

There is a limit to the rate at which an athlete can produce ATP through only aerobic means, a rate that varies according to training and genetics. When the muscles are told by the nervous system to work at a rate that cannot be fueled by aerobic respiration alone, the anaerobic system of ATP production kicks in.

In anaerobic respiration, the molecules produced are not ATP, CO_2, water, and a *little* lactic acid, but instead, just ATP and *a lot* of lactic acid.

Most of this acid is transported through the muscle membrane into the bloodstream and swept away to the liver for storage. But a great deal of it stays inside the muscle, where it interferes with the chemistry of the aerobic system. If the athlete continues to work hard, more pressure is put on the anaerobic system and more lactic acid accumulates. But not for long. The athlete is quickly overwhelmed by pain and the urgent need to stop everything and gasp. During this pause, lactic acid is cleared and blood pH is restored to neutral; the athlete can then resume, but at a slower pace.

Besides producing noxious by-products, the anaerobic system is not very efficient when it comes to fuel consumption, requiring nearly twenty times as much glucose as the aerobic system to produce an equivalent amount of ATP.

Because the signature of the anaerobic system is the production of lactic acid, it's easy for an athlete to know when that system is being taxed: A burning ache swells up in the most used muscles. Breathing becomes suddenly more rapid and urgent, but not just because the body is trying to get more oxygen; in fact, it has all the oxygen it can process. Rather, rapid breathing is needed to lower the pH of blood flooded with lactic acid. Anaerobic threshold is that point during vigorous, prolonged exercise when lactic acid suddenly increases in an athlete's bloodstream. It is the signal that anaerobic respiration has begun in earnest.

Expressed simply, AT is posted in heartbeats per minute. People who are not consistent aerobic exercisers will go anaerobic at heart rates significantly lower than their maximum. For example, a moderately active twenty-five-year-old woman whose heart will beat a maximum of 200 beats per minute (bpm) would typically go anaerobic around 125 to 135 bpm. Most elite triathletes and marathoners have anaerobic thresholds around 170 bpm, with some men approaching 185. That is very high.

At his peak, champion runner Derek Clayton could run each mile of an entire marathon 88 percent as fast as his best effort over one mile. In Clayton's case, that meant running for two hours and seven minutes with a heart rate of *at least* 185 beats per minute. That's endurance.

AT can be increased significantly through training—far more so than can VO2-max. Even after an individual has reached his or her best possible VO2-max, the AT can still be improved.

A high anaerobic threshold is essential for a top triathlete. But it isn't everything. Triathlons are not held in labs, but in living lakes, oceans and rivers, on roads and trails of all types, under insufferably hot August skies, and sometimes in the teeth of rainstorms. In these conditions, intangibles such as courage and desire become paramount. So too efficiency; lousy technique in cycling, or worse, in swimming, cannot be overcome by a high AT.

Mikki Yamamoto began his anaerobic threshold test seated on his bike in the big conference room of Newcombe's Ranch. The test design was simple and, while not as precise as a gas exchange test, reasonably accurate. His bike was mounted on a steel stand fitted with a friction device to simulate the road. When Mikki spun the pedals around, the device resisted the motion of his rear wheel with increasing force as Mikki's speed increased.

Mikki was instructed to spin easily for twenty minutes in order to exhaust the ATP already stored in his muscles. He was then to pedal at 12 mph for one minute, then at 13 mph for a minute, then at 14, at 15, and so on until it became impossible to hold the latest speed for a minute straight. At that point his muscles would be flooded with lactic acid. Somewhat before then, his heart rate would rise dramatically without a corresponding increase in speed. By relating speeds with heart rates, Mikki's AT could be fairly well estimated.

Mikki could read his speed from a digital display mounted between the handlebars of his bike. Attendants stood by to keep track of Mikki's heart rate, which was detected by the monitor strapped round his chest and displayed on a small screen fitted next to the speedometer.

At 18 mph, Mikki was hardly breathing. Then 19, 20, 21, 22. At 23 mph, drops of sweat formed at Mikki's hairline. At 24 mph, the drops fell from his nose. At 26 mph, his legs began to shine and, though his breathing was unlabored, his eyes showed greater effort as he endeavored to concentrate on the speedometer. At 28 mph, Mikki's jaw dropped and the skin around it stretched back, exposing his lower teeth. His T-shirt shook against his spine from the vibration of the friction wheel below. Mikki's stroke was smooth. His breathing was deep and steady against the growl of the load simulator. He opened his throat wider to let the air, laced with the vapor of his sweat, pour in.

When Mikki reached 29 mph, Paula Newby-Fraser walked over, stopped beside his shoulder and bit her lower lip. She stared quietly at the speedometer as Mikki pushed it to 30 mph. Mikki was visibly and audibly in pain. His once calm and boyish face was contorted and desperate for air. His thighs were quivering and the previously smooth spin of his feet began to break into pulses; he was blowing air rapidly and his face was fully flushed. He held it together like that for an entire minute. The testing crew drew in tight and said nothing until the one with the stopwatch and clipboard said, "Okay Mikki, go to thirty-two." With that, Mikki stopped peddling. Hunched and heaving over his handlebars, he devoured air for about fifteen seconds. Then he sat upright, smiled, mopped himself with a towel and began to spin again, apparently none the worse for his ordeal. (Knowing that the pain will be gone just seconds after stopping is what makes it hard for many triathletes to quit during the end stages of the run.) Mikki soon had his results. His anaerobic threshold was 175 beats per minute.

Just five months earlier, Newby-Fraser had beaten Mikki at the Ironman by five minutes.

When Mikki's test was done, Paula stripped down to shorts and a running shirt. Underneath she wore her swimsuit. She went to the far end of the conference room, stepped onto the black belt of a treadmill and started it moving, slowly at first, then steadily faster. Twenty-three minutes in she hit ten miles an hour, or six minutes per mile—roughly the pace she'd hold in the final leg of a two-hour triathlon. The tip of her nose, the smooth skin over her knees, and her knuckles turned pink from blood carrying heat to the surface. She was biomechanically sublime, round of muscle, and curiously appointed with curving red fingernails and totem jewelry.

Twenty-six minutes in, Paula reached down and turned the belt speed to 12 mph. She was running a 5:45 pace when she seemed to lose contact with the belt and just float there, grinning.

CHAPTER 5.

THE MACHINE OF THE GHOST

◆

Late February, 1989. Outside San Antonio, Texas

*P*aula Newby-Fraser was still on the treadmill at the opposite end of the room when Kirsten Hanssen pushed through the double doors into Newcombe's conference center. She stood five-foot-three-inches and weighed only a hundred pounds, if that. Perhaps it was her two-color nylon taffeta warm-up suit or her game-show smile that made her seem much larger. Whatever it was, for a size-four, blue-eyed, blond-haired woman, Hanssen took up a lot of space.

Out of her warm-ups, however, Kirsten appears significantly lighter and more wiry than *any* other pro woman on the circuit—a class of women who are themselves a bit shorter and *much* leaner than average. Among them, Kirsten was the thinnest, and for nearly three straight years she'd been the *winningest.* Some pros, including Newby-Fraser, were concerned that this only reinforced an unhealthy idea already widespread among young women athletes, namely, "The thinner, the winner."

"Women think they'd like to race in a swimsuit, but they

won't. They're worried," said Newby-Fraser, only half-jesting, "that standing next to Kirsten they'll look like a fat pig." To some extent, Paula was referring to herself as well; she loved the way her body worked, but like all the women pros, wasn't fully satisfied with the way it looked. Hanssen had it all—looks and success—or so many of the women thought.

Three years of tough training and successful racing had reduced Kirsten's body fat—as measured by calipers—to 4 percent. Of her one hundred pounds, only four pounds were fat, most all of it unseen padding around her internal organs. By comparison, at the peak of her career, Norwegian marathon and cross-country champion Grete Waitz lumbered in at 9 percent. The norm for American women is 20 percent to 25 percent.

Kirsten hadn't gone through a menstrual cycle in six years and she believes it was a direct result of life-style and athletics. After exercising and maintaining life functions, her body had no resources to maintain readiness for reproduction, which was just fine with Kirsten. Only recently had she begun hoping that someday she might "raise a family up with the Lord." But for the moment, Kirsten enjoyed feeling light and strong and was certain it was part of God's plan for her life and specifically, for her evangelism. It was characteristic of Kirsten to assign a religious purpose not just to the circumstances of her life, but to her actions as well.

Kirsten says she has a "relationship with God, who is Jesus Christ." [Her God is a definite male.] Christ's love for her, Kirsten says, makes her most always happy. Not even the sight of Paula running away on the treadmill could dull her smile as she beamed through the crowd of milling amateurs in the conference room. The last time she'd seen Paula's running backside was four months earlier at the '88 Ironman. Since then, Kirsten could only feel that He wanted Paula to be at the pinnacle of triathlon and Kirsten to be working for Him cheerfully in another department.

No one knew better than Kirsten Hanssen how quickly a triathlon career could rise, peak, and founder. While Newby-Fraser struggled through the 1986 season, Kirsten was busy using the sport as a personal showcase. With her mother, Susie, handling the business ("Mom's job was to hold my place in line at the Porta Potties"), Kirsten won the USTS championship. At that point, Kirsten decided she'd rather be a successful professional athlete than continue with her job as a computer programmer. She quit in December of '86 in order to train and race full time. The next season, 1987, Kirsten did twenty-two triathlons, a heavy schedule even by triathlon standards. She placed first in sixteen and took second in four more.

What set Hanssen apart in triathlon was not her swimming, which was merely excellent, but the same talent that enabled Newby-Fraser to crush the Ironman field in '88: she could build a big lead on the bike and then run as hard as she'd peddaled. Regulars around the USTS circuit had never seen a woman ride a bike as hard as Kirsten Hanssen. At the national championship race in September of 1986, Kirsten came out of the water with the leaders, then got on her conventional, chrome-moly road bike and swallowed the course in just under an hour. Her average speed was 25.2 mph.

Only Olympic and professional cyclists were then known to be capable of such speeds in what is, essentially, an unaided time trial. Using a bike unfettered by brakes or gears and riding on a track, 1988 Women's Tour de France winner Jeanne Longo set a women's record in the late 1980s, riding twenty-eight miles in one hour. (Longo's history of failing drug tests for stimulant usage is a factor worth considering.) Kirsten's effort, done on a heavier bike and in traffic was surely an equal achievement—if not for the 1500 meter swim she did at near-world-class time before it, then certainly for the ten kilometers she ran at six and a half minutes per mile after it.

In similar fashion to Newby-Fraser's spectacular long-distance debut, Kirsten's initial victories were grounded in a training program that most of her competitors considered light on mileage. Kirsten claimed to train only two hours on work days and four to six hours on the weekends. She resisted the temptation to turn training sessions into competition and, like Paula, seemed always to do her best work while racing.

Kirsten's training may have been unorthodox by existing standards, but it matched her conception of what USTS racing was all about. The 1.5k swim, 40k bike, and 10k run format was not, for Hanssen, a contest of endurance even though the races took most competitors as long as a good runner would need to do a marathon. Instead, Kirsten saw three middle-distance events done back-to-back-to back—then she raced each like a sprint.

Early training partners did not find her competitive, just highly disciplined and enthusiastic. But as her career progressed, the word *compulsive* came up more often. She allotted precisely thirty-eight minutes to running during lunch. The other twenty-two were for dressing and getting to and from the street from her eleventh-floor cubicle. "I tried to go a little farther each time, maybe only a half a block, but farther." Sometimes she ran the inside stairs and when she did, there was nothing haphazard about it. The steps were concrete, eleven to each flight, all the same. "I'd do one flight a step at a time, then double-step the next flight, then back to single." There was always a method, a plan to Kirsten's workouts.

Others saw madness. "I feel I'm goal directed," said Newby-Fraser, "but Kirsten is compulsive. If she goes out for a six-hour ride on the weekend and finishes her loop in five hours and forty-five minutes, dead tired, she'll force herself to go back out there for another fifteen minutes."

What Paula called obsessive-compulsive behavior, Kirsten felt as bliss. She was most tranquil when she was in the Rocky Mountains exercising near her anaerobic threshold. In those moments, of which she always wanted more, Kirsten was as close to heaven as she thought she would get in this life. She said she felt like she was "dancin' on those streets of gold," a reference to her conception of heaven as an "active place full of people just like me."

Kirsten Hanssen understands herself as a soul temporarily

hitched to a body—a body provided as an arena for moral development and a tool for spreading her religion. This "body as tool" philosophy was shared somewhat by Wilson, but not as thoroughly, at least not when judging by Kirsten's treatment of her body. Moreover, many of Kirsten's racing principles and training guidelines have a religious motivation as well as a physiological justification. She was once asked while out riding a mountain bike how she remembered which way to push the shift lever to downshift the rear sprocket. She answered quickly, without thinking, "It goes along with my mind and my faith," she said, "that down is for hell because that's the easy way." Such comments were not unusual for Kirsten, though she tended to make them most often when her heart was above 140 bpm.

Julie Wilson's husband, Jim, suspected Kirsten's religious zealotry was a fake or a cover. He'd seen plenty of them at Northwest Nazarene—young people so saturated with the gospels that they had no other personality—and didn't like them. He wasn't alone. When Kirsten credited God with her victories, some took it as saying, in effect, that God had wanted them to lose. That was a horribly unfair notion to many. But not to Robert Ames, Kirsten's fiancé.

Of medium build, buoyant in spirit, frank, strawberry blond, and fit, Robert Ames is Huck Finn with religion. When he met Kirsten, he was the young man every Christian girl hoped to meet. A young marketing manager in the Colorado skiing industry, Ames was also an avid amateur triathlete who had completed, by his estimate, "around forty-five races" by the end of 1988. In his late teens and throughout his twenties, he'd been a "bump skier," and one of the best. While living in Vail, Colorado, Ames twice won the U.S. Freestyle Skiing Championships. He was also outspoken about being a Christian, though not as much as Kirsten.

Ames says he pursued Kirsten Hanssen from the time he heard her credit God for her victory after the USTS nationals in 1987. He felt Kirsten's announcement of faith in her awards-banquet speech was exceptionally courageous even though, at the time, evangelical Christians were highly visible and outspoken in every facet of social life, from sports to politics.

Ames accompanied Kirsten to Newcombe's that February of 1989 and, whenever he could, he massaged her, held her, and whispered into her hair. He affectionately called her "my bow-legged bag lady," referring to the way Kirsten walked while lugging her huge athletic duffel bag. Kirsten loved it and knew Robert was her guy "the day I saw him washing his car windows in the rain, just like my dad would do."

Like Paula Newby-Fraser and Julie Wilson, Kirsten Hanssen first discovered her athletic talent in the water. At ten years old, she was ranked fourth in the nation at the breaststroke. She lived in Wichita, Kansas, then, and was the only child of Gary and Susie Hanssen. "We didn't raise her to win," mother Susie recalls, "but we demanded that she do the best that she could do." (The tone of her voice indicated that *demanded* was precisely the word she wanted.) Kirsten's father worked in the aerospace industry. "He was the youngest vice president in Beech Aircraft history," Kirsten proudly recalls.

Like Kirsten, Susie Hanssen is extroverted, positive, and athletic. But unlike Kirsten, she is outspoken and often critical of other people's shortcomings. She is also booked solid. "That woman hasn't worked a day since I've met her," said Robert Ames, laughingly, "but she's the busiest person I know."

Susie Hanssen was an English teacher when Kirsten was born. Possibly because there were no other children around to absorb the vigilance, Kirsten remembers constant correction from her mother, particularly concerning grammar and deportment. Susie worked hard to raise an upstanding daughter. She watched Kirsten's grammar and made certain she got to swim practice for three hours each day during the school year and for four hours a day during summer. Susie Hanssen believes in the vital powers of athletics, saying, "Athletics makes women happy and happy women make for happy homes; happy girlfriends make for happy wives and happy wives make for a happy country." Susie had it all figured out and was always there—enabling, directing, correcting, and advising.

But of her father, Gary, Kirsten wanted more. "One Christmas—I think I was thirteen—I got sick and didn't have to go to swim practice," Kirsten recalls. "I got to stay home and just play games with my dad. It was the best Christmas I ever had." After that Christmas, Kirsten didn't go back to swim practice and that marked the end of her career as a student swimming sensation.

Just before then, when Kirsten was twelve, she felt that her parents might split up. She remembers arguments over the role of Kirsten's grandparents in her upbringing, but Kirsten was not more specific. "There were angry telephone calls and long nights," Kirsten remembers. "It was frightening." In the midst of their family crisis, another couple came into the Hanssen home and led the family toward a religious conversion. "I made a decision when I was twelve to accept Christ into my life." Kirsten says this flatly, as though recounting a decision to eat more fiber or open an IRA.

Kirsten earned straight A's in high school, just as she had done in junior high, and graduated first in her high school class. Mother Susie is quick to downplay the accomplishment, "Kirsten's not a big intellect," she says matter-of-factly. "She just works very hard. She's an overachiever."

Kirsten enrolled at the University of Colorado (her parents' alma mater) in 1980. She studied hard, sang with the Campus Crusade for Christ, and pledged Kappa Alpha Theta. In her senior year, she was accepted into the Dance Line, an all-woman cheer squad that performed in sequins and tight white buckskin during the Colorado football games. Kirsten loved it more than she could ever have imagined. Showing her God-given legs, working out, being ogled, and cheered—"It was so much fun," she said.

Kirsten graduated magna cum laude with a degree in information systems and within three months found herself "in a little blouse, in a little dress, at a little desk" in the rates department of Public Service Company of Denver, the largest utility in Colorado. She stayed there for two years, writing and debugging computer programs; she sang in the company choir as well. Jody Townsend, Kirsten's boss, remembers a "fringe" employee who tested the limits of the unwritten dress code and never stayed late. "But when she was on the clock, she was persistent," says Townsend. "If she got something in sight and thought she could do it, she just hammered until she got it." Kirsten liked programming because, like triathlon, it could engross her completely. But programming did not give her an audience. Jody Townsend remembers, "The people contact—the little of it she got—was what she liked most. She had an easy smile and frankly I thought she was better suited to public relations."

Indeed, Kirsten's quest for a stage, for an appreciative audience, is constant. "I like being in the limelight," she says, "and not necessarily the competitive limelight."

"She loves appearing more than racing," says Robert Ames. "She'll come two days early if a race director asks her." Appearing and pleasing is Kirsten's greatest satisfaction; making others unhappy is her greatest fear. She remembers one swim meet in particular as she waited—her mother at her side—for her turn on the blocks. Another girl who'd just finished a race was standing nearby and was crying from disappointment over her performance. Susie Hanssen was mortified. Kirsten remembers her mother saying sternly, "If I ever see you back there behind the blocks looking so ridiculous, I'll whack you." Susie Hanssen explains comments such as these as timely efforts taken to teach Kirsten to, "Just accept what you have and go on from there." But the lesson Kirsten apparently learned was, "Keep all negative feelings to yourself."

Kirsten was a sophomore in college when she met a boy she thought she would someday marry. "We were so close. We would run together and play . . . and then he dropped me." It was just before Christmas. "It hurt a lot, but I pressed on. My family was going to Hawaii on this big vacation and I couldn't let my problem make things miserable for everybody else. I had to be in control."

Kirsten's ability to deny pain and to control its power is legendary in triathlon circles. What she did in Nice, France, in 1987 is a good example. The triathlon in Nice begins on a stony Mediterranean beach. The swim is long—2.5 miles—and cold. The finishing run is long—19.9 miles—and hot. Psychologically, the run course is very difficult. An out and back course, it is utterly flat, surfaced with concrete and from any point along it, seemingly endless, particularly because the heat waves eddying up from the road keep changing the sizes of the landmarks ahead. The bike course is seventy-five miles of long, aching climbs followed by fearful, twisting descents in the Maritime Alps. Traditional cyclists call it a "technical" course. "It requires good biking skills," said Kirsten, "or no brains." Some would say *and* no brains.

Two days before the race, Kirsten was bedridden in a Nice hotel, racked with stomach and muscle cramps. Between bouts of vomiting, she attempted to walk from her hotel to the race headquarters a block away. She didn't make it. The day before the race she could walk, slowly. Then anxiety set in. "When I get nervous, I eat. I said, 'Oh God, now I'm getting fat.'" The next morning, race day, Kirsten felt shaky and tender at the starting line, but she ran into the Mediterranean with the other seven hundred and came out with the leading women. It wasn't until she got on the bike that the effects of her illness—dehydration and electrolyte loss—hit her. Both legs cramped solid. With her legs hanging stiff, she coasted out of the transition area. Against great pain, she forced her left foot into the pedal cleat, then worked her leg manually around the circle, lifting and pushing it with her left hand. She pedaled grimly, guzzling replacement fluid all the while. Gradually, muscle fibers in her quadriceps came out of spasm and, as the electrolytes made their way into her muscle membranes, her leg began to respond to her will. Her right leg still hung like a prosthesis. Hordes of contestants whizzed by. Half a mile down the coast road, Kirsten got her right foot into the cleat and pushed it through the circle until it too came to life.

From there, she accelerated into the hills. She winced through the first thirty miles of ascents and spun through the descents to hold off the cramps. But by the time she came off the bike—three and half hours after starting the race—she was fully operational. An hour into the run she passed the women's leader, ex–Auburn University running ace Colleen Cannon. "I kept thinking I ought to be slowing down, but I didn't" says Kirsten. Cannon let her go, but stalked Kirsten for an hour, waiting for her to blow up. Race officials on motorcycles rumbled on each side as Kirsten ran, her knees rising high and her arms tic, tic, ticking from her shoulders. For the first time in more than six hours, Kirsten was scared. "It all started to catch up with me about two miles from the end. I didn't have anything left, but I was pulling away a bit more from Colleen. I was terrified of falling down. Even when I was in the finish chute, I didn't know if I was going to make it."

She won by thirty-five seconds.

If she could conquer Nice when ill, what could she do at the Ironman when well? Without question, Kirsten was near the peak of her ability and she sensed it. In 1988, she scheduled more long-course races, including the April St. Croix spectacular being organized by Rennie Roker. Roker was new to triathlon but not new to drama. He had recently worked on a hit TV series and his industry ties helped him land a wad of money from NBC for broadcast rights to the "America's Paradise Triathlon." Roker managed the touches, large and small. Much of the bike course was paved—for the first time—just hours before the race. Dionne Warwick was signed to sing the national anthem. To encourage the male athletes to greater performances, Roker procured the mighty talents of three Olympic-class female athletes and had them each do a solo time trial in their specialty—swimming, biking, or running—along the route the triathletes would follow. Their times were combined and Roker offered $5,000 to the first triathlete who could cover the entire course faster.

In advance of the race, Kirsten went to stay with her new manager, Charlie Graves, in Del Mar, saying, "It was a business arrangement only." A former collegiate swimming champion, Graves once sought a living as a triathlon professional, but (like Murphy Reinschreiber, Newby-Fraser's agent), had given up. When he signed Kirsten, Graves was in business with Reinschreiber, but they managed different pros.

Kirsten's stay in California was productive but uncomfortable. She trained in San Diego with Paula Newby-Fraser and the gang, but socially, her religious orientation clashed with the California singles culture. As a consequence, she did more distance than any of the top women training there or elsewhere: She averaged 475 miles on the bike, 50 miles of running, and 10 miles of swimming—each week. Surprisingly, her body did not break down, but got stronger. Before she left for St. Croix, her resting pulse was thirty-four beats per minute. Her VO2-max—the measure of how much oxygen she could metabolize in relation to her weight—was measured at 74.5 milliliters per kilogram per minute. (Grete Waitz, tested a few days after setting a women's marathon record, registered a VO2-max of seventy-three; Derek Clayton, the men's record holder, posted a sixty-nine.)

On the standard treadmill test of endurance, Kirsten lasted 29.3 minutes—3 minutes longer than any of the Olympic athletes tested earlier at the same lab. When they told Kirsten to get off, she was running six-minute miles up a ten-percent grade.

Kirsten won the St. Croix race in four hours and thirty-eight minutes, thirteen minutes ahead of Newby-Fraser. Moreover, after subtracting the three minutes she spent in transitions, she beat Roker's Olympians by a minute. Kirsten's parents stood just past the finish tape at St. Croix, waiting for their daughter to arrive. When she did, Kirsten first hugged her father. Then her mother stepped in and enveloped Kirsten in a bear hug. Kirsten kept one arm free and with it circled her father.

The remainder of 1988 didn't turn out as well. Kirsten had apparently pushed her body farther than it was willing to go and after St. Croix, it started pushing back. First she suffered tendinitis in her knees, then stress fractures in her legs; then she broke her left wrist in a bike crash in Texas (her second wrist fracture in two years). But she continued racing. By the time she entered her first Ironman race in October, she appeared emaciated. The foot-long blue cast on her right wrist was the finishing touch on a grim picture of athletic excess. Friends estimated her weight to be below 90 pounds—down from 105 in the spring of 1987. Newby-Fraser's agent remarked that Kirsten would "be carried off the course in a straitjacket" before the day was over.

She wasn't. Even *with* the cast, she swam faster than three others in the top ten. Her bike time was the fourth fastest and in the end, she outran Julie Wilson for third place.

By this time, many in the triathlon community—a culture not known for the practice of athletic moderation—were concerned over Kirsten's mental and physical health. "She's crazy," said Dave Scott, "she really abuses her body." Many of the women pros believed she was bulimic or anorexic or both. Kirsten's habit of eating virtually nothing during the day, then feasting at night caused more than one eyebrow to lift. "Nobody," said a close rival, "eats three peanut butter cheesecakes without gaining weight. Nobody."

"All she talks about is food," remarked another top male pro.

"She doesn't heal quickly from injuries, particularly from bone breaks and stress fractures. She's not absorbing calcium. She's too light," said a top woman.

Kirsten gave no ground on any of these subjects. "When you're lighter, you're faster. Yes, I love food and I do use my workouts as a way to eat. I just can't graze through the day like many of the other girls. I like eating one big meal at night. My mother's that way, too. I've never, ever done the throwing-up thing and never will. But people can hide it so well."

Kirsten suspected that much of what lay behind the talk about her weight was jealousy. "'I'm so big and she's so small,' I know that's what some of the other girls feel like racing next to me," she said. And no doubt many of Kirsten's competition who divided their meals into strict percentages of this and that, eschewing sweets of any kind, had to feel cheated when little Kirsten—epiphyte by day, glutton by night—sat down in her size-four warm-up suit to devour a quart of ice cream or an entire chocolate cake.

The signs of perfectionism were apparent, but surely weren't the whole story. She was too buoyant, too accepting of others, too aware of, indeed, too happy with her own pathology to be labeled "ill." Nevertheless, the signs of rampant compulsivity were everywhere. Her home was painstakingly color coordinated, the bedside lamps were painted to match the walls, and even the bathroom scale matched the wallpaper (her mother's touch). One hundred race T-shirts were stacked in her closet as neatly as coins in a banker's drawer. On her bookshelves were sixteen photo albums, time-ordered, jauntily annotated, and all devoted to her career. Was this narcissm or healthy self-esteem?

Robert Ames, sun bathing with Kirsten next to the pool at Newcombe's Ranch, knew all the talk and shrugged it off. He called her "my little brown-skinned beauty," and that she was. Laid out in a black two-piece suit, her blond hair wisping in the Texas breeze, she looked light and strong and in love—more than ready for the season's opener that would bring her, Newby-Fraser, and the best middle-distance triathletes back to St. Croix in just seven weeks.

CHAPTER 6.

NO DOUBLE-BUTTED CHROME-MOLY MAMA

◆

Circa 1989. Baton Rouge, Louisiana

"*T*he guy who says workin' out is bad for you is usually sittin' behind a desk with a cigar and a martini," said F.O. "Foxy" Denham, barely smiling. No one at Foxy's health club knows—or will say if they do—what the *F.O.* stands for.

Aside from his thinning hair, Foxy looks more like a teenage computer nut than a fiftyish community mainstay. "I've been in the fitness business for thirty years. Started as an on-the-floor trainer. I've gradually worked myself into a job for which I am completely unsuited—runnin' a business." The last part was pure southern self-deprecation.

Foxy's began in 1968 as, essentially, a big garage where LSU athletes could lift weights inexpensively. One of the early drop-ins was Jan Meador, the scrappy, athletic daughter of LSU sports legend Bob Meador. Today Foxy's is Baton Rouge's oldest operating health club and, with fifty thousand square feet of free weights, racquetball courts, treadmills, stair machines, pools, and steam rooms, it is certainly one of the largest. As for Jan Meador, she became Jan Ripple, the best all-around athlete to ever reach the top level of professional triathlon. Foxy gave Jan Ripple a free, lifetime membership in 1984.

Down the hall from Foxy's office, in a noisy, high-ceilinged room crowded with Exercycles and treadmills, Jan Ripple pumped a stair-climbing machine in front of the mirrors along-side nine other women similarly engaged. The group resembled a row of slot-machine enthusiasts.

Unlike the other women, who leaned heavily on the chest-high grips, Ripple pushed each pedal tread clear to the floor and didn't use the grips; she didn't hold on at all. "It's important to go all the way down," she said "otherwise, you'll cramp. The grips just keep you from developing balance." The readout screen between the grips registered her effort in a grid of red dots. There were twelve columns on the readout screen and each column could be a maximum of ten dots high; the more dots in the column, the greater the effort needed to keep up with the machine. Each column represented a unit of time. The leftmost column showed the effort for the current period and the columns to the right showed what was to come. Every column on Ripple's readout was nine dots high. "I'm usually up here," she said, pointing to the top line with her right index finger, "but I'm a little tired from my bike ride." She was referring to an earlier workout with the LSU cycling club. Ripple's index finger is crumpled, the result of a football injury in the seventh grade. The backs of her hands are ribbed in blue veins and her fingers are deeply lined from years of clenching and sun.

After a half-hour at level nine, Ripple seems no more tired than she was after five minutes. She rocks from side to side, her torso tight and erect, one knee rising up past her waist, then going down under the hump of her driving quads. Her buttocks are hard and pumped out under black, calf-length stretch pants. She's fudging a bit on Foxy's dress code. "Foxy makes the women wear tights under their shorts," she explains. "Not the men though. He doesn't want the men, you know, lookin'. I've been to some of these clubs in California. People are practically naked. That intimidates the bigger women. Not here though. People come to Foxy's to work. Look at 'em."

She was right. Everyone on the main floor exercised at a high aerobic pace: a fiftyish black-skinned woman wearing a pink sweat suit and listening to a Walkman slaps the treadmill next to a thin, red-faced balding executive who appears to be running for a personal best. Three young women spin the Exercycles together, chatting, but each of them is wet with perspiration. Sweat trickles down the tendons that rise up Jan's neck; she continues to rock the stair pedals. She wipes her cheek with the back of her hand and smears her eyeliner; the effect is to deepen her already-sunken sockets.

Foxy, the proprietor, continued, "Now, some of the best athletes are not involved in sports. I saw a guy in New Guinea climb a hundred-foot tree, then stay up there for hours, choppin' at it with a machete. Inside that tree was a nest with honey in it and he wasn't goin' down 'til he'd got it. Of course, he wasn't always that fit. He probably started out on a smaller tree."

It was difficult to believe that Jan Ripple had ever been up a smaller tree. More likely, she'd fallen from the big ones several times before making it to the top. Nothing else could explain how Ripple could take on triathlon's top talent while keeping up with three kids and a husband. In 1989, Ripple was the *only* woman professional to have *any* children, let alone three. Moreover, she was within a month of being the *oldest* female professional in triathlon. "Janripplemotherofthree, that's what the reporters call me," she sighs. "Some of the women out there say the nastiest things about me, like saying I got the coverage on television or whatever because I had a family." Jan's voice rises and her eyes narrow under a thrusting brow. Her short blond hair shakes. "I told those women . . . I don't call the reporters and tell 'em what to write about me! I can't tell 'em what to write!"

It isn't clear whether southern-bred manners or religious convictions prevent Jan from swearing at this point. She is a Christian and, like her parents before her, was born into it.

Jimmy Swaggert's Bible College sprawls a few miles from her home. She went to school with Swaggert's son at Tara High. Her kids attend a Baptist school. On the Sundays when Jan isn't racing, the family attends services across the street from the school. But in contrast to Kirsten Hanssen, Jan isn't a born-again convert and is not a fanatic adherent in her daily affairs. God doesn't affect her like a drug, as He does Kirsten.

Jan Ripple was born into a sporting family so rule driven and strict that it could reasonably be called an athletic cult. Discipline, religion, and athletics were not merely features of life for Bob and Mary Meador and their six children—they were life. "We didn't have toys when we were kids," Jan explains. "We played sports." Competition permeated their lives.

When Jan was old enough, she competed outside the family; first came gymnastics—she was Southern Regional Champion in the vault at eight years old. Then it was diving—she was Louisiana State Champion on the 1 and 3 meter boards. Then came track—she was Louisiana State Champion in the 50 and 100 meter dash. Then it was basketball—she was voted Most Valuable Player in five State tournaments. Then she swam, becoming Louisiana State Champion and AAU Champion in every distance up to 500 yards in freestyle and up to 200 yards in butterfly. Jan was one of the first five women at Louisiana State University to receive an athletic scholarship. She went to the Olympic Swimming Trials in 1972, but when she got there, she was too tired from overtraining to swim her best.

Outside of preaching, there is no activity more highly valued in Jan's hometown of Baton Rouge than athletics. LSU, the family alma mater, is the town's pulpit of perspiration. Jan swam for LSU in the early 1970s before construction of the current natatorium, a complex of swimming and diving pools roughly the size of a three-story K-mart. Jan's younger brother Rick, who made the Olympic swimming team in 1980 (the year of the U.S. boycott), is now head swim coach at the natatorium.

Facilities for LSU athletics are large, well-built, and cared for, particularly those devoted to football. Home games are contested in Tiger Stadium, a circular pit shaped like a strip mine with concentric rings of benches rising to the sky. Above the highest row is a large signboard that reads WELCOME TO DEATH VALLEY. The feeling on the field is primal. To preserve the turf for the rituals of the regular season, LSU football players have an indoor practice field as well—which they use when the outdoor field is muddy.

Basketball is played inside a domed stadium dedicated to "Pistol" Pete Maravich, who played basketball brilliantly for LSU and then for the NBA. He died at the peak of his athletic powers, of heart failure during a pickup game in a school yard. Jan Ripple's son, Kyle, at eight years, believed Maravich died during an NBA game. Despite frequent correction, Kyle insisted that it was so. The right time to die, he'd learned, was in serious competition.

Bob Meador, Jan's father and Kyle's grandfather, still holds the LSU record for most consecutive basketball starts. He started every game of four consecutive seasons—every game. He also played baseball and ran track, once doing them simultaneously. He was waiting to bat cleanup one afternoon when teammates saw him run out of the bullpen, jump the ballpark fence, and run to the adjacent track meet, then in progress. There he took his turn in the long jump, ran back, vaulted the fence, and returned to the bullpen. His long jump was good enough to win the Southern College Conference title.

Bob Meador played professional baseball after graduation with the Milwaukee Braves. He was a natural athlete who drove himself, and his six children, to the limit. Russell is the youngest. Today, although in his thirties, Russell still looks like a college wrestler—graceful, yet muscular from neck to narrow waist. Russell remembers his father as a paradoxical disciplinarian. "He was 'Sergeant Dad' to me. But not in the beginning. At first he called me 'my little baby boy' and I slept with him 'til I was three. They'd put me in my crib, but Dad would come in later and bring me into their bed. I didn't have my own bed until I was six. Then he changed. It was like he said, 'Here are the rules, son. Now you're on your own.'"

Of the six children, only Fran, Jan's big sister by two years, escaped the pressure to excel athletically. Russell explained why. "Dad called Fran 'Madame Queen.' She was his darlin'. He'd sing to her when she came down the stairs. And then there was younger sister Jan, doin' cartwheels, tryin' to get his attention. Jan wanted his affection, his love, and tried so hard to please him. But he didn't care. Or didn't show it if he did."

"Fran was the only one that was never spanked," remembers Jan. "Fran literally did everything Dad said, by the book. Once we were all on vacation and he told Fran, 'Watch the car, I'll be right back.' She must then have been about twelve, so I was probably ten. We'd been in the hotel room about an hour and all of a sudden everyone said, 'Where's Fran?' Dad went outside and found Fran in the car and he says, 'What are you doing out here?' and she says, 'You told me to watch the car.'"

"Because I was so completely different from Fran," Jan went on, "I had it rough. If I didn't agree with something he wanted me to do, I demanded his reasons. I wanted him to sit there and explain it to me, why I can't do this or that. I had a very strong will and I drove Dad crazy. Drove him particularly crazy. I had eleven-o'clock curfew 'til the day I married."

Jan was an active child, not easy to control. She was kicked out of kindergarten after three days. Her teacher said, "She won't drink the milk. She won't take a nap. She won't cooperate and she's extremely active and we think she's just not mature enough for kindergarten." Jan laughs about being labeled hyperactive and rebellious and knows people in the sport still see her that way. Triathlon pioneer Julie Moss said of Jan, "She's thirty-four going on sixteen." Jan would laugh at that, too.

Fran was the perfect one, the lady. Just like her mother, Fran went to LSU, became a cheerleader, and married an LSU athlete, in her case, a linebacker. Jan tried to do it all, too. She excelled at her mother's childhood sport—gymnastics, then she too became an LSU cheerleader and married an LSU athlete, another linebacker in fact.

Jan married Steve Ripple right after graduation and they immediately moved to Lexington, Kentucky, where Steve studied to become a pediatric dentist. Jan was a housewife who occasionally took outside jobs for spending money; for a while she chopped wood. The adjustment from a life of college athletics to full-time homemaker and mother of three small children was painful. Only exercise and faith, she says, saved her from abject depression. Toward the end of her six years in Kentucky, Jan experimented with triathlons and won every one she entered. Back in Louisiana, in 1986, she turned pro. Her father disapproved, saying, "Who's gonna take care of them babies, Jan?" but with Steve's support, Jan quickly won a reputation as a formidable competitor in USTS distance races and anything shorter.

Physically, Jan Ripple was born to sprint. Her muscles were heavily laced with white meat—fast-twitch fibers that contract powerfully and quickly, but fatigue early. Over four years of triathlon training and competition, she had done her best to raise her endurance for longer races. Her body fought her. She had an unbelievably high VO2-max—82 ml/kg/min—as measured at Duke University in 1989. But her maximum heart rate was only 178 ("my fallin' over dead rate"). Even if her anaerobic threshold was a record 90 percent of her maximum heart rate, it was still only 160 beats per minute. That was eighteen beats lower than Newby-Fraser's. With her high muscle mass and low exercise heart rate, Jan tended to accumulate heat and lactic acid faster than her cardiovascular system could wash it away. She sweated profusely and lost an abnormally high volume of sodium—a substance vital to mental coherence, the transmission of nerve impulses to the skeletal muscles as well as to heart function. In any race longer than two hours, sodium imbalances and/or dehydration would bring her to the verge of confusion and convulsions. Muscle cramps were normal for Ripple. The swim was not problematic—the water served as an external radiator, flushing away heat from her body. But on the run, she was always a quart low and ready to seize.

In a sport which favored slender frames powered by slow

twitching fibers that could ratchet all day, Ripple was an un-likely contender. But there were compelling reasons why none of her competitors would completely count her out, even from the Ironman. First, she always raced to win and knew how to gain advantage when it mattered most. There was a champion-ship race once, a sprint, that offered a special cash prize to the first person to finish the bike leg. Jan knew that the winner for this prize would not be the first cyclist into the bike-to-run transition area or even the first to rack her bike. Rather, the "prime line," as it is called, was drawn at the far end of the transition area. When Jan finished the bike course and stormed into the transition, Colleen Cannon, an excellent runner, was right with her. They racked their bikes not more than a blink apart. Colleen sat down to put on her running shoes. Jan didn't. Instead, she grabbed her shoes and ran off with them, barefoot, toward the prime line. Colleen saw Jan take off and gave chase, but it was too late. Jan crossed the prime line first. Then, a few hundred dollars richer, she sat down to put on her running shoes.

The second factor that made Jan a threat in any race was her twenty years of intense physical conditioning. "When Jan comes out of the water," said her agent, "her shoulders are pumped, she's big. Some say too big, like a man's." Jan's upper body made competitors talk, but her legs made them curse. She and Erin Baker were easily the strongest all-around cyclists and, like Baker, Ripple's quadriceps laid over her femur in two distinct rumps of muscle. One began on the outside of her hip, arched down and curved back to the outside of her knee. The other humped out from the midpoint of the first muscle and lay across, attaching to the inside of her knee. Her calves bulged under tight skin. Her legs were so strong that when cycling on moderate hills, she didn't bother changing gears or standing up. She just pushed harder and, over time, built up great, painful quantities of lactic acid. She recovered on the downhill, as best she could. "Jan never gets on a bike to do anything but mash big gears," said Kirsten Hanssen's beau, Rob-ert Ames. "Ooo man, does she fly hard."

In the water, Jan's power is palpable, particularly when she does 50 yard butterfly repeats or medleys of all the strokes. Unlike many triathletes who flutter kick lightly to maintain buoyancy, Jan has a big, two-beat crossover kick. It's kick, kick, cross—as she taps her ankles together—kick, kick, cross. The whumping kick keeps her hips near the surface and the crossover counteracts the sway.

Although Jan usually trains alone, her workouts are planned by her husband, Steve, who doesn't trust the job to anyone else. Steve believes Jan's discipline is so great that she would injure herself before quitting an ill-designed program. He is most careful with her around weight training; in the preseason he will often go with her to Foxy's to make certain that she's gaining endurance, not just bulk, from her workouts. He favors circuit training, which combines various lifts with aerobic conditioning. As a coach, Steve Ripple exhibits the characteristics that served him so well as a linebacker. He is calculating and dispassionate.

Thirty minutes into a forty-five-minute circuit-training workout, Steve stands next to Jan while she does her second set of bent rows with a thirty-five-pound bar. She stands straight legged with her upper body parallel to the mat. She lifts the bar to her stomach, then pushes it straight out to the full extension of her arms, lowers it, and repeats. After ten repetitions, her weariness shows in lengthening crows feet as she squints and grunts a little. On the twelfth repetition, she drops her chin a bit, just before thrusting the bar out. She smacks her chin with the steel. The blow pops her head up and her eyes fill with fatigue and pain. She lets the bar down slowly and rests, bent over. Steve holds his clipboard steady and shuffles a bit. Then he says flatly, "I know you hit your chin. You're losing concentration. Think of being on the bike when it's hard. It hurts and you tell yourself to regain concentration." He is her husband, but there is no pain in his eyes. There is empathy in his voice, but no sympathy. Jan pulls herself together and continues the set. Steve offers her a lighter bar, but she doesn't take it. She finishes the set with the heavy bar. When asked later about Steve's coaching style, she calmly explained, "I like to be pushed. Steve gives me praise when I deserve it. I don't deserve it now."

March and April, 1989. Baton Rouge, Louisiana

To prepare for the season opener in St. Croix, Steve and Jan stepped up the intensity of her workouts; they shortened the rest period between intervals on the track and in the pool. On the bike she did more jumps (simulated breakaways from a pack of riders) and increased the distance of her weekly endurance rides. All was going well but for one crucial part—hill training.

Louisiana is flat. The only hill with a road over it is about three miles from Jan's ranch-style house in suburban Baton Rouge. The hill rises all of six feet. The closest set of hills is in St. Francisville, forty-five minutes away by car. Over the winter of '89, Jan would sometimes drive there to train. "The hills there are little rollers, and that's big to everybody in Baton Rouge. But I had been to St. Croix and I knew what a hill could be."

The previous year, in 1988, Kirsten Hanssen came down from her Rocky Mountains and rolled up St. Croix's volcanic slopes like a pinball. Jan was left gasping and came in fifth. "I lost everything on the bike," she said. The run course is equally hilly. To do well in St. Croix, she knew she had to train there. That meant leaving Steve and the kids for at least two weeks. She'd never been away from Steve or the kids for more than two nights running, ever. Jan cried and didn't think she could go, but Steve was adamant. He poked angrily at the air and said, "No one is going to say we didn't give you the chance."

Jan knew he was right. It was important to prove early in the season that she could be a threat at any distance, that she could place highly at the Ironman. "I had to show 'em," she said, "that I can run long—that I can come off a long bike and burn for twelve miles."

Steve and the kids drove Jan to the airport the first week of April, 1989, and put her, crying, on the plane for St. Croix, where she would race Kirsten Hanssen, the Puntous Twins, Colleen Cannon, Paula Newby-Fraser, and Erin Baker on the twenty-third. Julie Wilson, unsponsored, would not compete in St. Croix. She was saving her money to race in Australia on April 30.

Foxy Denham leaned back in his chair. He thought about Jan Ripple and all she had gone through and then he said, "The average person thinks you just train real hard and one day you're there for good and everything's whippy. But you aren't. It's a process of adaption and decision, of getting used to what you've created. You reach that elite plateau and you make a decision, conscious or unconscious—are you going to work even harder to stay there, or are you going to relax and fall back?"

CHAPTER 7.

HER BEST

◆

Early April, 1989. St. Croix, the U.S. Virgin Islands

*J*an Ripple flew to St. Croix in the first week of April and was joined there by Mike Pigg, a boy-faced truck mechanic from Northern California who'd won the event in 1987 and hoped to repeat. Though married, it was natural for Ripple to share a place with a male athlete. She and Newby-Fraser didn't get along. And Colleen Cannon, Erin Baker, and Kirsten Hanssen, though friendly, were still rivals. And the other women just couldn't keep up.

Mike Pigg came to triathlon in 1986 and tore the sprints apart on the bike, just as Kirsten Hanssen had done in the women's field. Pigg didn't so much ride a bike as run on it, often standing out of the saddle and churning his largest gears. Traditional cyclists would laugh about Pigg's style. "He's all over the bike," they'd say. "He rides like a triathlete." But Pigg's style worked for him very well—in two races in 1987 he averaged close to twenty-nine miles an hour for twenty-five miles. By 1988 Mike Pigg had improved his long-distance running to the point that, unless he fell on his head on his way to the starting line, he was favored in any triathlon short of the Ironman. He'd won the St. Croix race the previous year by six minutes.

Pigg didn't impress easily, but Jan Ripple brought him to hyperbole. "She's an awesome biker. Why? Are you kidding, just look at her legs. They're as strong," he said, "as any man's." Such comparisons with men were inevitable for all the top women and inevitably demeaning; they implied that only by losing her femininity could a woman achieve distinction as an athlete.

Mike and Jan lodged together that April in the oceanfront condominium of a wealthy triathlon enthusiast and kept to themselves. They trained, rested, and spent a lot of time planning, procuring, and preparing what they ate. They took an oath together, foreswearing simple sugars of any kind until the race was done.

Jan thought nutrition might well be the determining factor in her race. As always, she was worried about losing the lead in the run—Jan called it being "run down"—in the hot hills east of Christianstead. To avoid it, she needed to be maximally hydrated and well-stocked with complex sugars that could be broken down into glucose at a steady rate. Simple sugars would go right through and not allow her to store up what she needed. "It's the toughest run course of any triathlon," she said. "There are hillier courses, but none that follow as tough a bike. Bodies are gonna be burnin' fuel like crazy. This is a big-money race with a deep field of top runners floatin'. It's gonna be fast."

Every day for two weeks, Ripple ran the run course midday, just as she would during the race—out of town, past the squatter's shacks of pressed dirt and tin, past the sprawling Buccaneer Hotel, and out to the turnaround in the leeward scrub, then back. Every other day she rode the bike course on a borrowed machine. Her titanium-frame racer had been lost on the way over from Baton Rouge, but she did not panic. She was a seasoned athlete and expected problems. She used the heavier bike for training and made arrangements to have another racing bike shipped if it came to that.

Six hundred triathletes, nearly all of Northern European descent, flew onto the island in the first weeks of April. Whenever they gathered in groups, they talked mostly about one hill—officially called The Beast—that lurked thirty miles into the bike course. The name was apt and made possible the race's tag line: The Beauty and the Beast.

The big hill switchbacks down an eroding cinder cone from which poured the western end of the fifteen-mile, volcanic island. What made The Beast so daunting was its combination of length—almost a mile—and elevation gain—a thousand feet. Its average rise of 20 percent (similar to Nob Hill in San Francisco) is plenty tough, even for excellent cyclists, but in places the hill is easily a third again as steep. The roadway is narrow; there is never more than twenty feet between the cliff and the side cut in the chocolate soil. Back and forth weaving, most triathletes decided, would be nearly impossible, and the general feeling was that even *if* one could weave, walking would be faster. The Beast was added to the course in favor of a less brutal hill through the efforts of a paying sponsor: The Carambola Resort. Named for the star-shaped fruit with yellow, waxy skin, the Carambola wanted the race to pass prominently through the grounds. Accordingly, the bike course was altered to include their mountainous access road. NBC, which had the broadcast rights, couldn't disagree that the inclusion of another dramatic focal point would pep up the broadcast.

Many of the seasoned pros felt used and threatened by the commercialism behind the course design. They liked the $110,000 prize purse, one of triathlon's largest, but generally felt the course was long on excitement and short on safety. They pointed first to the swim course, which, repeating the 1988 design, had a ninety-degree turn less than a hundred yards from the beach, exactly where the unseparated pack would be swimming the fastest. To avoid being socked, kicked and/or swum over, the pros knew they had to either reach the buoy first, so as not to be crushed in the pack as it went around, or swim wide and lose precious seconds. In the previous year's race, most fought to get to the buoy first. The violence started on the beach where Eney Jones, the fastest female swimmer in the bunch, was flattened and trampled on the beach. Jones swam with a bruised rib, but was the first woman pro out of the water anyway. None of the athletes wanted to see a repeat.

The Beast was the second issue. Kirsten Hanssen, not one to complain, and Dave Scott, ex-collegiate water polo All-American and six-time Ironman champion, explained their objections to race director Rennie Roker. "It's not that the hill is too difficult to ride up," they said. "It's too dangerous to walk up." They explained that few athletes would be able to ride to the top. Nearly everyone would be forced to dismount in biking shoes and walk—or run. Their cleats, the inch-high plastic buttons screwed to the balls of their shoes, would compound the angle of the hill, and put tremendous strain on Achilles tendons already tight from cycling. Season-ending pulls could well result. (The angles can be simulated by standing with one's heels on the floor and one's toes on the top of a dictionary. Imagine walking like that.) The slick plastic of the cleats, moreover, could easily slip on the steep pavement, bringing athletes down heavily on their kneecaps.

Roker said nothing could be done. If athletes were worried about walking up in their shoes, he said, they should take them off and push their bikes barefoot.

It was a classic conflict of interest between athlete and promoter: Roker, naturally, was concerned mainly about the success of one event, but the athletes had to take a longer view. In the end, Roker won. The course was not changed.

Each afternoon for a week before race day, while the steel drums played happy tinkle-bop in the streets, triathletes crowded the smoothie shops, drank iced fruit drinks, and talked about gears and recent attempts to climb The Beast. The word was that only Erin Baker was riding to the top consistently. Newby-Fraser hadn't and said she wasn't going to bust her ass trying. It was ridiculous, she said. Neither Colleen Cannon nor the Puntous sisters had been seen riding to the top. Kirsten Hanssen kept saying, "I haven't made it up that thing yet. I really don't think I can."

No one believed her. "Kirsten has much more confidence in herself than she's ever gonna let you see," said Jan Ripple. Others too, had noticed Kirsten's habit of underestimating her ability prior to races and when they were over, of downplaying the difficulty. "Oh, it did get a little tough out there" (Kirsten would chirp from the winner's platform) "but I just held my head up and told myself how lucky I was to be loved by God."

Kirsten's disclaimers sounded hollow to Steve Ripple, who would scowl and fold his big forearms over his chest whenever he heard them. "The thing that gets my goat about Kirsten," he said, "is how she'll never admit how much she hurts. When everybody else is out there sweatin' blood and wantin' to lay down on the road and die, she'll say, 'Oh, maybe it did hurt a little.'" It was impossible for Steve to believe that perhaps Kirsten didn't feel as much pain as his wife.

But about The Beast at least, Kirsten was telling the truth. She'd been on the island a week and hadn't made it up once. She was nervous about it and the anxiety was getting to her. She accepted the common wisdom that any contender who rode to the top would cross the finish line before anyone who didn't. Anyone who came off the bike once would never get back on, not on that grade, and would thereby lose five to ten minutes—and possibly their Achilles tendons.

On the Tuesday before Sunday's race, Kirsten called Robert in Colorado. "She was in tears," said Robert. "She kept saying 'I can't get up this hill, Robert.' She kept crying and saying 'I haven't seen anyone get up this hill, Robert. I don't think I'm going to make it.' I told her, 'Oh, Kirsten, you're going to make it. There isn't a hill you can't climb.' And Kirsten said, 'You don't know, Robert. This hill is *steep*. You better bring a forty-two-by-twenty-six gear for me when you come and you better bring one for yourself.'" Robert picked up two sets of 42×26's (a front chainring with forty-two teeth and a rear cog with twenty-six—the cyclist's equivalent of the trucker's compound low) in Miami on his way over and installed them on Friday before the race.

Jan Ripple wasn't concerned about making it up The Beast. She'd considered adding a smaller gear to her front chainring to make it a triple like a mountain bike, but hadn't. When her bike finally arrived two days prior to the race, she took it out to the hill and started up, just to see. "It was a struggle. But I did make it and figured I'd have no problem during the race because I'd have all this adrenaline pumping."

Newby-Fraser swore she didn't concern herself with what her competitors might or might not be planning, feeling, or thinking. She went to bed early.

On race-day eve, the streets of old Christianstead were packed until ten. Descendants of a hundred thousand slaves brought to St. Croix to make European sugar entertained the mostly Caucasian athletes with crab races and steel-drum calypso. Most triathletes were saving their legs for the race and danced little, if at all.

On the map, St. Croix is shaped like a cartoon whale heading for the western tip of Puerto Rico. The swim course began on a small island two hundred yards off the whale's back at the base of its hump. By 7:00 A.M. on race day, all athletes had been ferried out to the island; they waited on the beach under a banner of sponsor advertising.

In the final minutes before the start, Jan, Kirsten, Erin, and Paula adjusted their goggles. Unlike many of the amateurs who wore the expensive type with spongy foam gaskets and large eyepieces, all the women pros wore the cheap, rubber-gasket kind they'd used since childhood. They stood in the sugar sand and looked out through their goggles past the turn buoy lolling in the azure water. The women were placid and lost in contemplation, but the men were, by and large, agitated and anxious to go.

Dionne Warwick sang the national anthem. Someone blew

on a conch shell, the Caribbean equivalent of a starter's pistol, and the athletes plunged into the water.

There was no easing into it. The pace of the lead pack over the first 500 yards of the 1.9 mile course was an explosive one minute to one minute and five seconds per hundred yards. (The world-record pace for one mile is approximately fifty-six seconds per hundred yards.) The leaders swarmed round the first buoy, then pulled steadily away from the rest, denying them any draft whatsoever. After 500 yards, the lead pace slowed a bit, to 1:15 per hundred yards.

Eney Jones went to the women's lead again, with Ripple, Newby-Fraser, Baker, and Hanssen following at an initial pace of about 1:10 per hundred yards. After four hundred or so yards of that, they slowed to 1:20 per hundred—a pace they would hold for the duration.

Swimming effort cannot be gauged by any commonplace measure of speed. The fastest speed ever attained by a swimmer was just over five miles per hour—a record set by multiple Olympic gold medalist Matt Biondi during a 100 meter freestyle race. Depending on the distance of the swim leg, the best triathletes—men and women—average between 2.6 and 3.1 mph. The energy requirement of boosting the pace even five seconds per hundred yards, and holding it for 1.9 miles, is enormous, a quantum leap. But the gain from doing so would be slight—less than three minutes total—an advantage easily cut to nothing during a two-and-a-half-hour bike race.

Newby-Fraser and Hanssen swam in each other's bubbles and came out of the water a minute after Ripple, who had wobble-legged up the ramp to the bike racks when the clock read 43:23. There was fury in Ripple's eyes as she pounced, dripping, on her titanium-frame bike and heaved out of the transition area. "There were," she said, "two things on my mind when I got on that bike—get the lead and get the money." Baker was two minutes behind Ripple, having had "an 'orrible swim."

*   *   *

The bike course was a sideways figure eight. The right loop went out the whale's tail section and back to the base of its hump. This was the smaller of the two loops: seventeen rolling miles through sage and scrub brush on the dry end of the fifty-eight-mile course. The loops met at a hairpin turn in Christianstead, on a one-lane street with stone buildings rising straight from the pavement's edge. The first woman out of the hairpin would collect $1,250. Ripple planned on being that woman.

The big loop took the riders into the hilly, wet, and forested western end, where the second-prize point was set at mile thirty—roughly where the whale's blowhole would be, at the crest of The Beast. Jan wanted that money, too. So did Baker. So did Hanssen.

By mile six, Ripple caught the women who'd led the swim, rode through them and left them behind. Less than a minute back rode Baker, obviously recovered from her slow swim. She'd passed Newby-Fraser and Hanssen early and was spinning comfortably—her back twenty degrees off horizontal and her white helmet down. She wore no socks.

Ripple whizzed into Christianstead alone and as she rolled down the chute to the hairpin, she was right behind the NBC camera van. It blocked her view and she misjudged the turn; she entered it much too fast. Her bike rammed the mattress and hay bale barrier and Jan, still attached to the pedals, plunged over the bars and to the side, rear wheel up. As she extracted herself from her hay and bike tangle, Erin Baker banked deftly through the hairpin to take the prime.

Ripple remounted. Wild with adrenaline, she took off after Baker and caught her near the blowhole on the approach to The Beast. Baker was calm, but Ripple was steaming from the chase. As they started up, Ripple was slightly ahead; she gritted down on her silver bike and heaved her blue-suited muscle from side to side, wrenching the bars up and shoving the ped-als down. Black-suited Erin aimed her black carbon-fiber bike straight up the centerline and breathed with a *chuffing* sound. Her rear wheel was a solid black disk and it rolled steadily up with a *whuh ... whuh ... whuh* sound. Ripple struggled. The adrenaline she'd counted on for torque was spent. Inside, her legs flooded with fatigue. She tried to compensate by jerking the bike ever more violently from side to side, not dancing it up, but throwing it forward as best she could. The bike was barely moving when she twisted her heel too far out on the upstroke. Her shoe cleat broke free from the pedal; her momentum broken, she had to stop. "The hill was so steep I couldn't get back on; I had no choice but go up on foot." Baker kept riding, straight up the center of the roadway to the top without breaking rhythm. Jan walked, gasping, leaning into the hill as into a gale.

While Ripple walked, Kirsten Hanssen zipped by on what she called her "Pygmy bike" with twenty-four-inch wheels and mountain gearing. Jan heard her breathing. She made a *chi ... chi ... chi...* sound and she did not stop.

Hanssen's light frame helped ease the climb, but once over the top, as the mountain fell away under her little wheels, she lost ground to Baker—the frontal surface area of her body was not much different than Baker's, but the mass behind Hanssen was significantly less. Moreover, Kirsten was frightened by twisting descents ("I'm a chicken"), and the backside of The Beast was a doozy. She played it safe and waited for the run when the sun would bake the bigger women.

Newby-Fraser walked the hill a few minutes behind Hanssen, the speedster of Hawaii now just another pedestrian on that ridiculous hill. She was not in the mood for athletic heroics and figured she'd save herself for the last half of the bike and the long run in the midday sun that would follow.

When Jan Ripple got to the top of The Beast and climbed back on her bike, Baker had a five-minute lead. I'm still not very far behind, thought Ripple, you've lost a lot to Erin, but not to those girls (they all called themselves girls) who just went by; you gotta attack now; go after it. She did. "But," she said, "I forgot that at the bottom there's a sharp ninety-degree turn."

Jan didn't try to make it; she was going too fast for that. She hit the hay bales and flew, somersaulting with her bike attached to her feet. She landed on her shoulders and her bike seat in the field beyond. The impact broke three spokes of her rear wheel and crushed inward all features of her saddle. Her handlebars were twisted sideways. Surprisingly, Ripple's shoulders were only scuffed. The handlebars she twisted back. The broken spokes she tore away except for one which she couldn't. The seat was irreparable. But she wasn't planning on doing much sitting anyway. She gave chase. Her pace was furious and didn't bode well for a fast run. By the end of the bike course, Ripple had caught and passed all the women who'd passed her earlier except for Baker. Ripple's bike time was the second fastest of the top ten even though she walked The Beast and crashed twice.

When Jan racked her bike and pulled on her racing flats, Baker was a mile away. Jan knew that unless Baker blew up, (Triathlete slang for irreparable overexertion), something she'd never done at this distance, she'd win. Ripple shifted her focus to second place. So did Kirsten Hanssen, who ran out of the bike racks just one minute after Ripple. Newby-Fraser followed a half minute later behind long-legged Australian distance specialist Jan Wanklyn. Running sensations Sylvianne Puntous and Karen Smyers followed two minutes back.

Kirsten's ability to run hard immediately after cycling like a dervish caused anyone who led her off the bike to run scared. Kirsten was one of only a handful who assiduously trained for this critical transition. "You've got to leave your running shoes right by the back door," she'd chirp. "Otherwise it's too easy to just get off that bike and lay down."

Ripple's legs were slow to come back and Kirsten gained on her steadily over the first miles. She passed Jan at mile three and held her pursuit pace until she had a forty-five-second lead. Ripple chased her hard, but in eight miles Ripple never got any closer. That's how it ended—Baker, Hanssen, then Ripple.

Ripple was elated. Only Hanssen had gained on her during the run. She'd proven to everyone that she could trade blows with the toughest bike course round and still be a contender on a long run. "At that point I felt it—1989 would be my best season."

After cooling down, Jan found Mike Pigg and together they went to the store. "We bought three packages of Oreos and some other rich ones that come in foil packages—oh yeah, Pepperidge Farms. Mike wanted those. We sat on a curb downtown and ate cookies until we couldn't look at another."

Full of cookies and pride, she went to a phone and called her kids in Baton Rouge. Shelly, then ten, was the first on the line. She heard her mother's excitement. "Your mama got third, honey!"

Shelly was stunned. "You mean you didn't *win*?"

"No, honey," Jan said with her head a little lower, "your mama didn't win, but she did her very best."

CHAPTER 8.

WHEELS OF FORTUNE

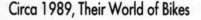

Circa 1989, Their World of Bikes

*T*he importance of the cycling leg—and its physical relationship to the run that followed—preoccupied most competitive triathletes after three-time Olympic cyclist John Howard raced the Ironman in 1980.

Howard was attracted to triathlon because, as he conceived it, "Triathlon is a pure test of horsepower." Unlike road racing, in which packs of cyclists ride wheel to wheel until the final sprint to the finish, triathlon does not allow drafting, which can cut the energy required to cover a given distance by as much as 30 percent. In triathlon, no competitor may ride in another's slipstream.

The bike leg in triathlon is what cyclists called a time trial: an unaided race against the clock over a set distance. Since the biking portion of the Ironman accounts for 80 percent of the total distance, Howard was confident he could compensate on the bike for whatever he lacked as a swimmer (which was considerable) or as runner.

When Howard emerged from the water in his 1980 Ironman

debut, the leaders were twenty miles ahead. He was an *hour* behind. Undaunted, he proceeded to set a record for the bike course by averaging twenty-five miles an hour for a hundred and twelve miles. He rode fast enough to take back the hour he'd lost to everyone who'd led him out of the water—except for one. When he began the marathon, Howard was still twenty-five minutes behind Dave Scott.

When Howard got off his bike to run, he had to struggle to walk. He had 26.2 miles to go. An indomitable competitor, Howard pressed on. After a time, he gained strength and was able to run somewhat, but in the end it took Howard forty minutes longer than Dave Scott to finish the marathon. Scott won and Howard placed third.

All the "rock fish" (triathlete slang for poor swimmers) in triathlon cheered Howard's performance, but in the end, the lesson drawn from his race was that efficiency and pacing on the bike are every bit as important as raw horsepower. (Interestingly, the best cyclists in the world cannot develop even one horsepower—the power needed to raise 550 pounds one foot each second for an hour. The elite level of racer operates between one-half and three-quarters horsepower.)

When winning triathlon performances are broken down and the time spent in each component is compared to the whole, the ratios keep repeating: swimming, 15 percent; cycling, 55 percent; and running, 30 percent. These proportions make apparent why races—which certainly can be lost on the swim—are usually won on the bike and defended on the run. Small improvements in cycling ability will result in greater gains than can be registered through improvements in any of the other events. For example, cycling a half a mile an hour faster will cut the time needed to complete the 112-mile Ironman course by 8 minutes. Cutting eight minutes off a marathon time means knocking almost twenty seconds (off each mile)—a huge improvement for a seasoned runner.

Nearly any triathlete could get faster on the bike; the problem was doing so without getting slower on the run. This is what made Paula Newby-Fraser's 1988 Ironman victory the watershed event that it was: She set a women's marathon leg record *after* cutting the women's record on the bike by half an hour.

When the cheering for Newby-Fraser quieted, attention turned to the instrument of her success: her bike. It was different and looked it, particularly to old road horses like Howard, for whom good bike design was two spiderwebs connected by Euclid. To the traditionalist, Newby-Fraser's bike looked straight out of a clown act, mainly because of the small wheels. Nearly four inches smaller in diameter than twenty-seven-inch conventional wheels, hers had only three spokes. The spokes were white, wide, and nearly flat—a sandwich of carbon-fiber laminates tapered to a knife edge. When she rode and looked down, Newby-Fraser saw nothing but the thin black line of her tire speeding through the V of her front fork. There was no silver triangle of spokes and no faint whizzing of air. Paula sat high above the wheels on a black saddle set on blue steel tubing, her feet pedaling circles around a chainring the size of a dinner plate. (The oversized front gear compensated for the smaller wheels, allowing her to pedal within the efficient range of 75 to 95 rpm.) The bike was equipped, naturally, with the latest aerodynamic handlebars. If it was part of a clown act, it was a *fast* clown act.

The bike was designed by Ralph Lewis, who was, like Newby-Fraser, a former South African recently settled in the States. Lewis raced bikes in Velodromes as a young man and took to human-powered wheels as many boys do to cars. Because top-flight production frames were in short supply in South Africa, Lewis began making them for friends. The bike he made for Newby-Fraser incorporated thirty years of experimentation, all of it toward one goal: blend the quickness of a track bike with the versatility of a road machine. Said Lewis of his new creation, "at anything over nine miles per hour, the performance just wipes out a big wheel bike." The bike was called the Hamilton, after Lewis's middle name.

The advantages of the Hamilton, Lewis said, derived first

from the rigidity of the smaller frame. More of the rider's power thus goes to moving the wheels round, he explained, than to flexing the frame. Second, the smaller wheels push less air, making the power transferred to the wheels more efficient in moving the bike forward. Finally, the bike was more responsive on hills. It accelerated faster and slowed more surely because the smaller wheels spun with less inertia than those of a big-wheeled bike. This also made turning easier. Gyroscopic effects were lessened, allowing the rider to throw the bike as much as steer it.

Wind-tunnel tests on his wheels confirmed Lewis's claims of greater efficiency. Compared to conventionally spoked wheels with aerodynamic rims, his wide, flat spokes would save a rider a minute over twenty-five miles. On the Ironman course, that amounted to four and a half minutes—a healthy but not prohibitive advantage. The greatest gains came from the rigid frame, the bike's lightness, and the biomechanical advantage of the whole when coupled to a woman's smaller body.

In Newby-Fraser's case, the fit was superlative. It has long been known that, at twenty miles an hour and above, a rider who makes no attempt to reduce his profile with respect to the passing air will put about 80 percent of his or her energy into simply moving the air out of the way. Of that energy, three quarters pushes the air that piles up around the body, and a quarter moves the air hitting the bike itself. What Lewis's frame did for Newby-Fraser was to offer less bike to the impeding wind, and enable her to adopt an extremely small, aerodynamic profile.

Her ballet training helped—no athlete is more accustomed to uncomfortable postures than a ballerina—but the bike was the right platform. Newby-Fraser was quick to say that no bike ever won a race, that only well-trained riders win races. She was right, of course. Among many well-trained riders, however, those with superior equipment usually, as would be expected, win—or at least finish with less wear and tear.

Newby-Fraser did not buy her Hamilton; it was a preproduction prototype given to her as part of a sponsorship package with Veltec-Boyer, a California sporting goods distributor. Veltec-Boyer would have preferred that one or several of the top men in the sport—Dave Scott, Mark Allen or Mike Pigg—ride the bike, but as one representative explained, "the top men would want thirty to sixty thousand dollars to ride it. Sponsoring the women was a much cheaper way to get the exposure."

Kirsten Hanssen was chosen to ride a Hamilton prototype as well. She called it her "pygmy bike" and felt something was wrong with it, but wouldn't know what that was until the middle of the season.

According to Veltec-Boyer, the distribution link between Lewis and the sporting goods' retailer fell apart at the peak of the 1989 season. The first shipments of 150 production wheels were found defective and none of the promised frames were received from Lewis's shop. Lewis did, however, sell custom bikes with hand-built wheels to a few long-distance specialists, including Brazilian up-and-comer Fernanda Keler and Texas sprite Amy Aikman, who had twice finished among the Ironman's top ten women.

Hard to get and expensive (up to $4,000 for a fully equipped, custom-fit model), Hamiltons were all but unavailable to unsponsored athletes. Still, Newby-Fraser's breakthrough performance on her funny bike tormented triathletes in the winter of 1988–1989. Everyone wanted a new bike, or, short of that, they wanted the latest wind-cutting wheels.

Julie Wilson wanted a new bike as much as anyone. Her red, aluminum-framed Vitus, the one she'd crashed in Australia and rode through the year following, had sixteen thousand miles on it, but still looked new. Julie did most of the maintenance on it herself while it hung from ropes her father had rigged from the deck of the upstairs apartment. Major servicing, like repacking the bottom bracket, which had to be done every three hundred miles because of the northwest rains, was done free at friend Kevin King's bike shop. In return for King's labor,

Wilson put a "King's Cycle" label on her race helmet. Neither expected this to net many customers.

Wilson often minimized the importance of bike technology in racing: "It's the one who pushes down on the pedals the hardest who wins," she'd often say. She believed this most when she had no money for new equipment. In the late winter of 1989, however, Julie knew her old Vitus wouldn't make it another season, no matter how hard she pushed it. When Jim Wilson called about getting a ride for Julie on a Lewis-designed bike, he was told "anything we might do will have to be a ways down the road." Jim and she didn't have the money to commission a bike from Lewis and, for that matter, they couldn't afford a new production bike either.

The problem ate away at Wilson through the winter and no affordable solution came forward. She and Jim figured they'd have a better chance of attracting a sponsor if they had photographs to show of Julie sitting pretty in fashion sportswear. Julie hated posing, but the prints turned out well. Jim took some around to local magazines after work and sent others to biking and sports-apparel companies. They received no offers. It looked certain that they'd be on their own again—with Julie on her old bike—at least through the early season and maybe longer.

On a rainy Saturday afternoon in late February, Julie and Jim sat down, as did triathletes everywhere, to watch the broadcast of the 1988 Ironman taped the previous October. It was painful. There was Newby-Fraser, chewing up the highway on that darn bike. There was Jan Ripple, not even finishing the race, but getting her five minutes of sponsor-pleasing fame. Wilson, who finished fourth, never appeared on screen, except by name in the final standings just before the closing credits. She took some comfort from that. "At least they showed my name," she wrote later in her diary.

When the broadcast was over, Julie was depressed. "All that work . . . and my career comes down to getting my face on this ridiculous show." She said it not with anger but with incredulity. "School kids could do a better job showing the race—

there's battles going on all over that course. And what do they show? Jan Ripple crampin' up. What'd she expect—she drank Coke and ate cookies, for Pete's sake." Her voice had turned angry. "The program has nothin' to do with the athletic story. It's just a freak show."

Julie was bitter, though she could little afford to be. She was already nervous about the hard weeks she'd start on Monday. She called them "death weeks"—three weeks of progressively faster speed work and longer distances.

Jim thought Julie needed some air and they left the apartment with the idea of thinking about something other than triathlons. Within an hour they stood in front of the display window of Angle Lake Cycle. Julie'd spotted a Trek 5000—a new carbon-fiber, one-piece frame-set fitted with Shimano Dura-Ace components and a bladed wheel up front and a black disc wheel in back. "What do you think they want for it?" Julie asked. Jim read the tag, "$2,300." Julie looked at the bike like a child. "It's a nice bike," she said, "but it probably wouldn't fit me. Let's go home."

Julie's parents, Andy and Thelma, had always done their best to support Julie. When they heard that sponsorship was not likely before Australia, they gave their daughter $500 to buy a new frame-set from a catalog company in Colorado. The money was a birthday present two months early; Julie would turn thirty on May 15. Julie and Jim pulled together some money of their own and bought new brakes, derailleurs, shift levers, a new crank assembly and headset, and a new bottom bracket. She ordered them from a catalog; the parts totaled $421. They couldn't afford new wheels. She needed what money they had left over for other essentials. Her running shoes were worn out ($75). So were her biking shoes ($100) and she thought she'd soon be needing new orthotics to keep her knee tracking straight ($220). Then, of course, there'd be the airfare to Australia and lodging for a week ($2,000 minimum).

Wilson knew her competition in Australia would have disc wheels and trispokes, but she figured she could beat them anyway. She'd heard Tour de France winner Greg LeMond say that bladed spoked wheels could do just as well as disc wheels on hills and she thought he was right.

Wilson drew strength from her role as underdog. She knew there was more to winning than having the latest equipment, the most efficient lungs, and the best mix of muscle fibers. If there wasn't more to it than that, what was the point of racing? Why not test the athletes on treadmills, have them pedal stationary bikes, and push water in swimming flumes. Why not test their equipment in wind tunnels and such, tote up the numbers, and award prizes? In such tests, Wilson knew she'd lose. She couldn't afford the equipment that Ripple, Newby-Fraser, and Hanssen had had given to them. Her VO2-max was probably lower because of her dented heart valve, but that hadn't kept her from swimming some record times for Nyssa and she wasn't about to let it stop her now. She could still be the best, she figured, and she knew how to do it. "There's a poem that Jim reads to me that goes somethin' like, 'You must believe and dream, but act you must too.' So many people in this sport do the believin' and the dreamin'; they want to achieve the highest, but they don't put in what it takes. They're full of excuses. They say, 'It's rainin' or, 'It's too cold,' or, 'I'm a little tired today, I'll do it tomorrow.'"

"If it comes easy," she asks, "What challenge was it? If somebody says, 'Julie, you can take this pill and win the Ironman without a day of trainin' *or* you can work and train and struggle and win,' well, I'd do the work."

The poem and hard-scrabble values helped, but couldn't bury Julie's lingering bitterness over sponsorship rejections.

Jan Ripple, who'd just signed to represent an electronics company at a base pay of $1,250 per month plus travel expenses, said, "I understand Julie's bitterness, but I know that if, like Paula [Newby-Fraser] she'd done the USTS circuit and got top three or top five, it would be different for her. Sponsors want your face out there. Julie should have said, 'Okay, I'm a distance racer, but I gotta at least show up at the shorter races.' That's what I did. We lost money [Steve and I], but I knew I had to get my face out there so people know I'm serious about my racing career. We thought, maybe a sponsorship will come from it. And it did." Wilson tried the USTS circuit in 1987, but missed Jim too much to continue traveling without him. "Triathlon is just for a few years," she would say, "but marriage is for longer."

Julie Wilson's dream of a bike sponsor was, for Jan Ripple, a reality. In addition to the cash sponsorship, Ripple had a ride with a Litespeed, a high-end bike manufacturer whose products filled a small study off the Ripple's kitchen. Two racing bikes hung from the ceiling; they were unpainted and the metal tubes of their frames shined like new dimes. The frames were titanium, actually a titanium alloy originally designed and largely sold as hydraulic line for jet aircraft and for which bike manufacturers paid $25 a linear foot. Each bike required about $400 of the stuff, before labor.

The titanium frames were light, strong, and flexible—capable of withstanding Jan's strength and the awful wrenching she could apply. Hanging with the bikes were two spare wheels—there wasn't room on the ceiling for the six other spare rims that leaned against boxes of shoes, gloves, water bottles, caps, and nearly forgotten trophies.

Most of Ripple's spoked wheels were fitted with bladed spokes laced radially, meaning that no spoke crossed another. She had one spare disc wheel in the room; the others were on the bikes. Five helmets, six pair of bike shoes, four tarnished loving cups, and rows of plaques crowded a floor-to-ceiling bookshelf behind the hanging bikes. Prize bottles of wine, Champagne, and cognac collected dust there too. (Neither Jan nor Steve drank the stuff—ever.) The books on the top shelf included: *Eat to Win The Sports Nutrition Bible, Psycho-Cybernetics,* and *Good News America—God Loves You.* On a wall adjacent to the bookshelf, twenty neck medals on ribbons hung in a clump next to a hook bearing nine tires and eight tubes. There was a short blue sofa in the room and an end table with two photographs—one of Steve in his college football uniform, and one of Jan in her bridal gown.

Apart from changing an occasional tire, Jan did no bike maintenance; she was a professional rider, not a mechanic. And with three kids, she had no time for it anyway. When her equipment broke—or, as happened more often, when she broke it—she sent it to the shop and pressed a spare into service.

Things were different for Julie Wilson, not worse, she thought, just different. "Yep," said Wilson, "that was my thing. They had their wheels but I could beat 'em." Self-confidence and the fruits of hard training are worth more than a good set of wheels, she felt and she did not dwell on the idea that some of her competitors might have it all.

CHAPTER 9.

PACKAGE DEAL

April 1989. Cardiff-by-the-Sea, Ca

*J*ulie Moss was one of the few professional triathletes racing in 1989 who could remember when top athletes entered the Ironman with the hope of just finishing. She was not like "the new girls," the ones Moss called "The Driven"; she'd been a competitor in the days before aero anything, before three-millimeter neoprene wet suits and complex-carbohydrate supplements. She was in it for the travel, the sunshine, the people, and not to become somebody else. Training was just her ticket to the show. It was not her reason for getting up in the morning. This is what she told herself and over the years she came to see herself as others did: as the most famous second-place finisher in the sport. Perhaps in *all* of sport.

Moss was twenty-four years old, a college student, and not a bad surfer when she entered her first Ironman in 1982. Her race went well all day, but as night fell she began to have problems running. Soon she was walking, then staggering, then lurching forward, desperately to maintain balance on legs that had gone dead to her will. A quarter mile from the finish, her knees buckled. She collapsed, and went down straight; her long body crumpling limb by limb into a heap on the road.

There on the pavement, between walls of bare-legged spectators, Moss was still conscious, quite lucid in fact, and she began to move forward once more by pulling herself down the centerline with her forearms; her legs, streaked with feces, noodled out behind her. After a bit of that, she got a foot forward and pushed herself up. There she wobbled, straddle-legged like a newborn colt. Heart-struck observers reached out to steady her. "Don't help me," she yelled and yanked her elbows away from their comforting palms. She pulled her bra strap back over her shoulder, lurched forward a short ways, lost her tender balance, and went down again. Network television followed Julie as she cantilevered down the dark street in a grim wash of halogen and sodium vapor light. When she got to her feet once more, Kathleen McCartney ran past to take first. That's when Moss went down for the last time. Twenty-nine seconds later, she pushed her hand over the finish line.

Someone scooped her up and took her away to the medical tent. She emerged a short time later, fully sentient, and as curious as anyone about the events just passed: "I laid in this tent here thinking, What is going on? Everything shut down. Just shut down and cut loose. It was a pretty scary experience."

Moss remained in the sport and became the candid doyenne of women's triathlon. She still competed, but in U.S. races was usually out of the top three. She performed best in Europe. "They treat me well there," she said, "and, to be frank, the competition isn't as tough."

At the eve of the 1989 season, Moss sat in her new home in Cardiff-by-the-Sea with a new attitude. "Winning triathlons is better than sex," she said. "At least that's what Mark says." Mark Allen was Julie's fiancé and heir apparent to the mantle of Dave Scott, the six-time Ironman winner. Allen was on a winning streak and had been comparing sex to triathlons frequently in jest. To Julie, the implication of many of Mark's jokes was that training hard enough to win a major race had a direct and negative effect on the male libido. Dave Scott had said the same thing some years earlier but had learned to keep quiet about what every pro knew: The world's "sexiest sport" was the sport that destroyed sex. "Mark ought to know," Moss said.

That sex was on Julie's mind, but not, apparently, on Mark's would be expected from studies which have shown that, generally, male libido drops in response to regular, intense exercise while female libido tends to increase with intense exercise. Some endocrinologists believe that testosterone, which is normally produced by women in small quantities, is responsible for female libido. Some endocrinologists also believe that intense exercise stimulates the female body to increase production of testosterone, and other androgens, thus increasing hair growth and libido.

Only recently had Moss begun to savor the joy of winning and thus appreciate the comparison. She'd won two long-course events in Europe in the '88 season. Instead of scaring her, the wins made her want to win even more.

This was true for Mark as well. After ten years of second-place finishes and mechanical disasters, Allen hungered for the title of world-beater. His appetite stimulated Julie and she felt her competitive desire build that winter and spring as never before.

"The bulk of my career has been built on fear," she said, "fear of having other women beat me. I've been swept along, getting attention for what I'd done, not for what I'm expected to do. I don't like that and this season I'm going to turn it around."

Moss began 1989 committed to race—and win—all season, having spent a good part of the winter in New Zealand training with Mark Allen, Erin Baker, Baker's fiancé Scott Molina, and Colleen Cannon. By late April, Moss was in the best shape of her life. She'd always been a strong runner, but consistent speed work on the track had made her faster and more confident that she could hold on at high beats per minute. As for cycling, after 1986 she'd been left behind by "The Driven" and their three-hundred-mile training weeks. But that winter she'd done her miles, her intervals, and her hillwork as well. Her swimming was fair, but now she understood that three or four minutes wouldn't matter. "I'm not afraid now to stand on the line with the other women," Moss said, two days before leaving to prove it at the '89 Australian World Cup. Her fiancé, Mark, had just signed a big contract with Nike and, as she put it, Moss was "part of the package." She would not be specific about what that entailed beyond requiring her presence with Mark at prerace clinics and press interviews.

Julie Wilson had signed with nobody and was still nursing sore legs when she and her husband, Jim, left for Brisbane. It would be Julie's first race of the season, the same race at which she'd crashed the year before: swim two miles in The Broadwater, bike sixty in the rolling bush, and run eighteen along the spit and through the Bobina to the finish.

April 25 to 29, 1989. Surfer's Paradise, Australia

Julie Wilson was glad Moss would be in the race. She admired Moss's honesty and delighted in her irreverent remarks. Moreover, Moss was never standoffish before a race like the other Californians, but always greeted Wilson by name and said things that Julie might think, but would never say, such as, "I accept what I can't change about myself. I have red hair and freckles and I'll never be able to get a good tan." Moss's presence eased Julie's nervousness and made her feel she belonged to the club. When Wilson looked at Moss, she saw a good, clean competitor and, one she thought she could beat. In last year's World Cup, even biking bloody for forty miles, Wilson had bettered Moss's bike time by thirty-four minutes. Wilson was certain Moss's superiority on the run could not close a thirty-minute gap over nineteen miles.

Wilson and her husband settled into their hotel at Surfer's Paradise in the middle of a monsoon four days before the race. There were ten-foot waves in The Broadwater. Heavy rains lasted two days more and kept Julie off the bike, which turned out to be good because her legs needed the rest. In the last days before the race, Jim massaged them for four hours each day.

While Wilson was kneaded by her husband, Moss and Mark Allen did star turns with the local press. "The Fittest Lovers in the World" were filmed strolling, surfing, and driving away in a rental car that had MARK ALLEN emblazoned on the right front quarter panel. To the press, Moss was just Mark Allen's fiancé and the one who crawled across the finish in '82. That annoyed her, but it came out pleasantly enough. Laughing, she said, "I really don't care how well Mark does here. I'm here for my race and I'll go on record to say I won't be happy without a top-three finish." It sounded good, but no one quite believed her.

Meanwhile, race favorite Paula Newby-Fraser was having trouble getting into the country. Her Zimbabwe passport was full—stamped solid with entry visas—and the Zimbabwe government was resisting reissue. To keep her Zimbabwe passport, she'd have to renounce any claim to South African citizenship. Two days before the race, the Zimbabwe consulate in Los Angeles released Newby-Fraser's new passport. The ordeal put her agent into the hospital for exhaustion the night before they left.

It made no sense for Newby-Fraser to race two long-course events in a week, but her pride and several thousand dollars were at stake. She had a contract to race in Australia and had accepted appearance money and airfare. She was a long-course specialist and there were few long-course events with good money behind them. She was the only woman pro in Australia who'd raced St. Croix as well.

The dark horse was Liz Hepple, an Australian cyclist who'd placed third in the Tour de France the previous summer and had raced in the 1988 Olympics. She'd taken up triathlon in her off-season and had won her last eight races. She was a fair swimmer, not as good as Wilson, Moss, or Newby-Fraser, but again, what's a minute or two deficit to an elite cyclist on an eighty-mile course? Nothing. *If* she came off the bike with a

five-minute lead and could stay on her feet through the run. ...
It was a scenario to consider, but neither Moss, Newby-Fraser,
nor Wilson gave it a thought because none of them knew Hepple from boo.

The major factor in the event, however, was not human, but
environmental. Wilson had formulated a race plan based on
what she knew of the course from the prior year—tough swim,
hilly bike, and a pounding run in high temperature. She
planned to use her strength in the water to emerge with
enough of a lead to vanish on the bike, and disappear in the
hills where she could build a lead without being a visible
pacer. Wilson thought Newby-Fraser might get to the lead on
the bike for a while, but felt it unlikely that she could sustain
that lead in the hills. Word was out around Surfer's Paradise
that Newby-Fraser had faded badly on the run in St. Croix, only
six days earlier. It was unlikely, they thought, that she could
recover by raceday.

If all went well, Wilson figured she might have enough of a
lead going into the run to hold off Newby-Fraser—and the Puntous Twins should they appear on race day. Judging from the
past, Moss would not be a factor.

Just one look at the swim course convinced Wilson that her
strategy was junk. The course had been changed and would
not repeat the arduous conditions of the previous year. There
had been many complaints from those who'd exhausted themselves against the tide and race officials were convinced to
move the starting point up the Nerang river, approximately
one mile upstream from where the river dumped into the bottom of The Broadwater. Thus, swimmers would be assisted by
the river's current for a mile and, upon entering the bay, would
be sped along by the flow of the outgoing tide.

The net effect was to turn the event into a float-bike-run.
Strong swimming would not be at an advantage and no one,
including Julie Wilson, would be getting away from swim-ex-
hausted, bike-run specialists. The currents would carry everyone to their bikes fresh. Worse yet for Wilson, forty kilometers
of hills—another of her strengths—had been taken from the

bike course and replaced with flats and gentle grades.

At dawn on race day Julie Wilson stood on the river bank upstream from the midchannel turn buoy. The brownish gray water flowed under high clouds in the dim light. White pelicans with black spots drifted on the current from right to left, deaf to the thrum of the television helicopter overhead. Julie looked out to her left at the orange buoy two hundred yards from shore and thought about her placement again. Yes, she said, this is the right place to be. She was far enough upstream to prevent the current from sweeping her under the buoy—an infraction punishable by time penalties or disqualification. She looked to her left, downstream at the hundreds of others and wondered how in hell they figured to make the turn against the current. Newby-Fraser, she observed, was among them.

When the gun fired, Wilson stuck to her plan. She swam out hard and, carried by the current, swept down on the buoy and cut it close on the outside. When she looked up and sighted downstream to establish her line, she saw a huge swarm boiling away hundreds of yards down river. Then the meaning of that hit her: Those standing downstream before the race had no intention of making the buoy; or if they had, they'd lost their resolve early and went with the pack and current. Whatever their intentions, they'd cut the course.

Wilson swam catch-up for the next twenty minutes. When she clambered out of the brackish bay past the Southport bridge, the clock read twenty-three minutes. The current had doubled her race pace to forty seconds per hundred yards, effectively cutting in half the energy usually required to do a swim of that distance.

Newby-Fraser had come out of the water a minute and twenty seconds earlier, the rising sun warm on her back. She ripped off her wet suit, hopped on her Hamilton, and disappeared onto the course before Wilson had put on her biking shorts.

Moss was one of the weaker swimmers among the women's pro field and Wilson expected her to be at least two minutes behind at this point, but she was only thirty seconds back. Wilson headed out onto the bike course confused and angry. "Calm down," she told herself, "and catch Newby-Fraser before it's too late." She had no idea how fast Newby-Fraser was going.

Moss intended to deny Wilson any lead on the bike. Her rear disc wheel, rolling black and thin behind her long legs, sounded like a beer keg rolling down a truck ramp. *Rummm, rumm, rummm.* Wilson was looking straight down between her aero-bars at the silver triangle of her spinning front spokes when Moss passed her on the right only six miles into the ride. Again, Wilson was jolted. The sight of Moss going away woke her up to the task redefined once more and she pushed hard to catch up.

Moss and Wilson soon rode side by side, six feet apart. Although they couldn't do as much chatting as they wanted, they spoke some and their few exchanges communicated clearly how terrific it felt to be friends and to be among the best in the world at what they were doing right now, so many thousands of miles from home. One pushed the pace, then the other. They dove and rose through the bush at a hard-driving 23 mph. They passed Australian sprinters Carole Pickard and Louise Bonham, but keeping their minds on catching Newby-Fraser.

"About thirty miles out," Wilson said, "Liz Hepple just blew by us. We didn't know who she was, but we let her go. With fifty miles left on the bike, we figured she'd burn up and die on the run." At that point, Moss and Wilson were tied for third.

Ahead in the hills, Newby-Fraser was feeling the fatigue of St. Croix. She was three hours into the race. The sun was high and white in a crayon-blue sky. Crickets buzzed and chirped loudly, but she didn't hear them. Hepple overtook her at sixty miles, spinning smooth circles and breathing softly.

A minute after Hepple took the lead, Wilson and Moss caught sight of Newby-Fraser. "Let's get her," yelled Moss. They steadily closed, then passed, riding in second place. Newby-Fraser kept her head down and her upper lip pressed tightly against her top teeth. No words were exchanged. When they were well by Newby-Fraser, Wilson settled back to her previous cruising speed. Moss didn't and pulled away. The fun was over. The two Julies knew then that they would finish their races alone, keeping silent about whatever they had left. But Moss had the advantage psychologically. She knew Wilson's legs were hurting. Wilson had confided this before the race in a moment of competitive weakness, recounting to Moss: "My legs just haven't healed since the Ironman last year. I've tried everything." Moss was her friend and Wilson knew she'd understand. She did.

Hepple led off the bike and came out of the changing tent in blue shorts and what runners called a singlet—a white running shirt with a U-shaped neck and thin shoulder straps. She had the equipment of the runner, but not the speed. She did, however, have what Newby-Fraser's boyfriend, Paul Huddle, called "The Look of Love," which meant, he said, that "you had to love it to be out there looking like that."

Running was her weakest sport, but Hepple was leading her country's richest race with eighteen miles to go. It was nearly noon, eighty-five in the shade, and humid. Heat radiated up from the road and Hepple felt it on rim of her nostrils when she inhaled through her mouth. Time to hunker down, she knew, and bear it.

Moss rode into the transition area in second place, three and a half minutes behind Hepple who was, at that moment, running in a quick chop toward the spit and into the wind coming off the ocean. Moss unzipped her one-piece cycling suit and stepped out. She sat down on the green indoor-outdoor carpet in her swimsuit and said about Hepple, "I hope all she can do is ride."

Wilson came into the transition as Moss was leaving. She got on her gear, slugged down some water, and began running. Her legs felt bruised from the inside out and Newby-Fraser was right behind her.

Newby-Fraser was now in her element—it was hot and humid, the run was long, and, except for Moss, her competition was weak. She'd tucked several packets of carbohydrate goo into her black-and-fuchsia racing suit; every five miles on the run, she would tear open a packet with her teeth, suck out the contents and get it down with a water chaser. At that time, the "squeezies," as they were called, were available only in San Diego–area triathlon and bike stores. Going by the brand name Leppin, the product came into the United States from South Africa through the United Kingdom.

Newby-Fraser ran hard out of the transition area and passed Wilson in the first mile. She caught Moss shortly thereafter and the two ran together until Moss pulled away at mile two. Seventeen to go.

Wilson made a deal with herself: Hold your pace for ten kilometers, then see how you feel. At ten kilometers the pain in her legs and midsection had subsided somewhat. She was breathing easier and picked up the pace. Soon she saw Newby-Fraser through the wiggling air, but she had nothing left for closing. Setting in for the duration, she hoped Hepple would overheat.

Moss ran beautifully. But for her elbows, which swung a bit wider than the book would want, her form was beyond reproach. Her long body was erect and when she passed Hepple with twelve miles to go, her freckled legs still had kick.

Hepple hunched ever farther forward as she hunkered through the miles, her knees rising less and less. With nine miles to go, Newby-Fraser passed her for second place.

Wilson closed rapidly over the last miles, cutting Hepple's lead from a mile and a half to a less than eight hundred yards. But she ran out of room. "Facts are facts," she said. "I couldn't catch her and just hung in there for fourth."

That's how it ended: Moss, Newby-Fraser, Hepple, and Wilson—in that order. Newby-Fraser wanted a comeback from St. Croix, but instead took what she considered another loss—this time from Julie Moss, the sport's most famous has-been. It was going to be a long five months until the Ironman.

For Moss, it was the biggest win of a long career. But was it better than sex? "Yes," she laughed, "because it was such a

novelty." Beyond the excitement, the win was a personal triumph she'd long desired. "I never wanted to go out of this
sport on my back," she said. "Now the door is open for me to
leave with my pride."

The massive course-cutting at the start of the race left Wilson disillusioned and angry. She was angrier still when she realized there had been no investigation, no attempt to penalize
anyone. An open-water swim is certainly difficult to marshal
because the possibility of misidentifying swimmers in crowded
water is so great. And there was a feeling in the air that the
race had ended too well, from a publicity perspective, to be
spoiled by talk of an uneven start. Moss and Allen, the package
deal, had won. Important people were happy.

CHAPTER 10.

CHEATING

◆

Early May, 1989. Seattle, Washington

*W*hen Julie Wilson returned to the Pacific Northwest from Australia, she found the rains had stopped. Alders, maples, and cottonwoods had burst like green fireworks against a blue sky that grew deeper each day. In the valley of the Green River, robins soldiered in the pastures and barn swallows swooped under bridges with streamers of string. The sun no longer skimmed the skyline but shone high above. The early season, so long awaited, had come ... and gone.

It had all happened too quickly and needed sorting out. "The season opener tells you where you are. It's a benchmark," Wilson said. "That's all." A good coach would assess her defeat in the same, detached way. But it wasn't how she felt.

Wilson didn't believe in reliving races, but she couldn't help it, especially when she rode her bike. While concentrating on her cadence and the shape of the road, her mind would float back to Brisbane and she would recall the other athletes standing on the banks of the Nerang.

She felt the closeness of the pack. She heard the starting

horn and then felt the bursting away, the coolness of water on her cheeks, and the strain in her heart as she pulled forward and against the shoving current. Then she saw a pack splinter off, cut the first buoy, and swim away.

Inside, her feelings would cycle from confusion to anger and then to acceptance tinged with despair. "I can't believe people would do that," she'd say. "Cheaters is what they are." And finally she'd sigh and say, "There's nothin' I can do about it. In every walk of life there are people who will cut corners."

The role of victim did not suit her, but she felt no less the chump for having raced fairly. It was not rational, but the longer she thought on it, the more she felt she could have done something, but didn't. Psychologically, the race had battered her competitive spirit and sense of fair play.

Physically, the race had torn muscle, stretched ligaments, and further irritated the fascia—sheathing around muscles and tendons—in her legs. Her right leg was particularly sore. She attributed this to a bike shoe cleat which, she discovered after the race, was five millimeters out of position. "Over ninety miles, it adds up," she said. Micro-capillaries in the plump bands of muscle that lay over her upper legs were swollen with fluids and they too throbbed from the pressure, a normal consequence of racing in hills and heat.

She felt broken and gypped. She was angry with pain, angry at her legs. On May 5, she stopped pedaling while on an easy forty-mile ride; she sat up, gritted her teeth, and punched her right leg hard between her knee and the hem of her yellow shorts. Then she did it again. "These darn legs," she cried. A red splotch grew on her skin. To Julie then, her body was a Broken machine; in her frustration she wanted to fix it with a hammer.

She ate lunch and dinner with ice wraps tied around her thighs and shins. She got a massage each week. Twice would have been better, but the expense was prohibitive. She took five hundred milligrams of naprosyn, a strong anti-inflammatory, twice a day. It was legal under the drug rules, but she didn't think it was safe. She quit taking it when a football player for the Seattle Seahawks sued his team doctors for encouraging him to take massive doses of anti-inflammatories—a routine, he said, that led to kidney damage. Wilson's sports medicine physician then recommended over-the-counter ibuprofen. Some days Julie took seven two hundred–milligram pills. Though even higher doses were legal, she couldn't stomach more.

Meanwhile, she continued to train and tried to reduce the pounding. She ran in the pool more often and did much of her bike work indoors with her bike mounted on a stand. There she could control her workouts more precisely and not have to worry about such things as getting caught hurting thirty miles from home, bucking a headwind. But there were trade-offs: sixty miles (three hours at least) on a bike trainer is a mental trial few can endure.

It was either this, or give up on a low-expense race with good prize money scheduled for the end of the month in Scottsdale, Arizona. She felt certain she'd finish Scottsdale somewhere in the money. She desperately needed the money and was unwilling to curtail training. But gradually, the pain and isolation wore her down. "How," she wondered, "do the others manage to train through injuries?"

Wilson's best friend, Linda, believed that in many cases, the secret was drugs. As a nurse in training and a former top-level marathoner, she knew why steroids were the preferred anti-inflammatory, pain killer, and pepper-upper of the run-down athlete. "I have no doubt about it. If they weren't on drugs, Julie'd beat 'em." She freely aired her suspicions with Julie and although the talk made Julie feel less defective, it was depressing to think that her own efforts might never, by themselves, be enough.

Jim suspected steroid use too, but thought blood packing was more likely. Also called boosting, blood packing is a procedure in which a few training-tired pints of blood are drawn out and replaced by blood brimming with red blood cells and hemoglobin. Jim's suspicion was not macabre paranoia. Boosting had been done with the U.S. Olympic Cycling team in 1984. Though not banned in 1984 (it was soon after), boosting was widely regarded in the medical community as a violation of the part of the Hippocratic oath that said "do no harm." In the cycling community, boosting was a dirty way to win.

The man who supervised the transfusions in 1984 was team physician, Dr. Herman Falsetti. Eddie Borysewicz (Eddie B.), United States Olympic Cycling coach at the time, assisted the procedure. Both have since left the Olympic program. But in 1989, Dr. Falsetti ran a sports-performance clinic outside Los Angeles. Eddie B. worked with him. Their clinic advertised steadily in leading triathlon publications. The banner of their advertisement read, "Train Smarter, Not Harder." They had professional triathletes as clients. Although there was no evidence that either Falsetti or Borysewicz were promoting improper performance-enhancing procedures to triathletes, their background inevitably aroused suspicion within the professional ranks.

Dr. Robert Voy, chief medical officer for the United States Olympic Committee from 1984 to 1989, was one of the first U.S. sporting officials to take the discussion of drugs out of the locker room and into the lab. "I'd be the last one to encourage drug use in any way," he said. "But the fact is, these drugs work. In any sport where endurance and speed are the critical factors, blood packing, steroids, and amphetamines will be there—because they work." Voy spearheaded the drug reform program inside the U.S. Olympic community.

Caffeine suppositories, stimulants, blood packing, and steroids had been used by professional cyclists for years. It was common knowledge. There had been many confessions. And some deaths. But those were the "failures." For every failure there were ten who would say drug use was not a problem, thank you. The drugs were available and so were physicians and users to advise on their use. For the cautious user, clandestine labs were available prior to competition to determine whether the drugs they'd taken in training could still be detected. If so, the athlete would withdraw.

All this notwithstanding, it was not until late 1988 that professional triathletes began to wonder whether their sport was "dirty." For one thing, there had never been, until then, enough money in the sport to serve as a believable motive. But more to the point, if a person wanted to cheat, there were less extreme ways to go about it. One could, for example, draft another cyclist, a ploy that could be worth up to a 30 percent energy advantage at the start of the run. In the early years of triathlon, few races employed many drafting marshals. But nothing beat course cutting, which was not uncommon in the amateur ranks for raw results. The most notorious course cutter was a wealthy, middle-aged man from Texas who infuriated his age-group rivals and was eventually thrown out of the sport.

Dirty tricks had been played, too. In a 1986 long-course event, race favorites Karen McKeachie and Laurie Samuelson, then a top amateur, were both victims of bike tampering. Some time after they left their bikes in the racks prerace, and before they emerged from the swim, someone loosened the stem bolts on both bikes, thereby disabling their steering. Samuelson was serendipitously unaffected . She'd recently obtained a new bike and had passed her customary machine to her husband, Roland, for the race. Roland made repairs immediately and proceeded. McKeachie, however, battled forward on her injured bike, steering largely by body language. She held together until the halfway point where, overcome by her misfortune, she got off the bike and threw it into a ditch.

Not all means of gaining advantage were illegal even though many had nothing to do with training the body. First came the racing wet suit. This $200 aid to buoyancy was good for one to three minutes in a fifteen-hundred-meter swim. After 1986, they were generally allowed in water cooler than seventy-two degrees. And most open water is. (Wet suits are not allowed at the Hawaiian Ironman, where the swim is done in 80 degree salt water.)

Aerodynamic handlebars and bar-end shifters came next. By making the rider more aerodynamic, they could save up to five minutes over forty kilometers. Cost: $100 to $200. "An aerodynamic water bottle," John Howard of Olympic-cycling fame told triathletes, "will cut five seconds off your best twenty-five-mile time." He wasn't joking.

Fast wheels came next—disc wheels, trispokes, and bladed spokes. The right combination could yield a gain of two to five minutes over an equally trained rider using thirty-six-spoke wheels with flat rims. Cost: $300 to $1,000.

Any one of these means—legal and illegal—could provide an insurmountable edge over the competition. And none of them required putting powerful drugs—often of uncertain composition—into an otherwise healthy body.

Two things happened in 1988 to make drug use more attractive to triathletes and promoters. First was the money. Suddenly, there was more of it than ever before—significantly more. Prize money was up and so were endorsement contracts. Top competitors who had been happy to win sunglasses and running shoes five years earlier were suddenly pulling down as much as $400,000 a year. Triathletes and their sport were hot cover stories in 1988 and 1989 for *Runner's World, Bicycling,* and *Outside* magazines. Once scorned as masochistic fools, triathletes had become trendsetters for the fitness sector. Aero-bars, clipless bike pedals, electrolyte replacement drinks, nutrition supplements, heat-dissipating running wear and flashy bike fashions, racing wet suits—manufacturers of all these products sponsored and used professional triathletes in display advertising.

In 1989, Erin Baker received a reported $90,000 to represent Le Coq Sportif, a European apparel manufacturer. Timex, purveyor of the official "Ironman" watch, paid Kirsten Hanssen $30,000 a year to wear the watch and the name. By 1988, the prospect of making a hundred thousand to half a million a year was not out of the question for a large handful of aspiring triathletes who found all other form of employment repulsive.

Drug use became less unpalatable as other means of gaining advantage were closed off. More prize money led to better marshaling, making course-cutting and drafting more difficult. Out-and-back swim courses—in which out-bound cheaters could, before rounding the far buoy, easily flip undetected into the home-bound lane—became less common as race directors grew savvy with experience. Easy gains from technology were no longer available; by mid-1988, most pros had aero-bars, disc wheels and/or aero-spokes, clipless bike pedals, and wet suits.

The easy ways of gaining advantage through equipment gone, and the opportunities to course-cut or draft diminished, triathletes were again forced to improve the old-fashioned way—by training and eating better. They learned about anaerobic threshold, about lactate tolerance training, about the different chemistries involved in ratcheting different types of muscles, about how to recruit a greater number of muscle fibers, about fuel for the body and spirit. When training guidelines based on heart rates were released by the American Heart Association in 1988, triathletes had already purchased thousands of wireless heart-rate monitors. While most turned to exercise physiology and exercise chemistry to improve their times, it was inevitable that some would look to the underground pharmacy.

Scott Molina, a pillar of the sport and a pro since 1982 (and then Erin Baker's live-in partner,) tested positive for anabolic-androgenic steroids in Nice, France, in September of 1988. Urine samples taken from Molina after the race (in which he placed second) contained, race officials reported, evidence of nandrolone, a synthetic variant of testosterone. Molina said he was innocent and argued, with corroboration from other athletes, that the test procedures were inadequate to prevent container tampering or contamination. Following his protest, a second test was made of the original specimen; positive again. Molina was suspended from racing in France for twelve months. He did not appeal. The results of the first test became public the day before Molina was to race at the 1988 Ironman.

Ironman race officials heard about Molina's positive test a week earlier and had been stunned by the news. The Ironman race was not just an athletic contest, many felt, but a spiritual offering, an act of personal atonement. How could anyone cheat themselves that way? they wondered. It was sacrilege.

Only reluctantly had many of the old guard tolerated the Ironman's transformation into an athletic spectacle.

"This drug business is really hard for me," said Bob Laird, medical director for the Ironman since 1982. "The whole idea of the race is to test what a person can do under his or her own power. That prohibits taking anything with the intent of gaining an advantage over somebody else. And I mean stimulants like coffee and even those herbal things the Japanese are into (Ma Huang, an herbal stimulant containing ephedrine). Even the nutritional powders and energy pills. Hell, if they take it with the intent and belief that using it will give them an advantage over the competition, then they're..." His voice trailed off before he said the inevitable last word, *cheating.* Laird's criteria for improper advantage did not, apparently, extend to electrolyte-replacement drinks which, although legal, were hardly naturally occurring liquids. In an Exceed advertisement/press release distributed at the 1989 Ironman, Laird is quoted as saying: "Exceed is what Dave Scott uses to be sure his body has the fluid and fuel it needs to make it to the finish line."

There was great room to quibble and equivocate about specific substances and procedures, but boosting, steroids, speed, and narcotics were universally decried. Nobody wanted to see in triathlon what had become too common in cycling and track and field.

The first post-race drug testing of a U.S. triathlon was done at the 1988 Ironman. It was an unmitigated, and thoroughly unintentional disaster. But it yielded some interesting results. A few weeks before the race, Bob Laird, the medical director, decided to run a kind of drug test, "not to catch anybody," he said, "but to see if we had a problem." He invited Keystone Laboratories, then of Columbia, Maryland, to manage the test, the nature of which he desired to be "voluntary and anonymous," as far as the athletes were concerned. Keystone agreed to do steroid and drug testing free of charge. This last part was important to Valerie Silk, chairman of the Ironman Corporation. The Ironman race was a business, and a business that Silk had just agreed to sell. Twenty-four days before the race, she accepted $50,000 in earnest money to seal an agreement to sell the Ironman that year for $2 million. Drug testing would simply eat up profit. The UCLA testing lab used for the 1988 Olympics (which just ended in Los Angeles) would have charged between $5,000 and $10,000 to test the twenty top finishers. The lab was available, but not used.

Joel C. Holt supervised the testing for Keystone. He recalls that the testing was to be done anonymously primarily because, "the people at the Ironman were worried about getting sued." Bob Laird confirmed that fear. "I didn't think we had the legal authority," he said, "to force anybody to give a sample."

"Valerie Silk's fear of lawsuits was not groundless," insisted Mark Sisson, soon-to-be director of the Triathlon Federation (Tri-Fed), the national rules organization for the sport. "There was nothing in the athlete's handbook in 1988 about not using drugs," Sisson remembers.

But the official Ironman Rules and Regulations that year were clear, reading, in part: "No contestant may use alcohol or any illegal, detrimental or dangerous drugs, stimulants, depressants or other substances with the intent to improve performance, eliminate the sense of fatigue, or for any other purpose." For Silk, however, this wasn't enough to justify enforcement penalties and it was Silk's race.

After finishing the 1988 race, Julie Wilson gave a urine sample to Keystone and was struck by the "loosey-goosey" procedures. "After I finished the race (in fourth place) I was walking over to the massage area—that's what I want first, a massage—and I passed this little table and a guy said, 'Would you like to take a drug test?' I said 'Okay.' He gave me a cup, I went into a honey bucket, closed the door, gave the sample, and came out. I put it with some others on his little table. That was it. Anybody who's been using isn't going volunteer a sample. So what's the point?"

Joel Holt sympathized. "It was quite irritating to me that a significant number of the top twenty finishers refused to be tested. That bothered me a lot."

Altogether, as reported to Bob Laird, Keystone took 151 samples. Laird was told via a telephone call weeks later that samples from 138 men and 13 women were tested for opiates, PCP, cocaine, marijuana, and amphetamines. No women tested positive. One sample tested positive for marijuana. "I was," said Joel Holt, "surprised that the concentration was so high." One sample tested positive for morphine.

Keystone's findings on the steroid testing were not reported in writing by Keystone or the Ironman Corporation. Nowhere was it recorded who gave samples or who refused. The secrecy only fueled rumors. Expectations within the triathlon community had been high that any testing of U.S. races would be state-of-the-art and air-tight. But nobody was happy with what happened that year at Ironman, not even Laird, who considered the "results" unpublishable in any medical journal.

Charlie Graves, Kirsten Hanssen's agent at the time, went much farther. "The test was an atrocity. It served no productive purpose. It only heightened unfounded suspicions. And worse. If they'd found something, it would have tarnished the entire sport and not just one individual. It was stupid."

The next spring, Tri-Fed assembled a $30,000 budget for drug testing. The money would buy only a handful of postrace tests and one—maybe two—out-of-competition spot checks of randomly selected pros. But Tri-Fed hoped it would be an effective deterrence. All testing would follow U.S. Olympic Committee procedures, including bathroom observers (shadows) to watch the urine go into the bottles. Everything on the IOC list of banned substances would be prohibited and published in the athletes' federation guidebook. All pros would be required to sign a testing consent form. Penalties were established.

Testing was done first at the season opener in St. Croix. Jan Ripple, Paula Newby-Fraser, Erin Baker, Sylvianne Puntous, and Kirsten Hanssen were all tested. Julie Wilson was tested in Australia on April 30. The results of these first tests were not known until June, well into the '89 season. All samples taken at St. Croix and Australia eventually were reported negative for banned substances, including one taken from Scott Molina.

The drug controversy swirled well into May. Still injured, Julie Wilson grew more certain that some of her competitors were racing dirty and she felt defeated. Her aggressiveness was slipping. She remembered how she used to yell encouragements to herself on the bike, things like, "Go get 'em, Gringo." The line was from *American Flyers,* a movie about a small-town boy who finds an identity as a cyclist. The boy trains hard and enters the big race. A moment comes in the race when, though battered and bloody, he must rally to catch an unethical rival. He gets mad and takes off in pursuit; as he does, a former rival yells to him, "Go get 'em, Gringo."

Julie hadn't yelled on the bike in some time. She was losing the desire to go hard and knew that unless her zest returned, the midseason was shot. Every swimmer, cyclist, and runner knows the principle of progression—to get faster, one must push steadily harder in training. Not every time out, but often and on schedule. When the time comes to go hard, the athlete must do it. Otherwise, no improvements will be made. For an athlete who is already in the top five at her distance, pushing harder requires total concentration and commitment. When the top women pushed themselves in running—doing VO2-max and speed work primarily—they would run six 1-mile intervals in a row (or more), each at 90 percent of maximum effort, with a 440 jog in between. On the bike they would ride at thirty miles an hour fifteen feet behind a car or a motorcycle, then pull out into the wind and work to hold thirty for a minute or two without benefit of the draft. In the pool, pushing it meant doing hundred-yard intervals, thirty of them, the last faster than the first. Or maybe six 400's at race pace with a minute rest in between.

Wilson used to enjoy speed workouts, but now she avoided them. Steroids, she knew, could change everything. In fact, were she not a professional athlete, many doctors would have encouraged her to use some to assist her recovery. Drugs could end her pain, curb her depression, and give her the appetite—and possibly the means—to win. At the very least, the drugs would make her feel powerful and wild again. She didn't have to inject them. There were water-soluble steroids in pill form.

Early in 1987, a bike component manufacturer's representative, who provided Julie Wilson with some free bike gear, told her that some of her competitors in an upcoming race would probably be boosting.

The U.S. Olympic Committee itself provided free information on the elimination times of various popular drugs. Some of Wilson's competitors were featured in display advertisements, endorsing capsules of pure ATP—the stuff which is made in the body and enables muscles to contract.

But Wilson wasn't interested. It was cheating, she said, and unhealthy. Medicines and transfusions were for sick people, not for people who claim superior fitness. To explain her feelings, she recalls visiting a friend in the hospital. "His bone marrow isn't functioning properly and he *has* to take steroids. His face is big and puffy and his eyes are yellow. The steroids are doing that; they're also weakening his heart and ruining his liver, which is just about gone. I look at this poor man and think, If this is how sick you've got to be for steroids to help you, no wonder it's a crime to put them into a healthy body."

But for Julie, all considerations of a drug-assisted performance came down to one question: What if I took them and won? Then I'd never know if I could have done it myself. I'd always be wondering, Was it me—or the drugs? I couldn't live with that.

CHAPTER 11.

THE RACING LIFE

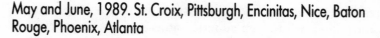

May and June, 1989. St. Croix, Pittsburgh, Encinitas, Nice, Baton Rouge, Phoenix, Atlanta

"Two workouts a day, max," exclaimed Colleen Cannon, a triathlete pro for seven years, "that's the life. A good friend of mine in Boulder," she continued with envy, "is Lorraine Moller, who ran, as you may know, for New Zealand in '88 [Olympic marathon team]. Lorraine runs once in the morning and once in the evening. She has the entire middle of the day free. She's fresh. She can do anything. Wow. I'm beat all day, trainin' morning 'til night, comin' and goin'. I have no time to shop. You look in our closets—Lorraine's and mine—and you'll see who's got it easy." Colleen laughed. They were good friends. For a wedding gift, Lorraine gave Colleen and her husband two round-trip plane tickets to New Zealand. Tickets in hand, Colleen left Colorado in winter and arrived in New Zealand's summer for preseason training with Erin Baker.

Baker and Cannon ran each other silly in March, thumping the trails out in the arid hills north of Christchurch on the South Island. They ran joyfully and hard, something Colleen hadn't done in years. A decade earlier, Cannon ran for Auburn University, where she'd once done a half mile in 2:11. She was still a good sprinter and a strong middle-distance runner. She routinely ran the last ten kilometers of a triathlon in thirty-six or thirty-seven minutes; Baker did them in thirty-five. To improve, each plotted their workouts according to time spent at different heart rates. Colleen's training base was lower than Erin's and she spent most workouts trying to catch up. Erin enjoyed Colleen's company, but even more so, having a competitor as a friend.

When Erin and Colleen left New Zealand in mid-April, two weeks before St. Croix, Baker knew she was running better than ever, and that was saying something. Her mate, Scott Molina, and Colleen encouraged her to pursue her fantasy of running for New Zealand in the 1992 Olympics.

There was also the money. Baker was not in triathlon primarily for the challenge, the camaraderie, or the excitement. Raised in a modest, working-class home among eleven other children, Erin had been earning a living since late childhood. Triathlon paid Erin's bills well enough, but she knew triathlon was a pauper's lot compared to marathoning.

With money and the Olympics in mind, Erin chose Pittsburgh, May 7, to make her professional marathon debut. Unlike triathlon, where the men nearly always took home more money, prize money at the Pittsburgh marathon would favor the women. The top ten females would collect a total of $128,000; the top ten men, only $33,800. The money drew a talented field, including several top Soviet women distance runners. This, Erin felt, would make it a proper test. She couldn't go wrong on the money—even *tenth place* would be worth $5,000, the same she'd get for *winning* a USTS race.

The weather in Pittsburgh fluctuates wildly during the spring, so few residents were shocked when it snowed during their May marathon. Twenty-mile-an-hour winds drove sleet and tiny shards of ice into skin. Runner's faces, knees, and upper legs glowed cherry red from blood sent to protect the front. A full third of the field dropped out.

Erin Baker, however, was used to difficult racing. She took third place, averaging 5.95 minutes a mile, missing second place by 15 seconds. She won $17,000.

Word of what Baker had done in Pittsburgh spread quickly. Baker's time of 2:36 was 15 minutes off Ingrid Kristiansen's world record of 2:21:06, but Baker was only moonlighting; she'd run just thirty seconds a mile off world record pace in a snowstorm. It got people's attention.

The net effect of Baker's performance on the professional women was that they all spent more time running, even Newby-Fraser. Though she would never say it, the idea of running a marathon shoulder-to-shoulder with Baker was distinctly unappealing. "I've always," Newby-Fraser said at the beginning of the season, "been intimidated by people with a strong running background."

At the time Baker ran the Pittsburgh marathon, Paula was moping around Encinitas trying to get in shape for the race in Nice on May 28, still stinging from the infamy of losing to Julie Moss, of all people, on April 30 in Australia.

"Those races were good for her," said Murphy, her agent, "they burst the bubble she'd been in since winning the Ironman last fall. She hasn't been taking her training seriously enough. She is now." Newby-Fraser's race card for the balance of the '89 season included six or seven long-course events and a clutch of shorter races where appearance fees and sponsorship tie-ins were good. Except for two races, she'd skip the USTS altogether. Victories in the long-course events would keep her sponsors happy. But they had to be victories. "There's a new race every weekend," she would sigh, "a new winner. People forget. Sponsors forget."

So far in the season she'd won not a single triathlon. Baker's running this well in the early season, Paula knew, only meant trouble further down her race schedule, if not from Baker, then from others who were training hard to match her.

Jan Ripple was one of Baker's pursuers who could conceivably catch her in the months ahead. Ripple's race at St. Croix proved she could hold a strong pace in heat after giving her all on the bike. Paula, Kirsten, Julie Wilson, and all the long-distance specialists were haunted to varying degrees by the thought of Ripple coming off the bike at the Ironman with a 10-minute lead and the ability to hold a running pace of 7:40 per mile. A race like that would break Paula's record, and, if Paula was on the course, it would break Paula, too.

Ripple was not thinking about the Ironman when she came home to "Battin Rue" from St. Croix. Instead, as captain of her sponsor's triathlon team, she was giving her full attention to the ten-race USTS production starting on May 14 in Phoenix.

"You'll have the best women at that distance, going fightin' each other every weekend," she said. "It's completely unlike running. Top marathoners only race each other once or twice a year. There's enough money in the sport so they can all make a good living without beating themselves up."

Jan believed her principal competition in the series would come from Colleen Cannon and the Puntous Twins, all experienced, well sponsored, and healthy. But of the three, Jan worried most about Colleen. The Twins just seemed to go along steady, but Jan felt Colleen had the fire in her belly. Moreover, Jan said, "Colleen didn't have such a great race in St. Croix, so she's probably home busting it."

The Twins, of course, were always a threat on the run. They raced well from the back, saving their long legs for the end when Ripple's legs would be crying. Then they would come on like the last nine bars of doom. Ripple was faster in the swim and certainly so on the bike, but unless she could drop at least a minute off her 10k, she knew she'd lead off the bike every weekend, then be run down over the last mile. It was a fighting thought. She'd have to get faster, particularly to compete against Baker in Avignon in July. Avignon would be the site of the first, certified international competition at the USTS, or "Olympic" distance. As such, the event would move triathlon closer to Olympic recognition. Most triathletes were for Olympic status, but not all. Newby-Fraser, not a sprinter in league with Cannon, the Twins, Ripple, or Baker, was cold to the idea and, at the time, thought the emphasis on "going for the gold" had turned the Olympics into a tawdry display—at least in the United States.

Ripple heaved through an additional track workout each week of May and June. The LSU Lady Tiger track team was then winning the NCAA track title for the third straight year, making everyone in Baton Rouge, including Jan Ripple, run a little harder.

Her husband, Steve, came to the track with a stopwatch to give Jan some technical support, but mostly he shouted and paced the sidelines with his arms folded across his chest. He took Jan's career and his coaching role seriously and was very much in charge of the workouts. Both of them felt Jan progressed best that way—with a male coach demanding her best effort. "Pick it up, Jan," Steve would yell. And she would, wringing out her guts again and again to make her interval. Where she had been doing one simulated triathlon each week, she now did two. Before St. Croix, she did one training race on the bike each week; she now did two.

Back at Foxy's Health Club, Paul "Sarge" Pendly, the seventy-year-old power lifter and fitness counselor, could have told Jan her program wouldn't work. Pendly stood in the weight room of Foxy's club and pointed to the mortar line between the cinder blocks on the blue wall. He said, "Your recovery is like this. You work and you work and if you don't go up [his plump index finger moved up the mortar line in a stair-step fashion] ... you say, I'm not workin' hard enough. And you work some more and still [he pulled his finger back] ... you go down. It's a losin' game. Your body needs rest and food. It grows when you rest and eat, not when you're workin' out."

Ripple overtrained. At the series opener in Phoenix on May 14, Ripple started the run even with Sylvianne and Colleen, but they dropped her and she came in third. "They were running five-minute, thirty-second miles," Jan recalled later, shaking her head. "I had to let them go."

"Next week in Miami," she said, "I blistered the bike. Had a two-minute-and-ten-second lead going into the run. Sylvianne Puntous ran me down with six hundred meters to go. Colleen ran me down with three hundred to go. I was exhausted, I was just beat up. It was at that point that Steve sat me down and he goes, 'You know what? Maybe we're working you too hard.'" Jan cut back on the frequency of her speed work, but kept up the intensity. It seemed to work because at the next race in Atlanta, she beat Cannon and took first.

Paula Newby-Fraser's training had apparently come together as well. On May 28 she won the long-course event in Nice, France. The hot weather favored her. Forty percent of the contestants dropped out, most of them during the board-flat run course that went for eighteen miles without shade. Paula finished in six hours and forty-nine minutes; Sylvianne Puntous came in two minutes later to take second place with sister Patricia behind her in third.

One minute of Paula's two-minute margin was earned in the transitions. Incredibly, her elapsed time for running out of the Mediterranean to her bike, getting out of her wet suit and into her bike gear, mounting the bike, and leaving the transition area was one minute and twenty-six seconds. It was like that all day.

Julie Moss placed fourth at Nice, six minutes behind Newby-Fraser. It was enough to make Moss's victory over Paula in Australia seem flukish. Still, the measure of Paula's performance was incomplete because Erin Baker hadn't raced at Nice—even though her sponsor, Le Coq Sportif, was a major cash contributor to the event.

Baker's refusal to race upset her sponsor, but Baker held her ground. She could not support a race, she said, for which prize money was unequally disbursed among men and women, particularly when women would be on the short end. She also told many that she was boycotting the race in protest over Scott Molina's positive drug test the year before. Colleen Cannon, who had won at Nice in 1987, stood with her friend Baker and protested the race as well.

Baker had always been vocal about her beliefs and didn't hesitate to act them out. It was a habit that won races, but angered many, including the U.S. State Department which, in 1985, banned her indefinitely from entering the country. They said Baker had proven herself a threat to national security by her role in a protest having to do with the docking of an American nuclear-armed ship in a New Zealand port. Allegedly, Baker had thrown a firecracker during the demonstration. For two years thereafter, Baker was angry that Newby-Fraser—whom she considered to be a South African athlete despite the Zimbabwe paperwork—should be allowed to reside and compete in the U.S. when she, Baker, was not allowed in the country. She had a point. Newby-Fraser, however, was miffed. "I'm not *from* South Africa," she'd huff, as if that should have cleared everything up.

When Baker, Ripple, Hanssen, and others got together later to protest the sex-based economic discrimination in prize-money distribution, the only top-ranked woman, Ripple recalls, who refused to sign the protest letter was Paula Newby-Fraser. As the highest paid woman pro, sponsorship dollars and appearance fees were good then for Newby-Fraser. She apparently had no time to reform the sport and little interest in doing so.

For Kirsten Hanssen, the season started poorly and then got worse. Like Ripple, Kirsten was bound by sponsorship agreements to do the ten races of the USTS. Hanssen came in sixteenth in Phoenix as the result of bike problems, a minute behind Ripple in Miami, third in Atlanta. With each race, the pain above her left hip, which had been around since St. Croix, grew more intense and lingered longer. She tried to ignore it and fought to keep up with her racing schedule (the equivalent of a marathon road race each weekend). Her life with Robert Ames had grown busier each week since they'd been engaged to be married. Robert had proposed on March 26 while on his knees, fourteen thousand feet up Mount Quandary. Kirsten said yes. They set the wedding date for November 11, after the Ironman.

Kirsten's relationship with Robert was flourishing, but her alliance with Charlie Graves, her agent, was unraveling. Charlie had decided that Kirsten was a low-yield property and her mother a pain in the ass. He said, "It got to where I wouldn't take her mother's calls. They wanted way more than we could get for them. Basically they had an unrealistic idea of what she was worth. For Christians, they were very, I can only say, greedy. The hours we spent on their business with sponsors and race directors were enormous, and the return wasn't worth it."

Charlie Graves was then thirty years old. He'd been pals with Murphy Reinschreiber back in Wisconsin before both moved to California where they sought to become professional triathletes. When neither succeeded, in 1989 they turned to the business side. "Until a few years ago," remarked Julie Moss, "none of them knew anything about being an agent. They're both sharp people and they've learned on the job. If they were doing it for the money, they'd be doing something else."

She had a point. There wasn't much money to be made representing the athletes of a new—and largely nontelevised—sport. To supplement their incomes, many athletes' agents also dabbled in event promotion. None of the principals thought this represented a conflict of interest. Or at least they didn't until Reinschreiber, in partnership with Graves, put on the Tri-Prix series in 1988. Toward the end of the first race, officials said they lost track of how many laps of the multilap course had been completed by each of the top contestants. The race was stopped and Reinschreiber, the race director, awarded first-place money to Paula Newby-Fraser, his client. Newby-Fraser also happened to be wearing the name of the race's principal sponsor—Jeep. The Tri-Prix series folded soon thereafter, as did the partnership between Graves and Reinschreiber.

Kirsten Hanssen and Robert Ames were not interested in Charlie Graves's business problems. They thought Charlie was slacking. "I was staying up until three in the morning with Robert," recalls Kirsten, "talking about how marketable I was and seeing that nothing was happening. We went around it a couple times, but in the end Charlie just said I was going to take too much time for the revenue I'd bring in. We got together at a breakfast meeting and cordially ended the relationship."

As for Graves, he thought Kirsten needed therapy. He felt she was hiding hideous secrets behind a mask of carefree joy. "She's inappropriately happy. Nobody is always happy. If her highs are that high, think of those lows that she allows nobody to see." Over the two years he'd known her, Graves said he'd seen Kirsten "go out and purposely inflict the maximum amount of pain to her body" many times. The last straw, for Graves, was when Kirsten did the Ironman in '88 with a cast on her arm. After that, he encouraged her to quit racing for the first half of '89. "She listened," said Graves, "and then did exactly as she'd been doing. She did not take a long-term view of her career. I saw her career as a ten year project. The way she was acting, it was only going to last three."

By mid-June, the excitement of the early season had evaporated. The anxiety over drugs, building since the last Ironman, began to ebb with the early-June announcement that everyone who'd been tested for drugs at St. Croix—including Newby-Fraser, Baker, Hanssen, and Ripple—had come out clean. No traces of steroids had been found. No stimulants. Nothing.

Naturally, some suspicions persisted. There were so many ways to mask drugs and gain advantage from substances or procedures that could not be detected by urine testing (or by blood testing for that matter) that the possibility of dirty racing later that season could not be dismissed. But of necessity, a truce on accusations was called. No one wanted a sport in which competitors had to prove themselves innocent. Triathlon was already tough enough.

Lack of sponsorship and aching legs kept Julie Wilson home and out of competition during both May and June. Moreover,

Scottsdale, the race she'd counted on for her midsummer paycheck, was canceled on short notice. The promoter, then one for three in actually holding the races he publicized, blamed the unseasonably high temperatures there in Arizona (110 degrees). Many athletes were stuck with nonrefundable airline tickets. A big race in Las Vegas was canceled as well.

Wilson felt in June that her last professional race could well be the Ironman in October. Financially, all signs were pointing to that. If she did not do well there, exceptionally well, she'd be forced out. Consequently, every race and every day's training hence would be preparation for the Ironman, starting with a middle-distance triathlon scheduled for Provo, Utah, on July 1.

CHAPTER 12.

RUNNER'S HIGH

June 30, 1989. Provo, Utah

*O*n the day before the race, the lobby of the Excelsior Hotel in downtown Provo, race headquarters for the Heritage International Triathlon, swarmed with athletes wearing running shorts and tank tops. Most were accessorized with rainbow sunglasses attached to neon-colored neck strings. Many sucked avidly on plastic sports bottles, stopping between sentences to take a nip of water or electrolyte-replacement drink. Outside, the ambient temperature was 100 degrees and humidity was less than 5 percent.

The automatic glass doors slid open and Colleen Cannon came in with the heat, pushing a mountain bike. Her long, gold hair was braided thickly across one side. Her eyes were deep blue and her face was lightly tanned and carried an enthusiastic expression. A cycling jacket was tied around her waist. Cannon continued on toward the elevators, but stopped when she saw Laurie Samuelson, a Brown University engineering graduate who raced with Colleen on the Pioneer Electronics team. Before turning pro, Samuelson worked for Pratt and Whitney as a test engineer; her job was to see how far jet engines could be pushed before they broke—good experience for triathlon.

"I just rode the run course," Colleen shouted to Laurie over the crowd. "It's tough—climbs two thousand feet in four miles, up to six thousand and something. Four miles of trails. Lots of rocks. I had to get off lots and walk the bike through the brush. It's so steep where the course leaves the road, I know people are gonna be walkin'. The elevation's gonna kill 'em. Where's Borcherds?"

Victor Borcherds promoted and directed the race with his wife, Suzanne. Both had emigrated from their native South Africa in the early 1980s and had quickly become prime movers in Provo's hospitality-tourism sector. One year earlier, they patched the end of their inaugural triathlon onto the end of the town's Fourth of July parade—a tribute to native Mormon efficiency as much as to Borcherds' boostersim. But the exposure garnered few fans—the last mile of the triathlon seemed exactly like a marathon finish, only slower and more painful, which it was.

The Borcherds's owned the Excelsior Hotel, which towered over the surrounding lowrise Mormonesque. The Borcherds also owned the sprawling water-slide park where, not coincidentally, the race would end. At noon it would be one hundred degrees in the finish area—a blacktop parking lot only seven dollars away from Borcherds's blue water wave tank.

Provo is swelling with families looking for a crime-free place in the sun. Brigham Young University is nearby, as are many growing software companies, like Novell. Salt Lake City, famous as the home of the Mormon Tabernacle Choir and the first successful cold fusion reaction (alleged), is fifty miles north. The Borcherds's supreme ambition was to build a ski resort just minutes behind Provo in the Wasatch Mountains.

The Wasatch hulk over Provo like a rocky glacier meeting a sea of sand, rising directly from the high valley floor six thousand feet and more and extending as far north and south as one can see—a considerable distance. At the foot of these mountains lies Provo, 4,500 feet above sea level.

The dry air and the elevation give nosebleeds to many new-comers, who may also tire quickly when walking the slightest rise of stairs. Towels dry unassisted. So does sweat, which made dehydration a serious concern for those entered in the triathlon. Following the one-mile swim would be a shadeless forty-mile bike race and then the toughest ten-mile run course in any triathlon in the country. For amateurs still out on the course after four hours, the run would be especially brutal. But what worried contestants most was the swim. The previous year, the water on Utah Lake was so rough that dozens were pulled from channel buoys where they clung in refuge from four-foot whitecaps.

All this made the race a logical qualifying event for the Ha-waiian Ironman, three and a half months later. Anyone who finished Provo in the top three of their age group could be one of 1,275 to compete in Hawaii, provided they paid the $300 entry fee.

Colleen had been riding the Wasatch foothills for two hours in the heavy sun, but was neither tired nor wet, just thirsty and worried. "Did ya hear they're planning a mass start?" she asked Samuelson before pausing to suck on her bottle. "They're gonna make us start with the tri-geeks," she said. Cannon was referring to the young amateur men who clogged the front and swam rough. Cannon had raced pro for five years. She wasn't into boxing and wanted the pros to start first and separately. She laid down her mountain bike on the burgundy-and-blue pinpoint carpet and went off to find Borcherds.

Cannon had flown to Provo from Boulder the night before with friends Erin Baker and Scott Molina. Of the thirty or so who would race pro, Cannon, Baker, and Molina were top tal-ent. The race paid their airfare and gave them rooms in the air-conditioned Excelsior. A hired man drove the five hundred miles from Boulder, Colorado, with their bikes and spare parts.

Such treatment certainly saved on athlete wear and tear, as

pros laboring just outside the winner's circle could attest.

Julie Wilson got to Provo the same way she had the previous year, eight hundred miles by car. Two days earlier, she and Jim drove the four hundred miles from Seattle to her parents home in Nyssa, Oregon, and spent the night. The next day, father Andy, mother Thelma, Jim, and Julie got into a camper and drove another four hundred miles across the Idaho desert and down the valley of the Great Salt Lake to Provo. It was early afternoon when they pulled into a campground on the shore of Utah Lake, walking distance from where the race would start.

About the same time, Colleen found Borcherds to complain about the swim. The mass start was distasteful to most of the pro women even though, once underway, the women were only a few seconds per hundred yards slower than the pro men. But in the congestion of a mass start, they could be boxed and pummeled by anyone who could swim the first two hundred yards in around two minutes. Many amateurs could do that and some of them were quite "physical" in competition. It was not uncommon for contestants to yell things like, "Swimming is a contact sport," just before the gun. The advisory in the contestant booklet read "Please trim your fingernails and toenails prior to the start of the race to avoid injury to other contestants." Newby-Fraser, who owned the most fearsome nails on the pro circuit, would not be racing.

Canon laid out the problem to Borcherds and asked for a three-wave start; the pro men could go first, then the pro women, then the amateurs. The timing system did not have to be adjusted, she noted, only the race results. Not wanting to whip up pointless hostility, Borcherds compromised with two waves—first the pros, then, a few minutes later, around four hundred amateurs.

Borcherds is a big-chested ruddy man with white hair and a booming voice. When he took to the lectern at that night's "mandatory" prerace meeting, he was hearty and expansive. And why not? He'd pulled it off another year. Well over seven hundred people—athletes, friends, and family—had come to his Excelsior Hotel in little Provo, Utah, from all over the country. They were sitting right there before him under the chandeliers. He spoke ebulliently to all present, congratulating them—the fittest of the fit and all that—for being part of a great athletic contest that would, to the enjoyment of all, end at the fabulous Seven Peaks Water Park.

Unfortunately, Borcherds explained to the athletes crowded into the ballroom, there was a problem. He and Suzanne were disappointed, he said, by the unexpectedly low turnout. Race registration was running short—around four hundred he said, far below the six hundred needed to pay out the advertised purse. "We have no choice but to cut the prize purse. Sorry about that," he said. Julie Olson, a longtime pro who'd come out from Minnesota, began to sob in her chair when she realized she'd need a fourth-place finish to break even on the trip. She hadn't placed better than fifth in a long while.

Borcherds said he had no choice but to cut back the first man and woman from $7,000 to $5,000. Further, he intended to cut off the cash awards at seventh place rather than tenth. The pros began to rumble. Borcherds back-pedaled and restored money for seventh through tenth. But he did it by reducing the smaller amounts set aside for the top finishers in each age group. This enraged the top amateurs, some of whom had come from as far as Pittsburgh. The dispute was symbolic.

"What these people [race directors and professional triathletes] don't realize is that triathlon is not a spectator sport," said Lew Kidder, publisher of the national triathlon tabloid *Triathlon Today!*. "It's a participant sport," continued Kidder. "The money doesn't come from people who watch it on television. Triathlons are hardly ever televised and for a reason: Triathlon is fun to do, but boring as hell to watch. The money in triathlon comes from the people who *do* it. They pay the entry fees, buy the magazines, drink the Exceed. If these people go away, the pros will have to go out and get a real job."

When the day ended, nobody who was there for the money was happy. But what could any of them do in Provo on a Sunday but race?

*   *   *

The sun popped over the Wasatch like a flashbulb on race-day morning and seemed to ignite all air to the east. Brilliant light flooded the valley and washed against the bike racks on the shore of Utah Lake where many athletes had been since before dawn, getting ready. The air was so bright in the direction of the sun that most everyone gathered on the shore looked down. Some stood with their backs to the sun and looked out across the chalky lake to the brown hills rising from the shore many miles distant.

In the space of twenty minutes, the temperature on the shore had risen fifteen degrees to about seventy. There was no wind and the water looked ruffled but calm. The athletes stood sleepy and squinting by the bike racks, doing their chores in the narrow spaces. Three women stood in a row applying sun-tan lotion to each other's backs. A bike pump was passed around. That was as far as teamwork went; most went about their tasks alone, setting out bike shoes, race bibs, visors, socks, and running shoes. Lastly they got into their skin-tight, neo-prene wet suits and walked slowly down the boat ramp to the water.

Jim Wilson stood at the water's edge a few yards to the right of the boat ramp and put the viewfinder of his camcorder on Julie, who stood knee-deep next to Erin Baker. A pale gray bottom sucker rotted in the flotsam at Jim's feet. The water stank. The lake was gaining color now, and texture too from the pin-head algae. But the pros said little about the fouled water. They'd seen worse. Lake Biwa of the Japan Ironman was always mentioned when talk turned to dirty water. People took home rashes from Biwa, and that was from just one swim. What was a dead fish or two? Many commented in relieved tones about how calm the water appeared, though no one could see as far as the buoy that marked the turnaround.

"Hi, Erin." Julie rested her knuckles on her hips and faced Baker and the sun. She stood slightly lower on the lake bottom than Baker and what she saw was only the sharp profile of Erin's angular face.

Erin turned. "Hi to you," she said. Baker was confident and unusually chatty. She was having her best season ever. She was the favorite to win the race, and felt ready to turn it on. "Haven't seen you since Australia in '88. Thought you'd win it this year."

"Thought so too," said Julie.

"Where have you been?" Erin asked. "Haven't seen you around."

"No sponsorship," said Julie.

"No ride yet?" Baker was surprised. "You're a good athlete. You had a great race in Australia. You should have sponsorship."

Baker's support meant a lot to Julie, but it got her no closer to sponsorship. She felt both proud and sad.

Fifteen yards from shore, a race official stood swaying in the aft of a powerboat. He gestured to the pros to swim out and get ready to start. Another boat joined the first. After much fumbling and groping with boat hooks, a line was strung between them—the starting line. Thirty or so yellow capped heads clustered in the boat gap, bobbing in their wet suits and talking in bursts.

When the starting gun fired, torsos rose up from the water and lunged forward with one arm extended. Then heads rolled and mouths gaped open at the waterline. White water flew and the burst of kicking sounded like surf. Those on shore were transfixed by the acceleration. After five seconds, the swimmers could no longer be told apart and for a hundred yards their yellow heads mingled like sparks from a campfire. Soon they settled onto distinct paths—thirty balls of spray, spitting across the water.

The amateurs were let go five minutes later. After ten minutes, nearly all the swimmers had disappeared; the others just dots blinking in the chop. Spectators took a break for coffee, sunblock, and film. Others hit the Porta Potties.

Twenty minutes after leaving, the fastest pros were back in sight, a few hundred yards from the exit ramp and closing slowly. They were swimming straight into the sun, as they had been for a half mile, alternately looking down into a bottomless cave of opaque water, then up into the boundless glare. They came in weaving, tacking into the light.

Jim Wilson stood next to the boat ramp and filmed his wife's approach. Julie put her feet down five yards from shore and rose out of the water in a black form-hugging, sleeveless wet suit and yellow cap. Her lips were stretched thin and she breathed rapidly through her teeth. The muscles of her shoulders and chest were heavy, swollen with blood and lactic acid, and shaped like teardrops. Halfway up the ramp to the bike racks and still striding, she began peeling off her wet suit. She took more time than usual in transition. Seven women were ahead of her by the time she left, but, in terms of time, the race was less than one third done.

Jim watched Julie ride away. "She knows the swim and the bike won't matter," he said. "It's a runner's race."

The bike course was a forty-mile loop that went south through Springville and Spanish Fork. But for three miles of concrete in residential neighborhoods, the road was two-lane, gravel-studded blacktop that took the riders through cash crops and horse pasture.

The temperature was in the high seventies when the first cyclists rolled down through Spanish Fork like a squadron of mechanical locusts. For the women, it was Colleen Cannon leading Baker, then wunderkind Lisa Laiti, who was back racing pro after recovering from a nearly fatal bike wreck. Paula Johnson of Florida came next, her brow furrowed, her teeth clenched. For a time in 1988, Johnson had held the women's record for an Ironman distance triathlon. The daughter of a pro baseball player, Johnson was once a tennis pro, but quit that for triathlon. "I wasn't quick enough to make it in tennis," she said. "I could go all day, but just didn't have the speed." After Johnson rode Laurie Samuelson, the ex-engineer, then Julie Olson, a five-year pro who built disc wheels in Minnesota. Karen Smyers was next. Tall and leggy on a bike, Smyers had run a 4:42 mile at Princeton and had captained the swim team as well. Julie Wilson rode two lengths in back of Smyers. The sun shone across the road and hit the women broadside as they rode against a backdrop of lush pastures, the towering Wasatch beyond them and a robin's-egg sky above. In the golden light, every working muscle was vivid on their bare flanks as they pumped their disc wheels round. Bike parts glinted like mirrors, muscles rose and fell; it was both beautiful and harshly mechanistic.

Behind their eyeshades, the women were thinking less about the ride and its artistic merit than about the grim run ahead. Cannon led Baker into the bike-to-run transition set up at the water park. Behind Cannon and Baker came a succession of fast runners. Paula Johnson, who'd driven eight hundred miles to Provo in a van with seven other athletes, was third. Karen Smyers, Beth Mitchell of Michigan, Julie Olson, and Laurie Samuelson got off their bikes next. Lisa Laiti quit the race in despair and frustration after cycling two miles off course.

Julie Wilson was around seventh at that point and when she started the run, she felt weak and her diaphragm had cramped; it ached as only diaphragms can. The thin air and lack of VO2-max running in training were exacting a stern price. Two miles into the run, when she came to the end of the pavement and started up the dusty hillside, her legs felt like Presto-logs and she knew she was finished. Jogging was all she could manage though her heart still thudded in her chest 150 times a minute. "I thought I was in eighth place about then," Julie recalls. "I wasn't going to finish in the top ten, I knew that. But we'd come all that way, I was healthy, and I needed the trainin', so I took it and finished. Lots of girls went by me." Wilson, like most of the other pro women, always referred to her competition as "girls."

Baker, meanwhile, was pulling the legs off her competition like a child might dismember a fly. She shouldered past Cannon early and built a two-minute lead by the third mile of the brushy trail. The tall manzanita kept her well hidden, but she

Julie Wilson takes a morning swim two days before Ironman. Hawaii, October 12, 1989.

Julie Wilson with husband, Jim, and his ever-present video camera. Hawaii, October, 1989.

Kirsten Hanssen says "Praise the Lord!" after crossing the Iron-man finish. October, 1989.

Kirsten Hanssen, flat on her bike. Ironman, '89.

Paula Newby-Fraser, pre-
season. Newcombe's Ranch,
New Braunfels, Texas,
March, 1989.

Kirsten Hanssen (right) and Paula Newby-Fraser about twenty miles into
the bike course. Ironman, '89.

Paula Newby-Fraser, fifty-two seconds after finishing Ironman '89. Supported by Paul Huddle (left) and agent Murphy Reinschreiber (right).

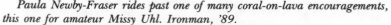

Paula Newby-Fraser rides past one of many coral-on-lava encouragements, this one for amateur Missy Uhl. Ironman, '89.

Jan Ripple is all business in the swim-to-bike transition. Ironman, '89.

Fifteen miles into the bike course, Jan Ripple heads for the lead. Ironman. '89.

(From left foreground) Katie Webb, Mike Farr, Paula Newby-Fraser, and Jan Ripple get last-minute instructions. Vancouver International Triathlon, August 13, 1989.

Erin Baker suits-up before the Heritage Triathlon in Provo, Utah, July 1, 1989.

Erin Baker in the lead, Heritage Triathlon, July 1989.

Swim start in Kailua Bay. Ironman, '89.

Jim Wilson (extreme right) points to the far buoy with Erin Baker (middle) and Julie Wilson (left) looking on. Just before the start, Heritage Triathlon, July 1989.

The race over, Ju lie Moss mingles on th Kailua pier. Ironmar '89.

could be heard coming from some distance away. The brush thwacked and rustled as she came; her feet thumped in the dust. She burst out of the bushes in a black one-piece swimming suit, aviator sunglasses, and racing flats with no socks. With her rounded breasts and hips that curved out from a chiseled waistline, Baker looked classically feminine and stunningly strong. Whipped forward on long strides, her feet landed surely on the rock-strewn trail and dust rose out behind.

Baker won and was merely tired. Cannon finished two minutes later, her face flushed, her eyes alert, but vacant, like an animal's. She'd been deeply drained by the race, but not as much as those who, unlike Baker and her, did not live and train at six thousand feet elevation.

Baker, Cannon, and third-place finisher Karen Smyers all won entry to the Ironman. Baker was already qualified by her second-place finish at Ironman the previous year. Smyers, who'd never done an Ironman distance race, declined the invitation. Cannon, who had done the Ironman once before, declined as well, saying, "I have more respect for my body now."

Julie Olson came in fourth, seven minutes behind Baker, visibly elated to have earned enough to pay for her trip. She would ache for many days thereafter.

Julie Wilson took her time on the run and finished fourteenth. Because, like Baker, she was already qualified for Ironman, her low placing was not a disaster. Although she knew her family would not be gravely disappointed, she knew they would feel badly for her. Knowing this made Julie feel disappointment too.

Around one in the afternoon, Wilson left Provo with her family to begin the eight-hour drive back to Nyssa, Oregon, where Julie had grown up. They were just passing Wendell, Idaho, when Victor Borcherds passed out the checks to the top ten.

CHAPTER 13.

THE WAGES OF SPIN

◆

July, 1989. Denver, San Jose, Shizuoka City, Japan; Baltimore, northern Minnesota, Chicago

*P*ain bit Kirsten's right waistline when she pedaled and it stabbed there when she ran, particularly when she lifted her knees. Changing her position on the bike to a more upright posture helped, but the increased wind resistance slowed her down. On the run, the stab was inescapable and incessant; because her legs were short, she needed to jerk her knees high like a sprinter and sustain rapid turnover to go fast.

As the season progressed, Kirsten grew accustomed to the discomfort and felt it would go away if she iced often and took ibuprofen. She did not consult physicians about it, partly because she did not think it was serious, but also because she hated going to doctors. She predicted they'd tell her to "rest and gain weight" and she felt this advice did not apply to her. Why rest if she was rarely tired? Why gain weight when it would only slow her down? Kirsten liked the way she felt and looked. "I feel light and strong," she'd say. "But I don't like being called skinny. I prefer 'lean.'"

Derisive comments about her physique originated in envy, she believed, and many—including Jan Ripple, Paula Newby-Fraser, and Linda Buchanan (from whom she wrested the national title in 1986)—did note, and to various degrees envy, the attention Kirsten's leanness drew. Many people complimented Kirsten on her thinness; few called it a health problem. Thin was in and Kirsten was the thinnest of them all; it was her trademark.

Kirsten thought the pain above her hip was the result of a poorly fitting bike. The top tube and handlebar stem were too long, she felt, making her overstretch. This would cause persistent and painful tendon inflammation where back muscles attached to her pelvic bones, among other things. She called Ralph Lewis of Hamilton and arranged to meet him in San Jose after the June 11 USTS race to consult about the bike. Kirsten placed seventh in the race, coming in just ahead of Jan Ripple, who was suffering from the stomach flu. Erin Baker, in a rare USTS appearance, outran Sylvianne Puntous and Colleen Cannon to win. Paula Newby-Fraser was fourth.

After the race, Lewis measured Kirsten's limbs and torso and agreed the fit could be improved. Kirsten's mother, then handling business in the wake of Charlie Graves's resignation, was pleased when Lewis said he'd charge them nothing for a custom bike. He later denied that he'd made such a promise.

Kirsten few home to Denver from San Jose, washed clothes, shopped, did some training, packed up, and flew to Japan midweek for a race on June 18. The race was the kickoff event of the Japan Triathlon Series; appearance money and sponsor exposure were good. Kirsten had raced in Japan before and relished the attention that Japanese men bestow on blond American women. She placed third in the Olympic distance event, ten minutes behind Erin Baker.

The following Sunday, June 25, Kirsten was in Baltimore for the USTS race. She felt tight and achy through the run and ended up eighth. In public, she took her defeat cheerfully and she consoled herself with the belief that it was all part of God's plan, somehow. She moved additional run workouts to the pool and iced her sore spots more frequently. Her mother, who then handled her race schedule, felt Kirsten's performances were suffering from romance. "Over the winter," Mrs. Hanssen said, "Kirsten was spending too much time playing with Robert. She rushed her training for St. Croix." Publicly, she was defensive of her daughter's talent. "Most of those girls out there," she was quick to point out, "would give their eye-teeth to come in eighth in one of those races." And it was true. Kirsten was racing slowly only compared to women whose speed had been built over three years of largely failed attempts to catch her.

Many competitors attributed Kirsten's poor showings to psychological issues. Word was thick that Kirsten Hanssen was an obsessive-compulsive with an eating disorder who was finally paying the bill for pushing her undernourished body too hard. "She's a ball of light," said Colleen Cannon, "but unless she stops racing soon—skips the rest of the season—her career is probably over."

Jan Ripple was certain Kirsten's body had begun eating itself. "She's losing muscle mass," said Ripple, "you can see it in her legs. If she'd have kept that muscle on, she'd have been awesome. As good as Baker, maybe better."

Robert Ames, Kirsten's fiancé, said he had no idea anything was wrong with Kirsten until the Fourth of July weekend. He and Kirsten had gone to Minnesota for a prewedding visit with Robert's mother, Dorothy. "We were running on a gravel road near my mom's place," Robert said, "when I passed her. That surprised me. I never pass her on the run. I asked her what was wrong and she said her hip hurt, right here, said it was real sore. She has such a high pain threshold anyway and we were so busy getting to races, doing the business end, and getting ready for the wedding that . . . well, she thought ice would handle it."

Five days later, Kirsten raced USTS Chicago. Robert raced too and, to his surprise, caught up with Kirsten just outside the bike-to-run transition. It was the first time he'd ever done that during a race. She was crying quietly as she rode. "It's my hip, Robert; it hurts so much." She began to sob.

Robert wanted her to pull over and quit the race. "You should stop, honey. You're hurtin' too much to race." But Kirsten insisted on continuing. She and Robert rode into the transition area together. As they parted to rack their bikes, Kirsten told him, "I'll just start the run and see how I feel." For six miles she winced, holding back tears to finish tenth and win a hundred dollars. When Robert found her in the finish area, Kirsten was ready to see a doctor.

Kirsten's Chicago-based publicist referred her to a sports medicine doctor in the suburbs, Dr. Karen Gajda. The doctor told Kirsten she'd had a fracture in her right iliac crest. The ilium is a large, curved bone shaped like a heart and made of two pieces. The spine ends at the junction between the two halves. The crest of the ilium is the topmost curve of the heart shape and is the point of attachment for major muscle groups of the back and butt, hips and abdomen. The cause of the fracture, she believed, was a combination of overtraining and a poorly fitting bike. Essentially, she said that Kirsten's muscles were pulling the bone apart.

It was a telling coincidence that Grete Waitz, seven-time winner of the New York marathon, was diagnosed just a month earlier with a similar bone injury in her pelvis. Waitz held world titles in the marathon, the 10k, and cross country throughout the 1970s and 1980s. It had taken Waitz twenty years of world-class marathoning to do to herself what Kirsten had done in four seasons of triathlon. Waitz is careful to allow plenty of time between races and does not race after a hard 10k for at least four weeks. At her peak, she did two marathons a year, maximum. In contrast, Kirsten had been doing a hard 10k nearly every weekend for three months—in addition to swimming and biking herself blissful.

In addition to the fractures in their pelvic bones, Waitz and Hanssen were alike in another possibly related respect: Each had stopped menstruating years prior to her injury, sharing a condition called amenorrhea. A woman's cycle will cease once her body fat drops below a certain percentage of her total weight. Apparently, there is a body fat trigger point at which the pituitary stops telling the ovaries to produce estrogen. Other factors, like stress, are involved, but the body fat trigger may exist because a certain level of body fat is a precondition for lactation—a primal precondition for successful reproduction. The trigger point varies among individuals. Waitz believed she was around 8 percent body fat (which included fat cells below her skin as well as those surrounding her internal organs). Kirsten wasn't sure, exactly, but immediately before starting her triathlon career, a fitness evaluation done in 1986 by the Public Service Company in Denver said 8 percent of her weight was fat. Three years later, her physical therapist measured 4 percent, but he had to extrapolate because Kirsten's numbers were not on the reference table that came with his calipers.

About the same time the fat-estrogen link was made, a more disturbing discovery was made for women athletes: A steady supply of estrogen in the blood is necessary for bone integrity and growth. Without it, calcium is not absorbed at an adequate rate to stave off osteoporosis. In "healthy" women athletes, bone density increases with the stresses of training; bones get bigger, stronger with the pounding. Not so for those low on estrogen. Some amenorrheic athletes in their twenties have been found to have the skeletal density of arthritic sixty year olds.

Kirsten's muscles were growing, getting stronger, but her bones were shrinking and becoming more brittle. It was only a matter of time before she pulled one of them apart.

When it did happen, one of Kirsten's competitors called to commiserate and give advice on recovery. Kirsten remembers her advising "Stay active and make certain you don't gain weight."

The pros—men and women both—were largely glad to have Kirsten sidelined and not simply because they knew Kirsten needed the rest. Many were simply tired of her cheerfulness;

they had endured her pious acceptance speeches and giggly, sing-song God praise longer than they'd thought possible. Moreover, Kirsten had become to many of the women a painful reminder of what they were not, but wanted to be. Julie Wilson wanted Kirsten's sponsorship and recognition; Jan Ripple and Paula Newby-Fraser wanted her legs and hated themselves for it. Overnight, Kirsten became a pariah, a mirror for their preceived inadequacies.

To many, Kirsten Hanssen was a grim object lesson in the rewards of treating one's body as a mere beast of burden. But that's what triathlon had been about—the will, the spirit driving the body on, ever faster. Kirsten's injuries gave triathlon a true demon to exorcise, as well as a false promise to live down.

Triathlon had been built on the illusion that it was, in addition to being great fun, healthier than running. Cross-training would keep an athlete injury free and could even improve a runner's times with less mileage on the roads—so went the promise. The idea was to take the six hours spent running each week and spread it out to one hour of swimming, three of biking, and two of running. In theory it worked fine. However, as soon as most converts had completed their first triathlon, they realized that if they wanted to finish even in the middle of the pack, they'd have to train just as hard in swimming and cycling as they had in running. So instead of holding their exercise time to six hours a week, they tripled it to eighteen hours a week and more.

John Krusenklaus runs a sports medicine clinic in San Antonio and also heads the medical support team for the annual Texas Hill Country Triathlon. Krusenklaus has done hands-on musculo-skeletal evaluations of hundreds of triathletes. He's interviewed dozens more and he laughs at the claim that triathletes suffer fewer injuries than runners. "They do three sports and pursue them all with intensity. As a result," he said, "they get three kinds of injuries, not one. That's not counting the bike wrecks." It was this propensity to athletic excess that met Paula Newby-Fraser when she arrived in San Diego from South Africa in 1986. Triathlon was not so much a sport contested by athletes, she observed, but a life-style of compulsive exercise.

Kirsten Hanssen was just the latest casualty—a once healthy, cheerful, young athlete who had, within eighteen months, been transformed into a sobbing wreck. She was not what the promoters of triathlon wanted the public to see. Charlie Graves had seen it coming and got out early.

The rules were different for the men. Dave Pulford, an agent with Dave McGillvray Sports Enterprises, which represented Jan Ripple and Erin Baker among others, acknowledged that sponsors were often taken aback by the oomph of Jan Ripple's shoulders. "When she comes out of the water, man, she's big." Jan was too thick, Hanssen too thin. "However," said Pulford, "we never get comments about the men—no matter how they look. For example, Mark Allen is like Kirsten in that he has trouble keeping the weight on. But nobody complains than Mark Allen is too thin. With the men, only their finish time counts."

The fear of being perceived as "unfeminine" or "too masculine" was a real and reasonable fear for all the pro women. The major triathlete publications were owned and published by men. *Triathlete,* the glossy monthly most heavily endowed with sponsor advertising, carried not a single race-related story or athlete profile in 1989 written by a woman. All the major race directors—with the exception of Valerie Silk at the Hawaii Ironman—were men. *All* the sports agents who represented triathletes were men. So were their sponsor contacts. How these men felt the sports' women should act and look defined the boundaries of financial success or failure for the women pros.

"Triathlon is the world's sexiest sport," said Newby-Fraser's agent, Murphy Reinschreiber. "The day of the athlete-billboard is dead. The start-to-finish-line people are suffering. Paula is marketable because she's so good with personal appearances."

Paula soon began appearing in display ads for nutrition supplements and pasta, showing plenty of bare leg, newly tinted hair, and freshly whitened teeth. She and Murphy joked about them, calling them her Vanna White ads, but neither protested their use.

Julie Moss summed up the women's plight with normal pith. "Until a woman crosses the finish line first," she said, "we'll remain captives of the men. Right now, it's a package deal and we're negotiable."

But it wasn't only men who enforced the sex code. Ripple, Wilson, Newby-Fraser, Hanssen—each had her own boundaries and codes governing on how they should look and act in order to remain, in their own eyes, feminine. Newby-Fraser kept her nails long and painted red. She wore many earrings, finger rings, and bracelets—even when racing. She gladly allowed her male housemates to change her flat tires. She openly derided the shape of her thighs.

Julie Wilson liked her muscular development, but only to a point. "My muscles are more defined than those of a lot of other girls, more 'cut.' I like that. But I wouldn't want them to make me look dykey." On saying "dyke," she laughed shyly.

Jan Ripple hated her shoulders, feeling they made her look "too masculine." She longed to be lighter and more svelte. Fed up with derisive comments about her "manly" shoulders and "powerful" thighs, she once made a desperate attempt to slim down by putting herself on a daily diet of 1,200 calories even though she was already lean and burning 3,000 to 4,000 calories a day. She did not become thinner, only weaker. After suffering numerous illnesses, she realized the folly of her gamble and ate more.

Womanliness in Louisiana means to most people who live there "being at least heterosexual." Homophobia is rife in Louisiana and was in Jan's community when Jan was growing up. A close relation once advised her not to continue in a particular sport because "The coach is a homosexual."

As a professional athlete, Kirsten too was zealously protective of her feminine self-image. She disliked most of her race photographs, feeling they made her look too much like a man, or simply not attractive. "Well, that one's not bad," she said, looking at one. "It makes me look like I have hips at least. But I don't like race pictures—something about how the skin looks so icky." She preferred softly lit, sports-fashion shots in which she appeared more rounded and less intense.

Their fight to maintain a traditionally "feminine" look was valiant, but essentially, it was a lost cause from the start. The natural course of their physical development as endurance athletes inevitably brought the female pros into conflict with cultural norms for femininity. The loss of subcutaneous fat from hard training revealed muscles with more definition, giving them the texture of men, whose skin fat is normally lower. The women's breasts, largely composed of fatty tissue, shrank. Their hips lost padding, and those athletes with narrow pelvic bones became even less rounded. Long hours spent swimming in chlorinated pools and running and biking in the wind and sun tended to wrinkle and toughen their skin and make hair brittle. Moreover, when fat levels drop far enough, the hormonal balance between androgens and estrogens changes enough in some women to create visible masculine effects, like facial hair. Indeed, endurance training would naturally give any woman a more masculine appearance. But that would hardly make her a man.

The subject of what made men intrinsically different from women arose frequently in triathlon in 1989, and not just because advertisers wanted feminine images. The reason had more to do with the revolutionary nature of the sport itself. For the first time in history, men and women had entered a major sport simultaneously and under the same rules. They raced the same course at the same distance and, usually, they raced together. The men were typically first to use the latest cycling gear, but generally speaking, the sexes competed on equal ground, indeed, on the same ground. In no other sport did male and female athletes race together across great distances, in full public view, dressed only in swimsuits and race numbers. People could *see* not just how women *differ* from men, but how much they are essentially *alike.*

What was going on *inside* triathletes was also studied with great interest. "We know with medical certainty," said Dr. Mary O'Toole of the Human Performance Laboratory at the University of Tennessee, "that while the best woman [triathlete] will always beat many of the men, the best man will always beat the best woman." This is true because women's hearts have a lower "stroke-volume," meaning that female hearts can't pump as much blood as male hearts. Also, female blood contains less hemoglobin than male blood, and hemoglobin is needed to transport oxygen to the muscles. Further, no matter how hard women train, they will always carry a higher percentage of their weight in fat. And they will always go slower with it than they would without it. The discovery that tied endurance—which depends on unbroken bones—to fat and estrogen levels changed many ideas about feminine "fitness." Before this research appeared in newspapers, no one saw irony in the fact that Kirsten Hanssen—who was to many the "best-looking" or "sexiest" woman pro because she was petite, blond-haired, blue-eyed, and handsome—was physically unable to conceive a child and had been for five years.

Word went around that Kirsten had quit the USTS and gone into recuperation for a hip injury—the colloquial description for any ailment below the waist and above the femur. She told few about the exact nature of her injury; those who knew Kirsten knew that whatever her injury was, it had to be serious to make Kirsten quit.

"She's probably out for the season," said Julie Wilson. "She can run in the pool and keep up her conditioning, but that won't help her on the roads. It's the poundin' that gets ya."

After her diagnosis in Chicago, Kirsten flew home to Denver and there she pursued recovery with the same methodical fanaticism she gave to training. She knew it would be months before she could race again. She also knew that the Ironman, her last chance for salvation in 1989, was two and a half months away. Time enough, she thought, to get ready.

CHAPTER 14.

LET 'ER RIP

August 11, 1989. Vancouver, B.C., Canada

*W*ith his baby face, slicked-back hair, and big chest pushing out of his dark suit jacket, race director Don Andrews resembled the English actor who played opposite Roger Rabbit—Bob Hoskins—except that Andrews is taller, six feet one or two. He carried a sheaf of papers close to his chest and paced among the round, linen-covered tables like a dyspeptic maître d'. It was his race and he'd called the press conference. It was just past noon on a hot Friday in August.

The press reception was held in a white room just off the mezzanine of the downtown Holiday Inn. An accordion room divider formed the back wall and a front table ran opposite, about three banquet tables distant. Laboriously, the room filled with athletes and reporters. The athletes found the fruit table quickly and loaded their plates; they took the carbohydrates—breads, fruits, and crackers—and left the meats and cheeses for the reporters. There was no mingling—the pros sat together in the corner nearest the door. Jan Ripple, Mike Pigg, Paula Newby-Fraser, and Paul Huddle sat at the same table.

They all wore the official race sweatshirt and all except Huddle hunkered low over plates, shoving piece after piece of fuel into their mouths, and mopping the plentiful fruit juice from their mouths and chins with linen napkins. Huddle sat upright and used his fork. Between swallows, Ripple and Newby-Fraser chatted. Ripple, expansive and smiling, did most of the talking while Newby-Fraser simply ate and nodded. Huddle and Pigg said little. Pigg, dehydrated from a virus he'd quartered for three weeks, carried a plastic gallon jug of water, which he hoisted often for a long draw. Most of the other pros looked equally whipped; they slouched at nearby tables and bolted fuel by the handful.

At 12:30, Andrews gave the cue to the AV guys who'd been crawling on the floor with patch cords in their teeth. The lights went out and a slide show of last year's race came up. It was a multiple-projector affair with a synchronized sound track of big-beat rock. *Thumpa, thumpa, thumpa* ... "I can feel it coming in the air tonight ... hold on," crooned Phil Collins. On the screen were nearly naked athletes—buffed, ripped, and cut—stretching in the rising sun. After a quick segue, the screen was filled with swim-start shots of tan arms amid spray—all of it accompanied by some purloined Kenny Loggins. Up next, cycling came in slow motion—teeth gnashed, thighs pumped, sweat flew, and bikes gleamed while someone sang/yelled "Highway to the Danger Zone." Runners had apparently not been as photogenic and the slide show slid tastefully through pathos and marched briskly to the jubilation of the finish. All the sporting emotions were aroused in about fifteen minutes.

Newby-Fraser and Ripple continued eating during the show with their backs to the screen, laying down their napkins only when the lights came up and Don Andrews summoned the most press-worthy to the head table. They rose from their plates of pits and rinds, beat their way through the thicket of chairs, then took their assigned seats at the head table. Wearing sweatshirts and tired expressions, they looked more like a gaggle of teenagers back from an overnight field trip than a cadre of the world's fittest athletes.

Ripple sat two chairs away from Newby-Fraser and listened carefully as Paula answered the first question put to her: "Does it bother you, Paula, that your season has been, so far, off the pace you set in last year's Ironman?" Paula leaned over the table on her elbows and sighed and did not smile. Her words, always pragmatic and well-spoken in complete sentences, were tinged with despondence. "My competitive will to win sort of comes and goes," she said. "As for this race, I'll go as hard as I can, but I certainly haven't been setting any standards in the sprint distance."

"When I heard her say that," recalled Jan Ripple, "I knew I'd beat her on Sunday. Right then in her mind, Paula was saying she was not a factor in the race. She still saw herself as a long-distance racer." Ripple knew that if she and Paula were together at any point on the run, Jan would break her. "I'd run next to her two times before in races this long," said Ripple. "I broke her twice. After you've been broken a couple times, you get it in your mind that's the way it's always going to be."

Ripple had arrived in Vancouver earlier that afternoon from France via Baton Rouge. Over the previous five days she'd traveled west eight thousand miles and had lost eight hours. She'd come without Steve or the kids, so the trip was something of a vacation, but she was bushed and knew she shouldn't be there racing. If it hadn't been for the contract she'd signed with Andrews and the possibility of TV coverage, she'd have stayed home and rested.

The weekend prior, on August 6, Ripple raced with the U.S.A. team in the first true Triathlon World Championship. Thirteen countries sent women's teams, forty sent men. Erin Baker, representing New Zealand, was undefeated going in, but Ripple was ready. In her previous two races, Jan had beaten every one of the top ten women sprinters but Baker. Her swimming was strong, her cycling unsurpassed, and she'd dropped her 10k legs down to the 35-minute range; she'd peaked.

The distances in Avignon were the USTS standards: 1.5k swim; 40k bike; and 10k run.

"I thought I could beat Erin in that race," Jan recounted quietly. "I was so fit. So strong. All I'd been hearin' about before France was how Erin had broken Joan Benoit's record for the seven-mile run. [And she had, by fifty seconds.] At first I didn't believe it. But I told myself, even if she did run that fast, she couldn't do it again a week later in France, not in a triathlon. My strategy was to go hard on the bike—to make her hurt, make her hurt so bad she'd never catch me on the run."

As it happened, Ripple led Baker through the swim and by the end of the bike she had a minute lead. Ripple ran powerfully and scared, just below six minutes a mile; Baker, doing 5:45 and better, kept closing. At two and a half miles, Baker caught her and for the next two and a half miles, Baker would surge and Ripple would go with her. At that point, they'd been racing for two hours and both were running a 5:30 pace. It seemed impossible, but both women held form; they were fluid and fast. At five miles, Baker surged again and Ripple could not go with her. Her face was flushed red, her pursed lips were white, she was going anaerobic and knew she couldn't go faster. Neither could Baker; after gaining two hundred yards, Baker slowed to her earlier pace and hung out there, just beyond Jan's reach. That's how they crossed the finish, one mile later. It was Baker by thirty-two seconds.

"I figured I was tougher," said Ripple, "not faster, but tougher. I think I was. I just ran out of room."

Paula Newby-Fraser knew she was not the sprinter Erin was and she knew Ripple too knew of her weakness. This affected Newby-Fraser's behavior, particularly when she and Ripple were in the same room, as they were now; Ripple jovial and expressive, Newby-Fraser withdrawn and blasé. Her lack of enthusiasm for the whole affair was palpable and not difficult to explain. Although she'd won USTS San Clemente the weekend prior, nobody seemed to care; all eyes had been on the World Championships in France, held the same day. Newby-Fraser did not race in France in part because the event wasn't her distance. But that was moot. She couldn't have raced there if she'd wanted to; Zimbabwe did not field a team and South Africa was not invited. Again, Paula Newby-Fraser was the outsider.

Her weekend before San Clemente had been equally bleak. After leading through most of the Japan Ironman, she was disqualified for drafting on the bike. Riders on the course reported that clumps of Japanese male pros, too proud to be passed by a woman, blocked her repeatedly. When she approached their blockades to pass, race marshals on motorcycles levied penalties for drafting. After twenty minutes of penalties, the race was lost. Reinschreiber, who was on the course, reported what he saw. "As soon as Mikki Yamamoto [whom Paula had instructed just four months earlier in Texas] passed her, they stopped giving her penalties. But there was no point going on and I pulled her off the course. I spent the next week on the phone trying to square things with Paula's Japanese sponsor." The race was won by Julie Moss.

This second loss to Julie Moss in a long-course event was demoralizing to Paula and it gave rise again to the suspicion that her '88 Ironman victory had been a fluke. The week before Japan, Paula won a short-course event in Oxnard, California. However, her win did not increase her stature because the race was easy pickings. Ripple, Cannon, and the Puntous Twins had all been in Houston that weekend for the eighth USTS race, (which Ripple won handily).

The week before Oxnard, Paula had come in second in a light field in Minnesota. She was lucky. Eighteen days earlier she had pulled a calf muscle during a short-course event and was forced to drop out. Her agent/manager, Murphy, had taken her to Tijuana for what he called laser therapy. "It's like space-age ice," he said. The treatment was apparently not available in Southern California, but they were desperate. Paula's lead sponsor, Aerodynamics Sportswear, had booked her for two days of prerace promotional appearances, most of them in consort with Dayton Hudson, the big, Minneapolis-based retailer. "Hey," said Murphy, repeating the gist of what he had told

Paula, "it's one thing to not show up at a race, it's another to shut down two days of saturated promotion." Paula's boyfriend, Paul Huddle, agreed with Murphy about sponsors. "You've got to please 'em. Sure, it's hard to go down to a store on a Saturday afternoon and stand there for hours when you should be in bed. But, I tell her, 'They aren't going to give you the money for nothin'".

By the time Newby-Fraser got to Vancouver, she felt the season was going quite badly. Unlike her previous year (1988), which had risen without abatement to a crescendo at the Ironman in October, this one was more like playing scales. It was tiresome. Murphy, on whom she depended for moral support as well as image control, had not accompanied her to Canada. At the briefing, she sensed a press partial to the local favorites and she felt that her status as the premier woman in the sport was slipping. She appeared not to care.

"Does your Hamilton [bike] give you an advantage over the conventional bikes of your competition?" asked a print reporter from the local tabloid.

Paula shot back, "I'm the wrong one to ask. I haven't ridden anything but the Hamilton since I can remember. Ask someone who's ridden both recently."

The press conference ended early when the reporters ran out of questions. Paula was relieved. "They ask the same things over and over," she complained. "Are you married? [No, never.] What's so different about your bike? [Ask the designer.] What do you think of your competition? [I try not to think about them.] Do you enjoy beating the men? [I just want to see how fast I can go.]"

With that, Paula stripped off her official race sweatshirt and left.

Four hours later, Newby-Fraser, Ripple and the others returned to the hotel for a mandatory, no-host press reception. Jan Ripple entered the mahogany-paneled sitting room on the thirty-fourth floor of the Hyatt in a red dress. Strapless and tight over her chest, it was layered and frilly below—good for dancing. She was hardly through the door before a group of admirers and editors overtook her. "How are y'all," she called out gaily. The group backed her onto a Naugahyde bench, where she regaled them with an animated account of her race in France.

Newby-Fraser, in jeans and a drab sweater, crossed the mauve carpet largely unnoticed and settled quietly in a window seat as far as possible from Ripple. She chatted somberly with a few people, then left early with a friend to catch a seven o'clock movie. The movie was distracting in every respect but for its title, *The Abyss,* for it described precisely, at that moment, where Paula Newby-Fraser felt her career was heading.

As all this transpired, Don Andrews held forth next to the floral display in the center of the room. He'd been drinking moderately since 5:30 P.M. and seemed to have a buzz on when he spotted Katie Webb—twenty-four years old, petite, and sunny—coming his way. Webb was a rookie professional who'd come up from Del Mar, California. Andrews hailed her down. "Hey, Katie," he boomed. "We got your swimsuit. It came in on UPS."

"It did?" said Webb, smiling.

"Yeah," said Andrews. "We took it out of the box. It's such a little thing. Wow. You're gonna turn some heads tomorrow. I think you should model it for us at the beach party tonight."

Andrews had arranged what he called The World's Largest Indoor Beach Party for a ballroom downstairs. It had already begun.

Katie Webb blushed and answered ambiguously.

Andrews turned to the crowd. "Hey, that's what we should do to get things going down there: Get the pros onstage in their swimsuits." Nobody said anything. Andrews went further. "Hey, I know how this works. I've got a Ph.D. in psychology. [Actually, it was in kinesiology]. First you get the women onstage and get the men excited. Then you get the men up there, and the women get hot. When that happens, you've really got things going. We'll do that tonight. Right?"

"Right, Don," said a woman who'd taken this in from the sidelines. "You get up there in yours first."

Mercifully for all, the conversation then changed direction. Andrews's comments to Webb were not unusual, but they were particularly inappropriate given his position as race director. They sexualized Webb's performance and thus diminished the importance of whatever athletic abilities she, as a professional athlete, brought to the race. Triathlon is not advertised as a beauty pageant, but a sport in which performance matters more than sexual attractiveness.

Except for English Bay, which was polluted (during the prior year's swim there was gasoline on the water) and cold (sixty to sixty-seven degrees), the venue was ideal. The start, the two transitions, and the finish were all on one plot of parkland.

And the organization was impeccable. There was a different swim-cap color for each age group. And a different color yet for the pros. Athletes were marked with a simple code on the back of their calves—a way to know if the person passing was in one's age group. Within hours of the finish, a report would be issued listing every competitor's time for each sport, their age-group rank for each sport, as well as their overall placing and age-group ranking. The entire bike course, with the exception of one bridge, was closed to cars and lined with hollering spectators. The run was flat and the scenery along it—Stanley Park on the left, the sea on the right—spectacular. Volunteers in official T-shirts were stationed everywhere. At five points along the seven-mile run they offered water, oranges, sponges, and electrolyte-replacement drink.

No race was better organized, and that was the problem. It was overorganized, overhyped, oversponsored. Andrews had squeezed it dry. Gone was the adventure and unpredictability that had drawn most participants to the sport. Every facet of the race had been buffed to a commercial sheen. This was matched by the promoter's interpretation of the triathlon movement. As Andrews intoned at the press conference, "If we cannot be heroes to others, at least we can be heroes to ourselves." He knew the triathletes wanted affirmation and he gave it to them. Sixty race sponsors, hundreds of volunteers, a four-color program listing every competitor's name, TV coverage, thousands of cheering spectators—all of it to make certain that no competitor left town unpraised.

Fifteen minutes before the pro wave was scheduled to go, Jan Ripple was frantic. She'd forgotten to tape over the stem-hole of her rear disc wheel, the space in the disc that allowed access to the tire valve. Nothing else mattered to Ripple but covering that hole. She held aloft a roll of packing tape and did a worry dance as she implored to spectators on all sides, "Does anyone have scissors or a knife?" She wanted a clean edge on the patch. A race official stepped out of the crowd to see about the commotion. Still no scissors, no knife. Jan put tape over the hole and tried to bite it off the roll. It didn't work. Seeing that Jan was heating up beyond reason, the race official kneeled and bit the tape jaggedly off the roll. "Oh," cried Jan, "but it's all wrinkled." Still stewing, she decided there was no time to fuss with it further.

Jan was excitable and explosive; everyone knew that. But could she really believe that a two-inch square indentation on her rear wheel, if left uncovered, could cost her the race? It was exactly this kind of thing that reminded people of the Ripple clan legacy: You always can try harder, be more prepared, do better.

Jan's behavior reminded some onlookers of the emotional side effects of steroid use—excitability and unpredictable outbursts of physical violence. But to those familiar with the athletic temperament of the Meador and Ripple clans, all Jan's outbursts were predictable: They happened whenever she raced, particularly in the transition area. Her motto was "Let 'er Rip," and it was stenciled on her black disc wheel in large, white script.

One or two pros rammed into the side of a lifeboat that was surrounded by thrashing swimmers and therefore unable to move. Aside from that, the swim leg was uneventful, and very fast. Leslie Fedon, a fine swimmer and rookie pro from Virginia, was the fifth fastest overall and the first woman to rise out of the gray water and hurdle through the shallows to the beach. Shannon Delaney of Del Mar was next and Ripple followed one second behind as they ran past the timing table next to the plastic baby pool set up for fast foot washing. Newby-Fraser was a minute behind Ripple and nearly seven hundred well-conditioned athletes were behind her.

A few minutes into the bike, as Ripple climbed the bluff to the university, she passed both Fedon and Delaney and then completed the rest of the bike course unchallenged.

Ripple came off the bike in first and ran seven miles without contest to the finish, beating Newby-Fraser—who finished third—by four minutes. A drubbing.

The postrace dance took place that night in a converted warehouse on a bayside wharf. Ripple arrived in her red dress and danced to six fast ones in a row, wearing out three partners in the process. As the night went on, she jumped higher and whirled faster. When the band played country, she took half the floor.

Newby-Fraser was not a sore loser. She drank a couple bottles of beer and danced twice. Then she and nine others went next door to a storefront recording studio. Showcased to the courtyard in their plate-glass booth, they laughed and sang a Beatles number to prerecorded music.

For as long as Paula could remember, her mother had told her she had a tin ear and couldn't hold a note. Paula closed her eyes, put her hands over her earphones, and sang along to an old Beatles tune about shaking it up and working it out. Her voice was strong and as melodic as it had to be.

Two weeks later in Cleveland, in a USTS distance triathlon on August 27, Paula Newby-Fraser raced the wheels off two of the sport's best sprinters, Lisa Laiti and Colleen Cannon.

CHAPTER 15.

COMING BACK

◆

July 3, 1989. Nyssa, Oregon; Pt Grey, British Columbia; Olympia, Washington

On her first day back from Provo, Julie left her parents' home on the corner of Walnut and 4th in Nyssa, Oregon, at 9:30 A.M. She rode her bike to a place where, as a young girl, she'd spent many hours on Lady, her mare. The place was called Cow Hollow, much to the amusement of her city-born friends. Julie stopped briefly and saw a red fox flying its bushy tail through the brush.

Later that day, Julie, her parents, and Jim packed the camper and drove out to Lake Owyhee (Oh-WHY-hee) at the southern end of which the family had a cabin—outhouse, oil lamps, no running water. On the map, Lake Owyhee appears as a skinny, blue, thirty-mile S laying north-south with a dam at the north end. The lake, the dam, the river that runs from it, the ridge above it, and the town downstream—all are named Owyhee. The nearest towns to the west and south are thirty miles away over sagebrush and broken-lava fields; twenty miles to the east is rural Idaho and to the north lies Nyssa.

Lake Owyhee is remote. And in the summer it is not blue, but green. A suspension of pinhead algae grows so thick that dogs running on boat docks to shore will jump off too early, thinking the stuff is solid. (They only do it once.)

The lake is not a smooth S, either, but has many fingers that go back like fjords into the sandstone. The canyon below the dam is deep, utterly still and hot. Rock buttes rise steeply from the wounds made by the water. Cross-sectioned, these formations look like giant slabs of multilayered cake, each skirted by mounds of flaky crumbs piled halfway up its sides.

The day after arriving at the cabin, Julie hiked to the top of Elephant Rock with her brother's teenage sons. They crouched on the "elephant's forehead" and rolled boulders over the "trunk." The rocks dropped silently away for a hundred feet or so before thudding in the dust and rolling randomly down toward the weekend cabins below. Once released, there was no telling where the boulders would stop.

Out in the Owyhee, Julie felt playful and happy. For the first time that season, she thought little about triathlon or of the ordeal it had become.

The next day, Wednesday, she and Jim drove down to Dry Creek, where a dirt road left the lake and headed into the rolling hills above. Jim got on his mountain bike and rode alongside Julie as she ran toward Twin Springs, an oasis six miles away. It was a hot "nothin' place," the surrounding land unpopulated for hundreds of square miles. The region was public property, a great expanse of sagebrush on dry, rolling hills, a home for antelope, and a summer pasture for grazing cattle and it was overseen by the federal Bureau of Land Management (BLM). They'd been on the dust road only a few minutes when the idea struck Julie to run naked.

"You know," she said to Jim, "I've always wondered what it would be like to streak."

"Now's the time to find out," said Jim. "Nobody's going to see you out here. Well, maybe a few cows."

"So," Julie recalls, "I took off my runnin' clothes and passed them to Jim. He was stuffin' my clothes in his pockets and I started streakin' and I was kind of nervous even though I knew nobody was out there. There was nothin' out there. Zip. I was runnin' along and lookin' all around and just getting into it when darn if here comes a car. It was a BLM ranger. I couldn't believe it."

"I jumped off the road and scrambled into the sagebrush. He drove on by and I climbed out of the brush, laughin', and got my clothes on. Jim and I laughed all the way to Twin Springs."

Running naked in Owyhee was the most fun she'd had all season and, for a time, Julie forgot how fast she'd have to run the closing marathon in order to stay with the leaders at the Ironman, just three months away. She'd run a 3:27 marathon there two years earlier and knew, if her 1988 injuries were healed, she could go at least that fast again in October. But that wouldn't be good enough and she knew it. Newby-Fraser's 3:07 in 1988 had boosted the pace of the contenders to a new level. The top three finishers would certainly run under 3:20. The thought did not scare her now, as it had in the early season. Somewhere in the Owyhee, Julie found confidence. A feeling of vitality and strength had returned; she felt ready to pick it up.

Her training emphasized speed work on the run, maintenance on the swim, and endurance on the bike. If her legs held together, she would peak for the Japan World Cup, a long-distance event with a good prize purse scheduled for August 27. Training for and competing in Japan would boost her endurance to the level necessary to mount an assault on the Ironman.

In late July, the Japan World Cup was canceled. The race's Australian promoters folded their tent when the local Japanese government announced the bill for closing the bike course to traffic: $4 million.

Wilson was stunned. So far, half her season's race schedule had been canceled, meaning she wouldn't earn a dime from May to October.

* * *

Ripple, Hanssen, Newby-Fraser, Cannon, and Baker all received monthly cash payments from sponsors in exchange for various promotional services. These payments ranged from a low of $1,250 per month to over $7,000. In addition, all had their race fees, accommodations, and travel costs paid for by race management more often than not. Most of them paid nothing for "product"—equipment used in racing or training.

In contrast, Wilson had no cash sponsor. Her entry fees were sometimes waived, but she was rarely "comped" for lodging, never for airfare or gas. As for product, Wilson was given sunglasses, bike pedals, and handlebars. A local bike shop tuned her bike in exchange for having its name stenciled on her helmet. For sponsorship in 1989, that was it.

Earlier in the season, the Wilsons had retained a real estate broker to search out sponsorship opportunities. Julie's two fourth-place finishes at the Ironman and her remarkable race in Australia would be strong selling points, she thought. But after five months, her "agent" secured nothing. To Julie this was intensely maddening, but expected. Significant cash sponsorship had eluded her since she'd turned pro in 1987.

Wilson's first agent was a car salesman who enjoyed the company of athletes. He took a $500 retainer and promised cash deals, clothes, and equipment. He delivered nothing, then disappeared.

Wilson's next opportunity came in late 1987. It began when a local medical group (EMS) gave a her a few hundred dollars to wear their logo. A few months later, Pioneer Electronics—for whom Ripple and Cannon raced—offered Julie a "spot" on the Pioneer team. But, unlike many of the other members, Julie would receive no more than she was already receiving from EMS. It was a trial offer, basically. But as part of the deal, Pioneer insisted that Julie downsize the EMS logo on her jerseys or get rid of it entirely. The Wilsons told Pioneer they couldn't do that. As far as Pioneer was concerned, that was the end of the discussion and word went around the team that Julie Wilson was not a "team player."

In mid-1989, Julie realized that her naïveté about business and Jim's underdeveloped sales skills were sandbagging her career. Only winning the Ironman, she thought, would bring her the support she needed to compete on an equal basis with her rivals.

Until then, sponsor or no sponsor, Wilson had to race; without the stimulus of competition, she would go stale and she knew it. She decided to do three half-ironman events, all close to home: Pt Grey in Vancouver, B.C., on August 7; the Troika in Spokane on August 20; and finally, the Black Hills half-ironman on September 10 outside the state capitol of Olympia. None of them offered prize money, which meant to Julie that they had a good chance of actually happening.

Jim Wilson accepted another teaching job after work and Julie buried her anxiety in training. Each week through July and into early August, she swam fifteen thousand yards; pedaled the bike three hundred miles in six workouts (seventy miles on the longest ride); and ran fifty miles. Her running was broken into speed work, recovery runs, and endurance runs in which she'd get off the bike after a long ride and immediately run hard for six to eight miles. Aside from pain in her left heel, training went well.

When she left for Vancouver, B.C., to do the Pt Grey half-ironman, Julie felt strong and unpressured. With none of the big names competing, she could relax and do whatever the heck she wanted. That suited her fine. She won the race handily and made Jim happy. This pleased Julie perhaps more than her time of four hours and thirty-five minutes. She'd been hungry for a win for so long. Her pace for the half-marathon run was seven minutes a mile. The training was working; she was getting faster.

Two weeks later, she did the Troika—the late-season qualifying event for the Ironman held in Spokane, the largest city in eastern Washington (and some would say in all of Montana). Called the "Hub of the Inland Empire," Spokane was built on hard-scrabble fortunes made in mining and logging.

The Troika drew top amateurs and aspiring pros from four northwest states as well as from two Canadian provinces.

Winning was not easy, but from the start it seemed certain. Julie was the first woman out of Medical Lake (site of two hospitals—one for the body, one for the mind) and by the end of the bike, she was three minutes ahead of her nearest competitor. She increased her lead to five minutes on the run and was still pulling away when she crossed the finish line. Julie's elapsed time of four hours and thirty-one minutes was half an hour faster than the previous women's course record and it put her in the race's top fifteen overall. On the run, Julie's pace was 6:52 per mile. Faster yet.

It was sobering, however, to realize that to win at the Ironman she'd have to go just as fast for twice the distance. But then, so would the others.

Julie attributed her running improvement largely to her diet and specifically to what she'd begun eating during the races themselves. Anyone who wanted to go fast for hours had to eat while racing. Eating was one thing, digesting another. Julie's on-board fuel supply—glycogen stored in her blood, muscles, and liver—accounted for only half the calories she needed to race four and a half hours. To go the distance at speed, she had to ingest and convert two to three thousand calories into ATP (the chemical that enables muscles to contract on command), and she had to do this while racing. Whatever she ate would be dead weight (or worse) unless it passed quickly from her stomach and into her small intestine for absorption into the blood. She'd tried a number of race drinks and energy bars over the years, but always felt they let her down on the run. So she'd begun to experiment with honey, a simple sugar. On the bike, in addition to energy bars, she carried a water bottle filled with pure honey, which she steadily sucked down with lots of water. One cup of honey equaled a thousand calories of simple carbohydrates—and sticky hands. "If I ever crash," she said to Jim, "they'll find me in the bushes, stuck to the handlebars."

On the run, she sucked Lifesavers.

Under normal metabolic conditions, such a diet would result first in a sudden burst of energy and alertness, then insulin production would quickly increase to sweep the abnormally high level of glucose from the blood, causing temporary glucose deprivation and a feeling of weakness and light-headedness. During intense exercise, however, insulin production is suppressed because all circulating glucose is quickly devoured by hungry muscles. Julie's body had adapted to the point where insulin suppression would last for at least four and a half hours, perhaps for an entire day. She absorbed the simple sugars and passed most of the water through—a lot of water. She peed on her bike three times and urinated down her leg on the run. This was mildly embarrassing to Julie, but all the pros did it if they could—and not all of them could. Like everything else in triathlon, doing it well took years of training. And it was worth practicing; the minutes saved avoiding the Porta Potties could easily make the difference between finishing in the money and out.

By late August, Julie weighed 117 pounds. Her jeans were bunched under her belt, her jawline was as sharp as the edge of a desk. She was taking in between four and five thousand calories a day (the equivalent of forty-five bananas) to fuel her training. "There's no way I can eat that much solid food. I've had to go to juices and liquids. I need six hundred calories an hour for training and another twelve hundred a day for life function." She was training between five and seven hours a day.

After Troika, Julie pushed her workouts to the next level. In the pool, her main sets were longer. Instead of doing just 10 100-yard repeats of freestyle, leaving every minute and thirty seconds (10 × 100 free on 1:30), she did the 10 × 100 on 1:30, then, immediately, another 10 × 100 on 1:20; then another 10 × 100 on 1:10. "In the Ironman," she said, "you have to push through feeling tired." On the bike, she motor-paced more frequently and increased her distance rides to seventy-

five and a hundred miles. She ran four days a week, often twice
a day, first doing aerobic work in the pool, then her speedwork
on the treadmill or track: four miles at 6:30 to 6:15 per mile.
Twice a week she ran six to eight miles hard immediately after
a long bike ride. Her heart monitor would read 150 to 160
beats per minute on these runs. Jim guessed her anaerobic
threshold was around 165, but Julie's heart never beat that fast
in training. Her recovery, however, was swift—her morning
pulse deviated little from fifty beats per minute all summer.

Her body was responding well to the regimen, but mentally,
the intense and prolonged training left her irritable at rest. Her
sense of humor turned from playful to cynical. At night she
worried obsessively about her weight and her bank account.
Jim did what he could to calm her down. How can someone
train from dawn till dusk on fruit juice, pita bread, and salad,
she fretted, and not lose weight? Do only idiots spend four
hundred dollars a month on athletic shoes and orthotics? She
had no answers. She was raw inside from the worry and waiting, and she felt that only rigid discipline in all aspects of training would keep her mind from bursting with anxiety. She
bought a new bathroom scale.

In early September, Wilson's bike routes were newly clut-
tered with brown leaves and the change in season brought
with it a change in her mood. She sensed the end approaching
and was deeply relieved. Her legs were healthy, she was winning, her times were good. Her voice was lighter in the afternoon. From now until the Hawaiian Ironman, she had only one
more race—the Black Hills half-ironman.

Thirty minutes before the gun, Julie Wilson crossed the parking lot to the beach with a gymnast's floating swagger. She
knelt at the shore and felt the water. Wear the thermal cap,
she thought.

The water was black and warmer than the cool morning air.
Thick vapors oozed up from the surface of the lake and hugged
the bordering firs and leafy alders. A few old-growth cedars
still stood in the park; underneath them about two hundred

contestants fumbled through their gear with fingers stiff from the chill.

None of the buoys marking the course were visible through the vapors until just before 8 A.M., when Julie and 185 others waded into the leaf-bottomed lake to await the gun. The 1.2-mile course followed the edge of the circular lake about 20 yards out from shore, just past the snags.

There was a lot of psyching up done in the water before the gun. Most contestants were old hands at triathlon and would not have given a second thought to doing a USTS event. But this—a four- to six-hour go—was another thing entirely. Julie moved toward the front with no sense of physical limits. Insulated by her wet suit and secure in the knowledge of her preparation, she was ready to cut all dogs loose. She joked with Jim before the race that she'd "squish 'em like bugs." Her aggression was back.

While waiting for the gun, Julie saw Alice Godfred, a swift swimming pro from Alaska, and decided to follow her. At the gun, Godfred burst away from the churning and Julie drafted her for a few minutes before losing her in a small school of men. Julie swam the 1.2-mile circle in the black lake in twenty-six minutes—1 minute and 20 seconds per 100 yards. "I caught Godfred somewhere in the last third and came out of the water right behind her. She beat me out of the transition on the bike while I was busy puttin' on clothes. I was so cold I had to put on a second jersey."

The bike course was moderately hilly on country roads. It was rough under the wheels and gave Julie a good shaking for two and a half hours. Mount Rainier loomed pink and white over the course behind a fringe of evergreens, but Julie never noticed. "I kept my head down and pushed; that's all," she said. She pedaled an average of twenty-three miles an hour and by the end of it she was in the top ten, overall. Godfred, the only woman within reach, was many minutes behind.

The last man Julie passed during the run was Richard Holloway, a top-ranked amateur who'd once run in the Olympic Marathon trials. When Julie first caught sight of Holloway, he was struggling up the last hill, a VO2-max hump on the flank of a hefty glacial moraine. The finish was about two miles beyond the crest. The longer Julie looked at him crawling up that hill, the more buglike he appeared. Get 'im; get 'im, she said inside and she fixed her eyes on his back and willed him closer. She caught him near the top, went by tall, and never looked back.

"I squished him, neahhh, like that." She ground her toe in the grass and laughed at herself as she told this to Jim after the race. They were both elated; Julie had run 6:45 per mile. If she could run 6:45s now in a half-ironman, there seemed to be no good reason why she couldn't do 7:25 in Hawaii. This would give her a 3:15 marathon and, if she held together on the swim and bike, a good shot at the top three. The way her biking was going, maybe better.

Jim took Julie to a sunny spot on the grass next to the finish chute. She laid face down on a blanket. Her skin was brown; her swimsuit was the color of a naval orange. Her hair, tied in a ponytail, lay shiny as corn silk over her strong neck. Jim sat down next to her and began to massage her legs. He took them in his hands and ran his thumbs broadside down her biceps femoris, rolling a hump of muscle from her butt to the inside of her knee. He worked her calf muscles, her iliotibial bands, her ankles and feet. She lay with her eyes closed and listened to the applause as the finishers trotted by. From time to time she lifted her head and looked up to Jim and smiled.

Her parents, Andy and Thelma, sat in camp chairs in the shade of the finish banner next to the announcer's stand. Julie and Jim were not ten feet away. Andy was ebullient. He leaned forward on his best knee and congratulated many. "Anybody who finishes this race is a champion," he said. Then he said it again: "A champion."

Shortly, Julie rose from the blanket and walked tenderly to the car to soak her feet in the ice chest. This was only routine therapy to cut the ache in her left heel. The cause, she discovered months later, was a bone spur. The bone spur itself grew in response to perpetual inflammation of the tendons and fascia which joined the muscles of her arch to her heel bone. As she iced her feet, Wilson thought steadily less about her victory and more about the remaining three weeks of training before Ironman.

July 6 to September 8, 1989. Colorado

During all this, Kirsten Hanssen was recovering in Colorado, dividing her time between Denver, where she had her tidy house, and Vail, where Robert had taken a job with a ski-equipment retailer. Going back and forth, Kirsten drove a gray, four-wheel-drive Subaru station wagon with no power steering. It was a practical car, a good deal purchased with earnings from her first job, but in no way elegant.

Getting through life economically was a point of pride and a source of comfort to Kirsten. She was a model home economist and a shameless bargain hunter. She scoured bulk mail for coupons; restaurant twofers were her favorites. These she would tear out, save in a commodious daytimer, and thrust forward to cashiers with satisfaction. Before races, while others stood out from the registration tables talking about the event, Kirsten often went through her competitor's goody bag, culling the coupons and examining the freebies. She was always searching for the quickest, most frugal way from here to there. Once she found the route, she would follow it happily, no matter how tedious or humbling others might find it.

Kirsten approached her task of recovering from injury in the same deliberate, intense, but paradoxically chipper and carefree manner. She parked her Hamilton racing bike in the garage and took to riding a mountain bike. The upright posture and easy gearing were kind to her iliac crest. She did her errands on the big-tire bike and wore no helmet when she rode to town. Her short, blond hair blew back from an ever-present headband. Her tan face and sunglasses gave her the appearance of a model for lip balm. In her own eyes, however, she saw the Wicked Witch of the West, thin wrists wide on the handlebars, legs pumping motorlike with Toto in the basket behind.

The image amused her. She was ever mindful of her appearance and often compared herself to images, attractive or not, that she had seen before in movies or on television. She thought of herself always as someone being watched—a possible role model, example, or inspiration to others. "Being the first to wear a dress at awards banquets ... yes, I was very happy to start that trend. Before I started changing that, the girls were coming onstage in shorts and tank tops ... ugh. And I made it a lot easier for the Christian triathletes to be public with their faith. I'm particularly proud of that," she said.

To maintain her aerobic base without the pounding of running, Kirsten bounced through hours of water exercise with the ladies group at the community pool. This, too, she thought, "must have been quite a picture." (Esther Williams among the hippos?) "I could only stay an hour and a half," she laughed. "After that, my skin would wrinkle."

Happy-go-lucky in other parts of her recovery, Kirsten was vigilant about not gaining weight. "You don't want to get down on yourself, feeling like you're too heavy," she explained. "It just gets you in a downward cycle where you don't want to work out because you feel fat. So you skip some workouts and you gain a little more weight—then you really don't feel like working out." Once Kirsten had the psychology of it figured out, she was confident she'd not succumb to overeating. She was in control.

Seven weeks after her layoff began, Kirsten competed in a short-course triathlon in Aspen to test her recovery. She won. Seven days later, on the Sunday Julie Wilson won the Black Hills event, Kirsten raced the National Long Course Championships in Texas. Graceful and swift, her swimming brought her to the shore first among a group of seasoned professional women. "I did have a pretty darn good swim," she chirped, "didn't I?" She biked without faltering through forty-eight miles of parched and heaving hills, littered with prickly pear cactus, live oaks, and baleful longhorn cattle. She held off Amy Aikman—who'd twice placed in the top ten at Ironman—and won by seventeen seconds. It was a 4-hour race in conditions as oppressive as Hawaii—95 degree heat and 90 percent humidity. If she could handle the heat and hills of Texas, she figured, she'd be just fine in Hawaii.

Those who'd followed Kirsten's decline were shocked to hear she'd come back so quickly, but doubted her recovery was complete.

CHAPTER 16.

GETTING LEAN

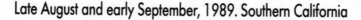

Late August and early September, 1989. Southern California

*B*y tradition, triathletes living around San Diego rode long on Wednesday. Those in town and training would shake down from the hills in the morning to join a procession of riders rolling up the coast from La Jolla to the nuclear plant outside San Clemente, about forty-five miles north. Scott Tinley, Julie Moss, Charlie Graves, the Puntous sisters, Murphy Reinschreiber, Ironman winner Julie Leach, John Howard, Scott Molina, Ironman winner Kathleen McCartney, triathlon original Tom Warren, Ron Smith, 1985 USTS champ Linda Buchanan, Mark Allen—all were periodic regulars on the Wednesday ride. "There was a time," reminisced one of the early riders, "when one truck across the centerline would have wiped out the entire sport."

As triathlon's early years of innocence went quickly by, the old-timers were joined by the MTV generation, bike-crazed gear heads, the driven, and groupies of both sexes.

Paula Newby-Fraser had been a regular on the Wednesday ride since 1986, but by late 1989 had quit it altogether, feeling she had too much to lose to brave the skills and road manners of an all-comers pack. Moreover, she shunned the spontaneous competitions that tended to develop among those who, she said with disdain, "rode their best race on Wednesday." She had no use for it, insisting that she would compete against others only on race day, never in training. Nor, she said, did she feel any kinship with "people who want to fart around on their bikes all day." By late summer, Paula's idea of a good time was not a chatty six-hour bike ride, but a beer on the beach or a "cuddle with my Huddle."

Training was a necessary evil and she did as little of it as possible. She had a particular aversion to what she called "garbage miles," the day-long rides, the eight thousand-yard swims, and the ninety-mile running weeks that the "masters of megamileage" (Dave Scott and Scott Molina in particular) had once established as de rigueur for Ironman contenders. No one, she felt, could do that kind of work in training and not be pooped on race day.

Instead, Paula preached speed and rest over distance and gruel. The over-distance fanatics might develop great range, she argued, but in getting it they sacrificed speed. "How," she asked, "can anyone expect to race at a certain speed without ever going that fast in training?"

An innovator, Newby-Fraser pioneered long-distance pace training and believed in it totally. Starting six weeks out from the Ironman she devoted one workout each week—in both biking and running—to going as fast or faster than race pace for a distance that built to just shy of the race distance. For example, on the bike she would, on the first week, do a seventy-five-mile ride averaging twenty-three mph—the pace she'd hope to hold during the Ironman. She did it again the second week. The third week she'd do a hundred miles at that pace, and again on the fourth. On week five she'd go back to seventy-five and then taper off completely the week before the race.

She did her pace runs faster than she'd race. The first week she held that pace for sixteen miles. She went farther each week until, during the fourth, she ran an entire marathon faster than race pace. Then she tapered. In swimming, her pre-Iron-man training was built around freestyle repeats of four hundred yards each. These workouts she'd do on Monday (with other, lesser sessions during the week), adding one more repeat each week until, four weeks out, she did eight repeats of four hundred at race pace. Then she tapered down to six 400's two weeks out. Her advice for the week before the Ironman: "Do nothing but keep moving."

With workouts like these on her docket, there is little mystery to Newby-Fraser's inherent aversion to training. It also explains why she usually trained alone as the Ironman grew near.

Dr. Mary O'Toole is an exercise physiologist at the University of Tennessee whose second laboratory is the Hawaiian Ironman. O'Toole has studied the physiology of long-distance triathletes since 1984 when LABMAN, her medical research group, first began pulling Ironman finishers into the tent. If what O'Toole now believes about muscle fibers is true—and many physiologists stand with her—Newby-Fraser was onto something big, early.

"There are," recites O'Toole quickly, "slow-twitch muscle fibers which use oxygen and are most in use for endurance-type events. Then there are fast-twitch fibers which don't use oxygen and fatigue quickly, but provide short bursts of great power—the Carl Lewis–type fibers. Those are the two main types of muscle fibers and, of course, successful endurance athletes have a very high percentage of the slow twitch variety. But," she says in a voice suddenly infused with curiosity, "in between is a category of fibers just recently discovered: fast-twitch oxidative fibers. These have the ability to respond quickly (like regular fast-twitch fibers), *but* they use oxygen. The important thing is that they can be trained to behave like slow-twitch fibers—but only by doing intervals of fifteen minutes or longer—at very high intensity. How fast is that? Well, let's just say that at the end, you keel over."

Paula Newby-Fraser, already a cardiovascular titan with an anaerobic threshold of 176 heartbeats per minute, was out building muscles nobody else knew they even had. She did her pace training alone or with a small group of her choosing. That September her group numbered five or fewer—herself, her boyfriend, Paul, her pal John Duke, and two friends, Todd Jacobs and Lisa Laiti.

Lisa Laiti was a classic, olive-skinned, dark-haired beauty. Reporters loved her, sponsors adored her exposures, Murphy Reinschreiber represented her. Like Kirsten Hanssen, Lisa had grown bored with a computer programming job in 1986 and had thrown herself into triathlon with abandon. She had great talent and quickly became the sport's star rookie. Then one day, she was riding her bike on a country road in Texas in 1987 when a pickup truck turned in front of her. She never saw it; her head was down and she was not wearing a helmet. Lisa T-boned the truck bed at twenty-five miles an hour. She suffered skull and brain injuries. Her hip was torn open on a tie-down cleat, then fractured by the impact. A large portion of her back was shredded by the pavement when she hit the roadway on the far side of the truck and slid. With loving assistance from Todd Jacobs, Lisa struggled and succeeded in regaining most of her athletic power and health. Lisa reentered competition the next season and won her first race. Though her speech was still unsteady, by late 1989 she could pedal the bike over long distances with unmatched ferocity. "I want to go fast," she said, and many wondered what Lisa was fighting.

As for Newby-Fraser, she admired Lisa's dedication and enjoyed having a companion who could push the pace. Todd and Paul got along well and were also well matched—both had placed in the top fifteen at the Ironman. It was a tight training group. John Duke, a thirty-eight-year-old amateur who owned an automotive business and did the Ironman as a hobby, kept things from getting too serious.

On Wednesday morning, September 6 (four days before Wilson and Hanssen won their respective races in Washington and Texas), the group left Paula's Willowspring Drive duplex in the hills above Encinitas and rolled down toward the El Camino Real. All the construction around them was fewer than ten years old, including Paula's home, one of the nearby hundreds built in the early 1980s; like all the rest, her house was beige stucco on plywood and roofed with concrete tile. Before construction, hundreds of acres of slopes and valleys had been stripped bare. All vegetation had been removed and the earth was homogenized—graded, turned, regraded, turned, graded, then rolled until the hills were as smooth as skateboard ramps. It was perfect for bicycles. Most towns of fifty thousand have one or possibly two bike shops; Encinitas has seven.

The sky that morning was a watercolor of blues, washed pale near the horizon and deepening to navy at the top of the dome. Below their wheels the roadway was smooth, perfectly crowned, and bordered by wide sidewalks of white concrete.

Paula sat high on her small-wheeled bike and nursed the brakes as she descended the long hill on Garden Avenue and neared the main intersection with the El Camino. The day was already warm and the countryside stretching north—tawny rolling hills speckled with tall eucalyptus and green acacia—was quiet but for a few cicadas buzzing. The tranquility of the day and the camaraderie of the group helped Paula forget temporarily that unless she won the Ironman, her greatest athletic achievement would always be remembered as a fluke.

The group turned right onto the El Camino, moved into the bike lane, and picked up speed. Car traffic was sparse. Two and a half miles later, they rolled past the white fences bordering the La Costa Resort. They continued north, toward the Palomar Airport turnoff and the Pacific Coast Highway beyond. Three minutes later, Paula rolled over a small piece of wood. The impact pushed the tire off the rim. When the flopping rubber reached the brake calipers, the bike stopped instantly. Paula flew over the bars headfirst and landed hard in the road on her side and elbow. She was certain she'd broken a rib and possibly an elbow, too. Both hurt like hell.

She was not, however, devastated. "Her first reaction," remembers Duke, "was that she could negotiate a deal to do color commentary on the Ironman for ABC." She lay on the road in stunned relief—the burden of repeating her landmark performance faultlessly lifted from her shoulders.

Summer 1969. Nyssa, Oregon; September 1989. Near Seattle, Washington

When Julie Wilson was ten, she went to the racetrack with her father. All those beautiful horses . . . When she learned that you could win money by picking the fastest, she knew she'd found her calling. "If there was one thing I knew," said Julie, "it was horses."

She was itching to bet, but had no money. Andy saw this as an opportunity to teach young Julie about gambling. He gave her a dollar and warned her not to get her hopes too high. Julie picked her horse. And it won. She took her winnings and ran to tell her father. "Go ahead," said Andy, "bet again." He was certain, but hoped as well, that the lesson was imminent. But Julie won again and was eager to place another bet. Andy could only suggest that since she now had a lot to lose, she'd better think it over a while. On the next race, he said, she might lose it all. Julie held her money tight and went back to Nyssa.

Julie had known from the start that triathlon was a gamble she might lose. After three seasons of racing pro, all her winnings were gone. Her family was still willing to bet on her, but she felt it was time to cut their losses. In early September she decided that if she did not win the Ironman, she'd retire.

Her need for a win, and not just a high placing, drove her to a training regime of heroic proportions. Her toughest days were Thursdays, which she called Death Days. They began at 4:30 A.M. in Kent and ended at 5:15 P.M. halfway up the side of Mount Rainier. In the course of the day she ran 16 miles, swam 6,000 yards, and biked 120 miles. In the process, she gained six thousand feet in elevation. The last leg was an eight-mile run up to the ski lodge immediately after dismounting from a six-and-a-half-hour ride. For ten and three-quarter hours, Julie's heart beat between 120 and 160 times a minute. On a scale of one to ten where ten reflected the greatest effort possible, she rated her effort between 8½ and 9.

She never gave herself a ten—not then, not once all season. She had a reason for that: She believed she was always capable of better. No matter how good she was, she could—and should—be better. Her attitude echoed the doctrine of perfection preached in her childhood church and practiced by her mother: Only those who strive toward Christlike perfection in body and soul will be saved. "Julie had this idea," said Jim, "that she wasn't any good unless she won the Ironman."

Somewhere along the way, the religious lesson had been twisted. Julie had confused worthiness with perfection, a mistake reinforced by the precarious economics of her infant sport.

On Friday, September 15, 1989, Julie rode onto a bridge above the Green River and looked down to the water. Spawning salmon were splashing in the rocky shallows, slapping their way upstream. Julie counted twenty-one. They were crimson and pieces of flesh hung off their battered sides. It was not right, she thought, that they would all die after struggling upstream so many miles.

The next day, Julie fought through her own "Death Day," her last before leaving for Hawaii. When she stopped in the parking lot of the Crystal Mountain Resort, she was lean as a raw-boned farm girl and glistened with sweat. At that point, she had no fear of the Ironman and, although she did not dare think it, she felt she could win.

Training for the Ironman was worse than the race itself—or so many who'd done it believed. That's where Julie felt she had the advantage. She did not have the speed of many of her competitors. "But I'm tougher," she said. "I know my training may not be good for me physically, but mentally, after what I've gone through, I know that no matter how hard it gets out there, I can take it. If you don't have it up here, all the fancy training and equipment won't help you—the Ironman will still break you."

Two days before she was scheduled to leave for Hawaii, Julie got up and ran twenty miles, then she mounted her bike and rode alone up to Paradise, on the south side of Mount Rainier, fifty miles away. The Douglas fir grow tall to the treeline on Rainier and crowd the two-lane road that winds steeply up to the lodge. Going down, Julie went into a tuck and let her bike run. She felt invincible. The sun flashed through the trees, blinking in her eyes like a strobe light as she plunged down the mountainside.

A cow elk, a thousand pounds of muscle and bone, ambled onto the road below, heard something coming and stopped. As tall as Julie on her bike and as long as a lane is wide, the animal stood sideways in the road and looked placidly uphill as Julie came around the corner. It did not flinch when Julie, screaming inside, missed it by inches.

Wilson knew she was tough; now she then felt lucky, too.

October, 1987 and 1988. Kailua-Kona, Hawaii

Jan Ripple had been broken by the Ironman twice. Her first attempt was in 1987. She came out of Kailua Bay in fifteenth position, pushed to the lead on the bike, and held it until Newby-Fraser overtook her at the bike-run transition. As she headed out of the Kona Surf parking lot and onto Alii Drive to begin the marathon, Ripple had three problems. Her first was Newby-Fraser, who'd won the event in 1986 and was now running away. Ripple's second problem was that she'd never before run farther than thirteen miles and thought she could simply gut out the last thirteen. Ripple's third problem was worse. Going into the race, she'd been justifiably concerned about dehydration, but she overreacted and drank too much. While guzzling water and electrolyte-replacement fluids on the bike, she retained twelve pounds of fluids. Ripple's body chemistry was such that the electrolytes she'd taken in were sweated out and much of the water she'd ingested stayed in.

The sodium concentration in her blood dropped lower and lower as she ran.

Her head ached, she was dizzy, her legs were cramping. She ran on, doing eight-minute miles and walking through the aid stations, drinking more. Her pace slowed. Soon she was walking more than running and began to double over. Steve stood on the sidelines and yelled at her as he did in training when he knew only anger and humiliation would move her forward. Things got worse. At mile sixteen he called in two medics. They checked her vitals and let her continue. She mostly walked the last few miles. Every few minutes another woman ran by. Coming into Kona, she pitched forward and fell onto her hands and face. She went on. Steve hovered, disbelieving and unsure what to do. He had no idea his wife would go through so much to avoid being called a quitter. He kept talking with her, trying to assess her brain function as much as to encourage her on. "What are the names of your children?" he asked. She didn't know. She went down for the last time a few yards from the finish. By that point, Steve had given up on the idea of pulling her out. It was too late for that now. "Get up, Jan! Get up," he shouted above her. Nearby spectators were aghast. "What kind of an ogre is this?" they wondered. But Jan just heard Steve trying to help her get across the line so she could stop. She finished fourteenth with a blood sodium level of 117. Doctors consider 135 to be on the low end of normal and anything under 120 to be life threatening.

Ripple finished an angel's wing away from seizures. She spent the night in the hospital and Steve told her later that he'd never go through it again.

In 1988, the Ripples came back. On the bike, Jan avoided the energy drink of which she'd so avidly partaken in '87. Instead she drank water and defizzed Coke. On the run she ate cookies. It didn't help. The big muscles in her thighs began to cramp even before she finished the bike. With twenty miles left to go in the marathon, Jan looked at Steve and said, "I can't go on. I'm one big cramp." And she pulled out.

Late August Through September 1989. Baton Rouge, Louisiana

Ripple swore that '89 would be different. Steve was willing to go once more, partly because her season had gone so well and partly because Erin Baker was coaching her by phone from Colorado.

Baker decided in August to skip the Ironman and run the Chicago marathon instead. She said, sensibly, that she couldn't do them both because the marathon followed the Ironman by only a few days. Baker's withdrawl improved prospects for all the top women at the Ironman.

With Baker's coaching, Jan's confidence and workload increased. She experimented with different foods on the run: jam sandwiches, jelly sandwiches, candy bars. She did weekly bike rides of six hours' duration, largely on the urging of Scott Molina, Baker's fiancé and legendary over-distance training machine.

Jan did her long rides on River Road, the antebellum two-lane thoroughfare that follows the Mississippi levee between Baton Rouge and New Orleans. Jan couldn't see the river, just the sloping levee and the long slab of baking roadway that ran on as sluggish as the river above. It was not unusual on these rides for her to encounter fewer than ten cars an hour. Occasionally the superstructure of a freighter floated by, but she didn't notice.

When Ripple got off the bike after these rides, she ran sixteen miles at first. After the next ride, she ran eighteen, then it was twenty. Always, the humidity was crushing. Steve and the kids drove just ahead of her. They kept the lift-gate door open, transforming the family van into a mobile fuel station. When Jan wanted water or electrolyte drink, she ran up to the back of the van, grabbed a bottle from Kyle, Shelly, or Kate, drank it, and threw it down. Steve would then stop the van, the kids would shag the bottles, and they would press forward as a family.

During that last month, Ripple did all her swimming in the fifty-meter pool inside LSU's natatorium. She swam no intervals, but concentrated instead on distance. "I did long, long swims. The pace in Hawaii is not as fast as a USTS race," she said, "but the course is terribly long. There are so many people swimming in a line that you just kill yourself trying to get around them so basically you just train for the distance."

By the end of September, Jan Ripple had it all: speed (only Erin Baker was faster in anything under five hours) and endurance (she could ride for six hours in ninety-degree heat and ninety-five percent humidity, then get off and run seven-minute miles for twenty miles). She was ready to rip and everyone who'd followed her season had no doubts whatsoever that when she got off the bike in Hawaii, she'd be leading by several minutes.

September, 1989. Colorado

Kirsten Hanssen, the human hummingbird, flew through the balance of September on sugar water and the love of a good man. Her injury under control, she divided her considerable attention between training for the Ironman and planning her wedding to Robert Ames.

Robert had moved during the summer from Vail to Steamboat Springs to take a new job. He also was in training for the Ironman. The move, the new job, the wedding, the Ironman . . . "It was," he said, "nuts."

Kirsten liked it busy. She loved change and the pressing adversity of so little time and so much to do. "A true champion," she said, "enjoys a challenge."

On her bike, Kirsten ranged throughout the northern Rockies breathing hard in bright colors, working the back roads, snacking her way from one mining town to another. In her high-altitude heaven, Kirsten saw the work of her God and felt Him near.

Kirsten was inspired by nature—she believed God created nature for man's needs and enjoyment—but she did not study it. In the small backyard of her Denver home grows one tree. It is a large tree, at least sixty feet tall. In the summer, it shades the entire yard and, in the fall, fills it with leaves. Kirsten had lived in the house for three years—and did not know what kind of tree it was.

Kirsten trained on a conventional twenty-one-inch racing bike with eighteen-spoke wheels. The custom-built Hamilton promised by Ralph Lewis (the bike's inventor) in July was held up in a disagreement over terms with Kirsten's mother, Susie. Lewis wanted full payment before he'd ship it. This was news to the Hanssens, who understood that Kirsten riding it at the Ironman would be payment enough. But Lewis already had Paula Newby-Fraser on a Hamilton; from Kirsten he wanted cash. Mrs. Hanssen told him, "Fine. When we get the bike, you'll get the money." And there it sat until it was too late.

Kirsten swam mainly in the community pool in Washington Park, a facility paradigmatic of every underfunded municipal water hole. Inside the front door, chesty guys in tank tops and Lycra hefted big black discs in a weight room lit by bare bulbs hanging on long black cords; the floor was covered with layers of disintegrating carpet remnants. The air stank. Bored teenagers hung over the entry desk, flirting with the cashier. There were no lockers in the locker rooms. Instead, army green mesh bags on wire hangers were provided for clothes. People carried these out to the pool deck by the dozens and hung them on a towering rack next to the shallow end.

The pool itself, twenty-five yards long, was usually crowded, choppy, and always in need of paint. Kirsten liked it there. She was the light in the darkness.

Two weeks prior to the race, Kirsten's fracture still hurt and she favored her right side. She was counting on the slightly slower pace of the Ironman (compared to the sprints which broke her) to cut the jarring just enough. On the bike, if the winds were light, if she could spin and not have to push in a tuck too long, she'd be all right.

Newby-Fraser's X rays revealed no breaks, but her ribs had been bruised and some intercostals, muscles between the ribs, had been ripped in the fall. They jabbed hard when she breathed deeply. She was back on her bike in six days, although with her elbow torn up, it would be weeks before she'd be able to lean down on the aero-bars. She was also unable to swim comfortably for weeks; it hurt too much to reach out. But that didn't worry her. No Ironman race had ever been won on the swim. It always came down to the run.

CHAPTER 17.

CHILDREN OF SHAME
ON THE ISLE OF GUTS

◆

Early October, 1989. Kailua-Kona, Hawaii

*F*our days before the race, Jim Wilson picked up his brother, Jerry, and Jerry's wife, Nancy, at the Kailua-Kona airport. They'd come to vacation and cheer on their sister-in-law, Julie Wilson. As Jim drove the rented Toyota down the Queen K highway back to Kailua, nine miles away, Jerry looked out his open window. The sensation was that of a campfire blowing in his face. For miles on either side of the road he saw only rigid lava wobbling in the heat lines and clumps of grasses that seemed more mineral than vegetable. Jerry looked at it for some time and said, "Now I've seen the one place that's uglier than Nyssa."

Between Kona and Hawi (fifty miles away), the Queen K rolls over a predominantly barren, wind-blasted inclined plain of jagged brown rock that rises to volcanic summits on one side, and falls gradually to the sea on the other. Toward Hawi (Ha-VEE) the hills begin—a long series of low-gear rollers that slowly level a few miles from town. Except for the green miles near Hawi, the highway's dominant views are of tortured textures and hues that children discard early from their crayon boxes: burnt umber, raw sienna, and brindle. Although the start and finish of the race are in town, a seaside oasis of green and blue, it is out in the volcanic slag that the Ironman is truly contested.

Julie Wilson had been on the island for nearly two weeks and had spent much of her time on the Queen K, training. Most other contenders rode and ran near town where it was cooler, but Wilson preferred the highway, the heat, and the wind.

On Thursday night, thirty-six hours before the race on Saturday, Julie squatted on the sofa in her rented condominium and tried to sit still. She'd just returned from the pro meeting at the Hotel King Kam, where the race director had announced that there would be no postrace drug testing. Julie wondered at first whether she'd heard correctly: "No drug testing at the Ironman this year." Incredibly, it was true. Tri-Fed had run out of money for testing and the Hawaii Triathlon Corporation—which would sell the race two months later for $3 million—would not part with the $5,000 to $10,000 required to test twenty of the top finishers for everything from steroids to stimulants. "After analyzing the results from last year's pilot testing," a race official said, "we decided we did not have a drug problem at the Ironman."

Dr. Bob Laird, medical director for the race, was deeply disappointed in the decision, which had come down from Chairman Silk through race director Debbie Baker. Laird later revealed that in the anonymous, purely voluntary testing done of samples taken from among the top 150 finishers in 1988, they found "one positive for opiates and one for marijuana." Although marijuana would not enhance anyone's performance in an endurance contest and neither, one could argue, would opiates (because they depress heart rate), both were banned substances. Moreover, the positives came from people who'd volunteered and most people would assume that volunteers would be cleaner than those who would participate only under duress. Moreover, fewer than a third of the samples had been tested for steroids, and most of the top twenty finishers had either refused to give a sample or weren't asked. Nevertheless, Ironman officials insisted that there was no evidence of a "drug problem" at the Ironman.

Wilson had counted on drug testing and was outraged. She wanted to run outside and scream or jump on her bike and churn down Alii (Uh-LEE-ee) Drive in the dark. But she had to save herself for the race and found that very difficult. She prowled the couch like a cat in a rowboat and when she could stay in one place, she folded and unfolded her legs beneath her as she talked, laughing nervously. "The pro triathlete," she said, "is just a piece of meat—just something for people to make money from." She was breathing hard, excited. Her flat stomach, bare below a short, elasticized top, wrenched in, then out. Her hands flew away from her shoulders as she tried to keep her erupting thoughts in order. "I don't need 'em. I don't need any of 'em. I've got it just as I want it. Nobody expects me to do well here. I'm completely free. It's like I've got a secret and I can just go out there and play my game." A bitter, angry confidence escaped from defenses weakened by fear, anxiety, and now again, betrayal. Jim sat calmly on the floor in front of her. Outside, the sea crashed next to the pool and the breeze hissed in the palms. Julie grew quiet for a time.

"I know this is really strange," Julie continued, her eyes bright blue and drilling, "but there's a time before the race when everything's crazy and spinning and I feel like I'm just sucking everything out there into my head. [Her hands went wide, then closed in on her skull.] And then, it's like I just shut everything out and I'm in here alone. Just me and Jim and everything that Jim's told me becomes so clear."

Kirsten arrived in Hawaii ready to do business, but her position was not strong. She had no sponsors lined up for 1990, only three months away. For two years running, Timex had retained Kirsten (for $30,000 a year) to promote its "Ironman" watch—but the company had decided not to renew. (The Hawaiian Triathlon Corporation owns the "Ironman" trademark and licensed it to Timex for a reported dollar a watch.) "The watch sold so well," recounted Robert Ames, "they figured they didn't need to pay Kirsten anymore to help sell it."

Kirsten had no sponsor and worse, since Graves had quit in March, she had no agent. On Friday morning, she and Robert called Dave McGillvray, who represented Jan Ripple and Erin Baker, among others. Robert asked him, "Would you be interested in representing Kirsten in 1990?"

McGillvray was noncommittal. He said, "I am interested. But let's talk after the race." After the race.

Kirsten looked grim around Kona during the final days. Robert said she'd "put on her race face."

The night before the race, Kirsten stayed in the hotel with her parents. Kirsten's mother cooked. Susie enjoyed cooking for Kirsten. She liked to be involved in her daughter's nutrition. When Kirsten was young and swam on the juniors team in Wichita, her mother brought her food after practice. "She always brought me two eggs Benedict—toast, tomato, eggs, and cheese. Yep. That's what she did all right."

The Hanssens sat down at the table together and they prayed that God's will would be done.

Paula made an appearance at the bike check on Friday afternoon. She'd been "comped" into the Royal Sea Cliff, two miles from the pier. During the final two weeks, she trained with Lisa or Paul, or alone. She was massaged. She did her nails and painted them silver. She decided she was a Buddhist, like her brother Stuart, and she replaced the crystal on the pendant chain around her neck with Murphy's gift: a small jade Buddha.

As she often did, Jan Ripple arrived at the race with a male traveling and training companion, this time Cristian Bustos, a pro from Chile who spoke no English. Jan was more comfortable around men than with her female rivals and Steve, who could not leave his dental practice for another week, was happy Jan did not have to travel alone.

After getting Bustos oriented, Jan settled into her rented

condo, went about her training, and did whatever she could to avoid the many reporters out there searching for one more interview with Janripplemotherofthree.

Steve Ripple flew in to take charge of final preparations in the last days. Principally, he looked after Jan's bike, seeing that it was tuned up, cleared by race officials, and checked in at the pier on Friday afternoon.

After that, there was nothing more to do but get through the night and get down to the pier by dawn, ready to race.

CHAPTER 18.

LET'S GO HOME NOW

October 14, 1989. Kailua-Kona, Hawaii

Before dawn on race day, Kim Wilde huddled with his fellow mechanics near the bike racks. Wilde was a lean, muscular man in his early thirties with big forearms and wore sunglasses shaped like old silver dollars. He had the presence of a platoon leader—which he was.

Wilde and his crew of mechanics provided what was called "neutral bike support" for the Ironman. Their job was to fix broken bikes wherever they lay along the 112-mile course and do anything possible, short of welding a frame or providing a new bike, to get the rider—amateur or professional—going again. It would be Wilde's second year in charge at the Ironman although he'd been a bike mechanic for twenty-five, working time-trials and stage races throughout the U.S. and abroad. He'd been yelled at, stepped on, bruised, cut, greased, and run over—all in the service of cyclists, a large number of whom treat race support crews like indentured servants.

Over the years, Wilde had learned not to fly with a metal tool box and was angry that morning because one of his mechanics had. "He was a young mechanic," Wilde said, "and he didn't know that metal tool boxes tend to break open in baggage compartments—they don't flex. You have to use plastic. The poor guy lost two bottom drawers of his box—all his major tools." Among other things, the mechanic needed a crank wrench.

"Here," said Wilde, "Take mine for the race."

Wilde's crew had been wrenching on bikes all week; most had worked until 3 A.M. Now, with two hours sleep behind them, their toughest shift—seventeen hours of racing—was about to begin. They broke the out-and-back bike course in pieces, two stretches of roadway, each about twenty-eight miles long. There would be two teams, each responsible for breakdowns among comers and goers along their assigned strip. Wilde would be with the second team. His crank wrench would be with the first.

At 5 A.M., Jan Ripple stepped into her racing suit—a skin-tight, blue-and-white body-sleeve that resembled a wrestling leotard, only more colorful. She walked into kitchen, turned on the lights, and poured grape juice into the blender she'd set out the night before. She plopped in a banana, some strawberries, a glop of strawberry yogurt, and one heaping scoop of Dyna-Carb powder. She whipped it into a slurry and drank the calories slowly.

At six, she and Steve left the Kanaloa in their rented sedan, turned onto Alii Drive and headed for the pier, six miles away. There were no streetlights; it was utterly dark but for the cars ahead, each moving like a flashlight along a black path between the jungle and the sea. There was no wind; small waves lapped gently in the dark.

As they drove past the beach homes and condominiums on the outskirts of Kona, the Ripples reviewed strategy. "Come out of the water with the leaders, go to the front on the bike, and stay there. Dictate the pace. Hurt 'em. Hang tough on the run." They entered town, a promenade of shopping boutiques, restaurants, historical markers, and more condominiums. Steve parked the car in a place he could leave quickly. They grabbed Jan's athletic bags and headed for the bike racks on foot.

The television lights mounted high above the finish line burned a corridor of hazy blue daylight between the bleachers and the seawall. Hundreds of awakening athletes with bags on their shoulders shuffled down Alii toward the light, spare clothes trailing, looking like refugees from behind. Moving on, they stepped carefully through the snaking power cords that fed the finish tower and entered the compound of bike racks. Lighting was poor in the racks and dark figures rose and fell in the thicket of wheels and handlebars.

Julie Wilson hadn't slept much. She'd drunk fluids constantly the day before and had to get up many times that night. At 5:15 A.M. she ate two bagels and drank more water. After Jim massaged her legs, they headed for the King Kamehameha Hotel and Julie's hideaway inside—a leather bench set against the wall opposite the registration desk. It was dark there and close to the restrooms.

Julie laid down on the bench and cried. She felt vulnerable, scared, and small in the face of what this race had come to mean. She wanted so badly to do well. She and Jim had worked so hard.

Crying helped; it always did. After another massage from Jim, she was ready and they left for the bike racks.

Kirsten Hanssen and Robert Ames rose at 5 A.M. and, after joining in prayers for the day, Robert said, "Let's get to the Jungle."

Kirsten had little to do in the racks but stick her fluid bottles in the cages and check tire pressure. Unlike all the others, Kirsten had no computer on her bike and thus none to start or reset. Timex, her sponsor, had subtly but firmly discouraged her from using one. Timex did not manufacture bike computers, but their rival in the timepiece market—Casio—did. The upshot for Kirsten was that without looking at her wristwatch and calculating from known mile-posts (few can do it in the heat of racing) she had no idea how fast she was going. While others followed their rpms as assiduously as their heart rate, Kirsten never knew her rpms—and didn't care.

Robert kissed Kirsten and said, "Have a good race, honey," then left for his bike in the amateur racks.

"You too, hon," chirped Kirsten, without looking up.

Paula Newby-Fraser and Paul Huddle arrived at the bike racks together. They traded a floor pump to get their tires to 160 pounds pressure. Paula tied back her hair with a rubber band, laid her fanny pack and race number over her bike, and left to get in the water. She was calm and focused.

Julie Wilson finished her chores in the bike racks quickly, then walked with Jim toward the sea. All in one moment they were coach and star athlete, husband and wife, childhood friends. They made goofy faces at one another and Julie left to join the Puntous Twins in the water.

Dawn broke soft and blue at 6:40 A.M.; the black-and-white grimness of the bike pits was gone, replaced by a brilliant tropical morning. The mood of the athletes brightened as well, as self-doubts gave way—at least on the outside—to boisterous self-satisfaction. The race would start in twenty minutes and hundreds of athletes were funneling into the horseshoe bay down a narrow flight of stone steps. The beach was short and narrow, and because the rocks near the pier and seawall are home to spiny sea urchins, most contestants swam out immediately to tread water—a task made easier by the high salinity of Kailua Bay.

Jan Ripple and Steve were still in the racks, swarming over Jan's bike. They ripped the wrappers off five brown Power Bars and molded them like plastique explosive around the top tube. A little box with a trapdoor on the back end hung below—a pill dispenser stocked with sodium pills, potassium pills, ibuprofen, and some enzymes designed to help her mitochondria pull oxygen from her blood. Two spare tires were taped behind the saddle and a pressure canister of Quik-Fil was taped to the down tube.

Jan struggled with last-minute adjustments to a thin, black water bag she'd wear on her back during the bike. She was taking no chances with electrolytes and hydration. She adjusted the straps, found the plastic tube that led from the bottom end, and bit the mouthpiece. Water squirted into her mouth. Satisfied with the fit, she took the whole thing off, rummaged in her bag, then shouted, "I can't find my pills [her enzymes]. My race caps, I can't find them." Her hands were shaking.

"Oh great, Jan," Steve barked. "Where are they? They should be with your gear. Oh great, Jan."

Steve ran off into the dawn and returned a few minutes later with a white plastic bottle full of pills. He shook some into Jan's hands and said, "It's time. You'd better get in the water."

Helicopters whumped overhead. A thousand yellow-capped men and two hundred and seventy-five orange-capped women treaded blue water. Spectators crowded the seawall; above, every balcony facing the bay was jammed with people waiting to see 1,200 swimmers start at once.

During the warm-up, many athletes swam out far past the starting line—a rope of flags strung across the bay—and a good number didn't come back. It was 6:55. Helicopters roared low over the water but the announcer's voice was still clear. "We will not start the race until everyone is back. Get back behind the flags. Everybody must get back behind the flags." Despite the repeated warnings, about fifty pros and top age-groupers remained a hundred yards and more beyond the starting line. Jan Ripple and Julie Wilson were holding their position under the flags in the middle when a woman treading alongside Wilson said, "Hey, look at those people way out there." She'd just opened her mouth to continue when the starting cannon boomed.

Two acres of blue water turned instantly to boiling white and the turbulence and shouting and clapping from the pier, the seawall, and the balconies roared across the bay. Hundreds of birds shot up from the seaside palms. Nobody thought seriously, and with good reason, of declaring a false start.

The top competitors who'd started behind the flags swam furiously to catch up to those who'd started beyond them. Ripple was pulling so hard that most of her back was out of the water. Julie Wilson accelerated alongside Sylvianne Puntous until Puntous was hit square across the shoulders by a descending forearm and then swum over. "She just disappeared," said Julie. "I looked around for her and then she popped up, okay. It was a very aggressive start."

Ahead of the angry swarm the bay was calm—no wind, no chop, no rolling swell. Nothing but fast water. Twenty-five minutes into the race, the women's leaders stroked past the turnaround boats anchored 1.2 miles down the coast. Their pace: a minute ten seconds per hundred yards.

As they began the long push to the pier, Newby-Fraser swam close to the lead, drafting Mark Allen, who in turn swam in Dave Scott's bubbles. Kirsten was only a few seconds behind in another pack of pro men. Julie Wilson and the Puntous sisters swam two minutes farther back, pulling their way along at a steady 1:15 per hundred.

When the pack slowed after the turnaround, Ripple swung out of the lineup. She passed Newby-Fraser and went after Hanssen, who'd gained a full minute on Paula over the second third of the course. Wilson and the Puntous Twins held their pace.

Hanssen was the first of the race favorites and the fifth woman overall to raise her pumped-up shoulders out of the water and run up the Astroturf to the bike racks. Her swim time was six minutes faster than she'd posted in 1988, the year she'd swum with the cast on her left forearm. Kirsten was breathing hard but she ran right through the fresh-water showers, grabbed her transition bag from a volunteer, then plunged into the changing tent.

Ripple heaved out of the water thirteen seconds behind

Hanssen. Bare feet slapping, she did a small-step run straight to her bike. She did not change clothes, having decided earlier to bike in the same blue-and-white skin-suit she wore for the swim. Her jaw was clenched, and her lips were just a dark line below her blazing eyes. "I try," she said, "to relax on the swim, but once I start the bike, I get intense."

In one unbroken motion, Paula rose from the water and drove a long, painted thumbnail under her swim cap; she clamped the rubber between thumb and forefinger and threw the cap down. She was only twelve seconds behind Ripple and made all of it up in the transition. As Jan struggled with her water pack, Paula slipped into her bike gear and rushed away.

Ripple pushed her bike clear of the racks and got on. As soon as she put pressure on the crank arms, she felt a clunk in the bottom bracket, where the pedal arms attach. At the same moment, the trapdoor in her pill box swung open and her pills—sodium, potassium, enzymes, and all—tumbled down and bounced on the road. She kept going.

Back in the changing tent, Kirsten pulled her suit down and off, then stepped into another; it was identical but newer and dry. She gripped the side panels and pulled hard against the friction of her wet body and the elastic of the suit. As she did so, her left wrist brushed her eye, dragging her contact lens across her eyeball and out. She found it, thinking, "Paula and Laiti are getting away." She licked the lens off her wrist and held it on the tip of her tongue as she pumped up Pay 'n Save Hill all the while saying to herself, "On the highway ... put it in on the highway."

As Newby-Fraser, Laiti, and Hanssen attacked the hill, Wilson ran up the swim ramp with the Puntous Twins, then stopped to dress, putting on cycling shorts and a sleeveless top over her orange swimsuit. She did not show the urgency that possessed the others. She had great confidence in her biking skills and felt, at that point, that Ripple would blow up on the bike and that Kirsten's hip would cripple her on the run. She didn't know what to expect from Newby-Fraser. Nobody did.

Kirsten turned onto the Queen K highway with her contact lens still on her tongue. Leaning down on her aero-bars, she took off her sunglasses, stuck them in her suit, and tried to poke the lens back in her eye, but could not. The wind and the bouncing made it impossible. She flicked the lens off her finger, stood up on the pedals, leaned out over the bars, and pumped.

Newby-Fraser, Wilson, Hanssen, and Ripple had all made it through the swim more or less as planned. Not all the pro women, however, were so lucky. Terri Schneider, who'd placed sixth the year before, ran out of the water two minutes behind Wilson. But no one could find her transition bag in the racks. It had mistakenly been placed in a room at race head-quarters by someone who believed Schneider had withdrawn from the race. Ten minutes later, when the bag was brought to the pier, Schneider was close to a nervous breakdown. She chose to continue the race, but her concentration and compo-sure had been destroyed. She tried to make up the time, forgot to drink enough fluids, and wound up in an aid tent out on the highway. She would finish the race eleven hours later, sobbing.

Twenty miles up the highway, Ripple had established a fast pace and was leading with Laiti and Newby-Fraser riding paral-lel a few yards behind. "I wasn't thinking at all about what was gonna happen next," said Ripple, "I just kept askin' myself, "Are you goin as fast as you can?"" She concentrated on the discom-fort in her legs, using that as a kind of tachometer to measure her level of performance.

Laiti felt lousy. Her head was light and it ached. Paula felt fine. Three motorcycles, each with a camera operator in the second seat, rolled effortlessly alongside the lead group of three. Kirsten Hanssen was a quarter-mile back and closing. A helicopter drabbled overhead. The winds, which had been blowing viciously across the road all week, were still. The tem-perature was in the low eighties; the humidity was 10 percent.

Kim Wilde, chief bike mechanic, remembers what happened next: "Jan Ripple started experiencing mechanicals around mile thirty-five. She was pulling the lead pack at the time, heading for the Waikoloa turnoff to Hawi."

Ripple's pedals and crank arms were wobbling in and out and she realized that the clunk she'd felt back on the pier had been a warning of something about to go terribly wrong. She lifted her head toward the open rear end of the ABC camera van, and she yelled to the crew inside "Where's the mechanics?" "I need the mechanics."

"Okay," someone yelled back. "We'll radio Shimano."

Jan was worried, but not panicked. She was confident that the bike guys would have her going in a couple minutes or less. She could make that up. She could hear Hanssen and Laiti breathing hard and knew she'd been taxing them.

Kim Wilde drove alongside in the Shimano repair van just thirty seconds later. Jan rolled onto the shoulder. Paula, Lisa, and Kirsten sped past.

Wilde remembers, "I got out of the van. Jan was there, the press was there, and the moment I looked at her bike, I knew she was screwed. The crank bolt was loose, about to fall out. It's a bolt with a fourteen- or fifteen-millimeter head, but it's recessed and you need a special wrench to tighten it—the wrench I'd given away that morning. It should have been a fifteen-second delay. Instead, when Jan saw me coming, she was looking at the end of her race. The bottom line is, it was my mistake. It was a stupid, rookie mistake. There are certain things that you never live down. This is one of them."

Wilde tightened the bolt as much as he could with his fingers and told Jan, "It's only gonna hold like this for a mile or so. I'll be back with a wrench as soon as I can." Wilde got back in the van and pushed his driver toward Kona at 80 mph. At that speed, his crank wrench was nine minutes away.

Jan got back on her bike and made it another mile before her crank bolt fell out. She pulled over into a crowd of ABC people, spectators and aid-station volunteers who commiserated as she paced next to the road and felt the bikes whoosh by.

"I stood there, expecting the van to come any second. And then," she said, "when it didn't come and it hit me that everything I worked for was racing down the road without me. That's when I lost it, lost it totally."

Ripple shrieked, "Where's the truck?" again and again and again.

Wilson and the Puntous sisters rode by. "Ooops," said Sylvianne. "It looks like Jan." Wilson could see that Ripple was "real pissed off" and thought she must be out of the race.

Jan kept screaming, "Where's the truck?" But as the minutes went by, her anger was blunted by despair.

On the road outside Kona, Wilde and the other crew executed a rolling hand-off with the crank wrench. Wilde turned around and floored the accelerator. The van wove in and out of the procession of bikes and cars, at times hitting 90 mph on the two-lane road. Reaching Ripple, Wilde jumped out of the van with the wrench and went to work, kneeling in the gravel, his heart pounding. Jan's anger welled up and she kept screaming, "Where were you?! I've been standing here for twenty minutes! Where the hell were you?"

Wilde had no excuse and said the only thing that came to his mind. "Don't worry; calm down. It's a long race, it's going to last all day."

This enraged Ripple. "If you think it's going to be so damn easy," she screamed, "let's see you try to make up twenty minutes on Paula Newby-Fraser."

Wilde was silent as Jan stormed away. He'd done his best. It wasn't his fault her bike had broken down, but he knew Jan had the only point that mattered—the Ironman was no longer a race of distance and attrition, but of time, of pace. Anyone out there could see that the pace that day was the fastest ever.

Jan Ripple was no longer a contender. She couldn't win. But she couldn't quit either. She rode mad for the next seventy-seven miles and passed hundreds, often forgetting to eat and drink.

*   *   *

As she rode alongside Sylvianne Puntous, Julie Wilson was confident. Sylvianne was the only woman other than Newby-Fraser to have won the Ironman twice. Puntous had more experience with the race than any woman, could beat Newby-Fraser handily in any race under five hours, and of two chances to beat her in Hawaii, had done so once. If, Julie figured, she was close to Sylvianne, she was in contention. Her average speed—22 mph—was on target. She felt strong and knew she'd gain time on the leaders when she hit the hills and headwinds twenty miles south of Hawi.

But when Wilson began climbing toward Hawi, there was no wind. The great sapper was gone. The temperature off the road was a good 10 degrees below normal, where normal is 110 degrees and "really hot" is when the metal sign posts warp.

Up ahead, Paula and Kirsten rolled into Hawi alone, leading the race. They'd dropped Lisa Laiti in the hills when Lisa's head ached badly and she'd begun tossing her head, trying to shake her eyes into focus.

Soon, Julie and Sylvianne entered Hawi together and threw their empty water bottles on the road. Volunteers ran out from the roadside tables and socked new ones into their reaching hands. Sylvianne coasted and drank and when Julie saw this, she knew it was time to let her horse run. Now! She stood on the pedals and burst away. There was a tailwind and it was suddenly quiet. With no wind rushing, she engaged her biggest gear and spun it down the road. "I felt great. Did the whole back fifty like a bat out of hell."

At the aid station just south of Waikoloa, volunteers knew the leading women were coming when they saw a helicopter rise from the heat waves some two miles away. Below it, the lights of the pace car pulsed and a camera van shimmied behind, the distance and the heat belying the furious pace of the riders approaching. Paula and Kirsten came through so fast that volunteers, who'd begun running at full speed a conservative

while ago, barely got the bottles up in time. *Whack!* . . . *Whack!*
And they were gone.

They'd ridden eighty miles. Their sides were rippled with
white waves of evaporated salts from the sea air and the sweat
wicking through their suits. Sweat ran off their noses and into
their mouths. The taste was of bike helmet—metallic and
slightly bacterial.

Paula's form was faultless. Her back was flat, her head was
down—it was wind-tunnel perfect and she'd held it for nearly
four hours. The task was similar to what she'd learned years
ago in ballet: Assume an uncomfortable posture, hold it, and
smile. Kirsten couldn't match Paula's efficiency. She rose ever
more frequently from the saddle to reduce pressure on her
burning iliac crest.

Julie Wilson was gaining a bit and feeling fine.

Jan Ripple was seven and a half miles behind Wilson, pushing
a big gear and pedaling as fast as her quads would allow.

Twenty-five miles from town, Kirsten could hold the pace
no longer and Paula pulled away, seemingly undiminished by
five hours of racing. When she rolled down the long hill to the
bike-run transition an hour later, Newby-Fraser led Kirsten by
four minutes.

Less than two minutes after Paula pulled in, she ran out of the
transition area, having changed only her fanny pack and her
shoes. Running fully erect, she started the marathon just two
minutes off her record pace in '88. On Alii toward town, Paula
was breathing hard and felt a panic welling up that she might
have gone out too fast. She centered herself by pushing away
thoughts about the uncertain future, and concentrated instead
on how she felt at that moment, and why.

She was doing seven-minute miles outside town when she
met the ambulance carrying Lisa Laiti. Laiti had been just a few
miles from the bike-run transition when she passed out, fell
from her bike and slid, unconscious, into a parked car. The
impact fractured two vertebrae in her neck. [She would recover completely.]

Julie Wilson started feeling weak about ten miles from town and labored harder to hold her pace. *What's happening to me?* she wondered. When she tried to reason the cause, she couldn't keep her thoughts in a straight line. Fighting to be optimistic, she thought, *I'll be running soon. I'll be using other muscles. My legs will come back.*

Julie stripped off her cycling shorts and jersey in the bike-run transition and left wearing only her orange swimsuit, shoes, and a white visor. It was one in the afternoon in Hawaii and she was going to run a marathon. She was in third place. Hanssen was ahead by four minutes, and Newby-Fraser by eight.

Julie felt lousy and could no more run seven-minute miles than fly. She settled for seven forty-fives. *Okay,* she bargained with herself, *just go easy through town. Give the legs time to recover. Anything,* she reasoned, *can happen in three hours.* But the excitement of side-by-side competition on the bike—the rushing landscapes, the wind whistling in their helmets, the distractions of gear changes—all of that was gone now, replaced by a grinding self-awareness and the loneliness of pain.

Jan Ripple arrived in the bike-run transition area determined to get back in the race. Her husband, Steve, knew the race was lost, but Jan heaved out of the transition area and bravely jogged up the long hill to Alii—a hill which could not be more cruelly placed. Steve followed her out and soon both were going down Alii Drive—Jan running, then jogging, then walking, and Steve shadowing her with the car, stopping periodically to confront her, coach to athlete.

Jan was out of her head. Her core temperature was too high; she was dehydrated and swimming in lactic acid. She could not breathe without pain—abdominal muscles on her right side were in spasm and her gasping only shoved her diaphragm into them like a boot. "I've got appendicitis," she cried to Steve. "It hurts so much. I know it's appendicitis." Had he not known how much she was hurting, Steve would have laughed.

"It's not appendicitis, Jan. It's not," he said. "You're just cramped. You're going to be okay, but you've got to stop. The race is over, Jan. You've done all you can. It's time to stop. Get in the car, Jan." He reached out for her.

Jan was doubled over and barely moving when she felt Steve's hand on her shoulder. She pulled away. "Don't you touch me," she cried. "Get away from me. I'm gonna walk. I'm gonna get back." A spectator stepped out of the crowd and stood at Jan's side. "Just walk with me," he said. "Just walk with me a little."

This infuriated Steve. "Jan," he barked, his eyes blue and blazing at her, "I made a promise to myself—I'm not going to let you go through twenty-five miles, doubled over, just trying to finish the race. We've been through this before. It just isn't worth it, Jan. We've talked about this and I'm not going to let you go on."

Jan pushed him away and went on, jogging slowly. Fuming, Steve inched the car down the avenue lined with tropical flowers and cheering spectators rooting Jan on. A mile later, Jan stopped again and stood in the road, doubled over, wincing.

Steve got out and slammed the door. "It's over, Jan. Get in the car."

"Don't touch me! You just don't touch me!" she yelled.

Steve stepped in front of her. "It's over. Don't you see? It's over." He pleaded. "What is it, Jan, to go out there on that highway and struggle? You have nothing to prove to me. You've done your best. It's time to go."

Jan tried to run around him, but she didn't make it. Steve's big arms enveloped her and he took her away, broken and weeping.

Most all those who'd witnessed the final scene felt Steve Ripple was the meanest man in Kona. He'd broken the oldest Ironman taboo, and he knew it and was glad.

"All these spectators, they just think [Jan's] struggle is great. They want to see it. They say, 'You can do it. Just walk a little bit. Hang in there, you can do it.' They're nothing but encouragement. Well, ninety-eight percent of the people in that race enter just to finish. That's not what Jan's here for. She enters the race to win. I'm her coach. I decide whether fourteenth place at the Ironman is worth blowing the USTS finals and going to the emergency room. It's not. Most of those people out there don't understand that."

Jan agreed. "As my coach," she said later, "anything Steve says to me needs to be said. People who say he's abusive don't know Steve, don't know me. I have the kind of personality where you got to get really down and dirty."

At 1:30 that afternoon, Jan Ripple was out of the race. Lisa Laiti was in the hospital and Paula was running comfortably through town on her way to the highway. Kirsten Hanssen was one mile behind her, running with the form of a sprinter but not the speed. Julie Wilson was another three-quarters miles behind Kirsten, not improving and worried about the Twins who, alongside Julie Moss, were coming up quickly.

The weariness in Wilson's legs had come on without notice and was, like most forms of exhaustion suffered at the Ironman, completely unresponsive to mere acts of will. In years prior to 1987 any contender beset with such fatigue would stop and consume great quantities of jelly sandwiches, defizzed Coke and water. Fifteen minutes to a half-hour later when the glucose kicked in, they'd continue recharged. But after 1988, stopping was out of the question. The pace was too fast. After 1988, anyone wishing to place in the top ten had to do his or her recovering on the move.

Toward 1:45 P.M., the top age-groupers amateurs began rolling down the hill to the bike-run transition. There were no smiles. All of them had a vacant intensity in their eyes. In various states of repair, they kept coming, some fully functional and others showing clear signs of diminished function—the knee that wouldn't bend as well as the other; the face too red or the face too pale; the arms that wouldn't pump.... But they kept going, hoping for the best.

Paula Newby-Fraser, meanwhile, was churning up the Queen

K like a training tape—erect, hips forward, relaxed hands carving perfect arcs from waist to breastbone. She looked strong, in total control of her race and she ran like that, mostly in the company of top men, for seventeen miles. Only when she leaned through the turnaround nine miles from the finish did her weariness show. Like a fighter hit by a body blow in the late rounds, Paula's shoulders sagged, her arms dropped, and her lower jaw fell with a deep, low sigh behind it. But, with the lens of an ABC minicam three feet from her face, she straightened and went on. She'd averaged 6.8 minutes per mile over the first 17 miles. If she could do the last 9 in 7.7, she'd equal her 1988 record.

At the next aid station, Paula pulled a small, clear plastic pouch from her fanny pack and ripped off the end with her teeth. She sucked out the contents—a clear, carbohydrate polymer goo—and followed it with a cup of water. The one hundred calories of high-test body fuel tasted like cake frosting; in fifteen seconds she'd eaten the equivalent of one banana, predigested.

Out in the lava fields a mile behind Newby-Fraser, Kirsten Hanssen was also concerned with nutrition. Back at the transition she'd shoved a couple unwrapped Power Bars under the elastic of her Lycra shorts, just above her knees. Usually stiff like a Big Hunk candy bar, the stuff was now melting, making rectangular, oily stains across her thighs. "Oh, those silly things," she said later, "they made me look like I'd totally pooped my pants."

Even under the most disorienting of circumstances, Kirsten could see herself clearly in her mind's eye. But at that point she could discern little else. Her missing contact lens distorted her vision. The heat murmuring off the road and the asymmetry in her gait caused by her aching left hip made her balance precarious and forced.

Set against the languid highway and the broken shuffle of competitors farther back, Kirsten ran like a mechanical doll with an overwound main spring. She knew her style was "choppy," and wished she had the long, gliding stride of Sylvianne Puntous, but settled for what she had—a spine straight as reinforcing rod, high knees, and a rapid turnover. It worked, propelling her down the road a full minute per mile faster than Julie Wilson.

Patty Loverock looked down at Kirsten from the bed of a moving press truck. A senior editor for a women's fitness magazine, Loverock had sprinted for Canada in the 1976 Olympics and had come to Hawaii to do a piece on the Ironman, but was having second thoughts. "You know," she said, "doing this sport tends to make the men look better and the women worse." Nodding at Kirsten, she said "Look at her, she's a running skeleton."

Sylvianne Puntous ran through the turnaround gate two minutes behind Kirsten. She, her sister Patricia, and Julie Moss had gone by Julie Wilson long ago, back in town. But now Sylvianne ran alone. Patricia had walked off the course at mile thirteen, cooked by the pace.

When Julie Moss saw her fiancé, Mark Allen, running alongside Dave Scott, as the pair led the race with just four miles to go, she quit. Moss felt her race was of no importance in the face of Allen's struggle for victory. "I was in eighth place, heading for fourteenth," she said. "I just didn't see any point in finishing that way when Mark needed me with him." It had been seven years since Moss had crawled across the finish for second place—a long time ago. She'd proven she could finish the Ironman; but that was nothing compared to winning it. Unable to win herself, Moss figured the next best thing was to be with Allen as he struggled to win his first Ironman. She jumped onto the back of a press motorcycle, caught up with the ABC camera van, and climbed aboard. From there she shouted encouragement to Allen, who, two miles from town at the bottom of a low grade, pulled slowly away from Dave Scott's shoulder—where he had been all day—to take the lead. Allen finished fifty-two seconds ahead of Scott, and Moss was there to hold Mark when he won.

Meanwhile eight miles from town, Sylvianne Puntous passed Kirsten Hanssen for second place and continued to pull away. Puntous had been closing steadily for sixteen miles and when she went by, Kirsten had nothing left for acceleration. She'd heard Sylvianne had been walking through the aid stations and hoped it was a sign she was overheating, which Puntous in fact was. "My hope," said Kirsten, "was that she would break down."

While running painfully to the turnaround, Julie Wilson saw Newby-Fraser come toward her and go by. Then Puntous, then Hanssen. Wilson knew exactly how far ahead they were and doubted any of them would crash. She ran on with no hope of doing better than fourth and every reasonable fear of worse. She was getting fuel into her muscles, and lactic acid out, at too slow a rate to move her body faster than 8.5 minutes a mile. Soon, Fernanda Keler, a fleet-footed up and comer from Brazil, passed her too. Julie went on knowing her career was over and that this was her last triathlon.

Jim Wilson rode alongside on a mountain bike as Julie struggled over the last few miles. She stopped often and stood on the shoulder and cried. As she did, three other women, formidable athletes all, went by. The years of sacrifice, of dreaming and believing she could do it all went through her mind and came out as tears. She ran forward, drained and confused. What went wrong? she asked over and over again. Did I overtrain? Didn't I eat enough? She had no answers and knew there were none to be had. But damn it, answers or no answers, she was going to finish.

In her last miles, Kirsten talked to God. Help me to hold myself up so that I might better glorify your name, she prayed. She thought of the Christian summer camp where she'd been taught the Total Release Concept—that racing to one's limit is a way of releasing Christ's love for others. She sang hymns in a breathy whisper. She encouraged the age-groupers who plodded on the other side of the road. She looked for beauty in the scruffy plants clinging to the lava. "It's so important to remain upbeat out there," she said later. "If you don't, if you let in any depressed thoughts, you begin to spiral down. I thought of heaven above and how you have to keep pluggin' away, little by little. It's just like life."

To Patty Loverock looking down from the press truck, Newby-Fraser seemed stronger over the final miles. "Unless she falls on her head," pronounced Loverock, "she's going to win this race. Nobody else out here is even close."

A bit farther on, Newby-Fraser stopped. She took off a shoe and the sock beneath it, then ripped off an injured toenail like an old Post-It note and went on. When she got down to the last quarter mile and the fans were cheering ten feet deep on both sides of the road, she took off her sunglasses, uncovering her eyes for the first time all day.

She hit the tape with both fists high, exultant. She felt it was the best of all possible races. She'd beaten her old record by five seconds, and her boyfriend, Paul Huddle, had beaten her (unlike 1988, when she beat him by three minutes). "No one can say now that my race last year was a fluke," she said. And no one could give her grief about beating her boyfriend, either. Sylvianne Puntous finished next, twenty-one minutes later. She crossed the line running, but immediately slumped into the arms of two volunteers. They took her to the medical tent and treated her for dehydration and heat exhaustion. Kirsten finished two and a half minutes later. "Praise the Lord," she said, holding up her palm in witness.

Julie Wilson came in twenty minutes after Kirsten in eighth place. Her finish time of nine hours and forty-five minutes would have won the women's race through 1986 and it was eight minutes faster than she'd done in 1988.

Wilson was happy it was over and she walked to the medical tent for an IV of saline and glucose. When the bag was empty, she rose from her cot and rejoined Jim. They found Julie's cousins and the four of them walked off through the milling crowds to search for the rental car Jim had misplaced eleven hours earlier. Julie's back ached and her legs were sore to the bones and quivering. When at long last her group found the car, the others were hungry and wanted to get a pizza. Julie leaned wearily against the car and said, "Listen, you guys, I've peed in my suit seven times today. Let's go home now."

EPILOGUE

Kirsten Hanssen

Kirsten Hanssen married Robert Ames that fall and began taking estrogen pills in December in hopes of rebuilding her bones. She kept her home in Denver but moved to Steamboat Springs, where she and Robert drew plans for a house overlooking the valley.

In February of 1990, Kirsten Hanssen-Ames set a women's record for the Mountain Man Triathlon in Avon, Colorado—a cold-weather version of the Ironman consisting of a 15-mile cross-country ski, 9.1 miles of snowshoeing, and 12.4 miles of ice-skating.

Kirsten retired from triathlon in the spring of 1991 and took a job with a bakery/delicatessen in Steamboat Springs.

Jan Ripple

"It was the longest night of my life," Jan said of the night following the Ironman. "I lay in that bed in the dark asking why. I was so fit for that race. So fit."

She and Steve rescheduled their flight and left Kona unobserved the next day. Shortly after arriving in Baton Rouge, Jan received a letter of apology from Shimano, but she did not think one was due.

Three weeks after the Ironman, Jan Ripple led the USTS National Championship race until the last mile of the run when she was overtaken by the former National Pentathlon champion Joy Hansen, who won by seventeen seconds. Afterward, some of the regulars at Foxy's teased Jan about being beaten by "such a little girl."

Five weeks after Ironman, Jan won the National Triathlon Sprint Championships. She ended the 1989 season in first place in the professional rankings and in *Triathlete* magazine's annual reader's poll.

After two more seasons of racing, Jan set her sights on making the U.S. Cycling Team.

Erin Baker

Erin Baker, who won every triathlon she entered in 1989, returned to the Ironman in 1990 to race against Newby-Fraser. On a brutally hot and blustery day, she beat Newby-Fraser by five minutes—the approximate period of time that Newby-Fraser lost to a malfunctioning bike chain. Urine samples taken after the race revealed no banned substances in either athlete. Ironically, Baker went through much of the 1991 season without a sponsor—a consequence, she believed, of speaking out against sex discrimination in triathlon prize distribution and endorsement contracts. In 1992, Baker concentrated on making New Zealand's Olympic track team.

Paula Newby-Fraser

Paula renewed her endorsement contracts and spent much of 1990 plugging bikes, shoes, clothing, energy drinks, and Polish cheese dumplings. "She's now a bit of a commercial property, you see," said her father.

On April 4, 1990, Newby-Fraser's U.S. immigration status was changed from "temporary worker of distinguished merit" to "lawful permanent resident."

Murphy Reinschreiber, her agent, sought "to promote her in a more mainstream way" and Paula attributed her success to "a life-style based on fitness and moderation."

In 1991, the Women's Sports Foundation fêted her as "1990 Professional Sportswoman of the Year." In October of 1991, she won the Ironman for the fourth time.

Julie Wilson

A small retirement party was held for Julie Wilson one month after the 1989 Ironman. She was happy through the evening, but wept openly and without embarrassment when she thanked Jim, "my masseuse, my sponsor, my husband, my coach, my friend." She said she would miss "the anticipation, the excitement, and those days in the sun whippin' down the road on my bike."

Two months after the Ironman, Julie was pregnant and Jim said, "Call me Thor." Nine months later, on October 17, 1990, Julie gave birth to a son, Zachary James.

Jim and Julie brought Zach home to a house they'd purchased (barely) in the spring; it was their first house in ten years of marriage and though it was small and needed work, it was no match for their energy.

Julie stopped swimming entirely after retirement, but kept up her running and biking, "detraining" as she put it, through her pregnancy. She was offered a job as a dental assistant in a friend's pratice, but turned it down, taking instead a part-time job with the Boeing Company as a fitness counselor.

When Zachary was five months old and kicking the air from a blanket at Julie's feet, she watched a videotape of her 1988 race in Australia. Toward the end, she laughed, saying, "This is what your mama used to do, Zach ... when she wasn't so tired."

She was still running, fifty miles a week.

Index